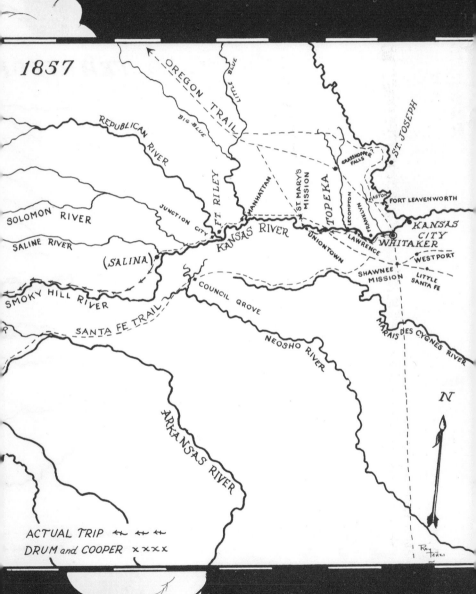

1857

ACTUAL TRIP ← ← ← ←
DRUM and COOPER × × × ×

PILLAR OF CLOUD

PILLAR OF CLOUD

JACKSON BURGESS

G. P. PUTNAM'S SONS   NEW YORK

To D. M.

respectfully and gratefully

PILLAR OF CLOUD

1

WHEN I came West, in 1858, Whitaker, Kansas Territory, looked to me like the end of the world. It wasn't, quite, for there were about a dozen towns just like it strung up the lower Kansas River valley; some of them are still there, but the rest died or were blown away. Whitaker is gone. It was one of the ones that dried and shriveled and disappeared. At the time, though, everyone around the town was sure it would soon be the biggest thing in the territory. It must have been the noisiest, anyway. There was hammering and sawing all around the clock, blacksmiths at work, a steam sawmill shrieking and snarling, wagon wheels squeaking, harness chains jingling, and, down by the river, men firing rifles.

I used to go down and watch the target practice. The riflemen were some sort of militia got up to protect the Free State settlers of the area from raids by pro-slavery guerrillas. Anyway, I was told that they were militia and that that was their duty. Most of them just seemed to like shooting off guns and a few were roughnecks hoping for trouble.

"Trouble" was what everyone talked about in Whitaker. Men in the hotel or around the stable told you, like preachers crying "Judgment Day," that there was going to be trouble. If you stood long enough among the loafers watching the militiamen someone would be sure to shake his head and tell you that trouble was certain. The notion was never very clear:

just a solemn, pious vision of turmoil. After I'd been in Whitaker a few days I learned that the way to make friends was to agree that, yes, there certainly *was* going to be trouble. The Kansas Territory was without a governor just then, as it was off and on during its early days, and everybody set the arrival of the next one as a likely time for the Apocalypse.

I had come down to Whitaker from Fort Leavenworth with a boy named Bob McVey, from Tennessee, whom I met on the boat coming upriver from St. Louis. McVey was an engineer by profession, although he'd never built anything. He was going to, and he used to tell me all about it. He had his mind full of bridges and roads, and he used to sketch some of them for me as we sat in the hotel at night. I didn't know a thing about engineering or bridges, but I could see that Bob's were out of the ordinary run of bridges. Maybe it was the way he drew them: full of sweeping, soaring lines and proportioned like birds or girls or running hounds, light and swift and airy. Most days McVey spent riding up and down the valley, shaking his head over the haphazard, swampy roads; muttering at the graceless bridges; sneering at the flimsy wharves and the tumble-down buildings. Wherever he found construction going on or, better yet, work projected, he would try to talk someone into letting him do the job. Every night, almost, he came back to Whitaker with a fresh snub rankling in his heart and a fresh idea to pencil for me.

"I'm ready to move on," he'd say. "I give up."

Bob was a blond boy about my own middling-thin size but with an air of uneasy, fidgety strength about him. He had an orange beard that would make you stop and stare in the street. Despite his youth it was full and thick and wiry, but the startling color of it was its grandeur. It was as orange as a sunset, a tangerine, or a marmalade cat. When he sat sprawled back in a chair, his muddy boots crossed in front of him and his chin sunk reflectively into that glittering beard, it made me twitch with envy. All I could manage then was a mustache, and a rather light one at that. I made the most of it, though. It was trained straight out and I waxed it into curling points that came almost all the way around. I knew, however, that it didn't have the simple, wild vigor of McVey's orange brush.

"Come along west with me, Cooper," he'd say. "We're both in the wrong place. I'm not getting any building done, and you're not practicing any law. Around here they're using blacksmiths for engineers and gunmen for lawyers."

I would sigh guiltily. I had come to Kansas to get into the anti-slavery fight and now I'd got a look at the fight and I'd lost my nerve. Besides, it was all so confused and wild. The Free Staters weren't real abolitionists. The slavery men were seldom slave-owners. All kinds of other things were mixed up in it: national politics and money interests and land deals and power grabs. Violence overlay it all. Besides that, no one noticed me. I had planned a grand entrance into a new life, coming out here to bring law to the frontier, and I'd found the territory had more lawyers than Washington and no more law than the bottom of the sea.

One May day, chilly and clear, Bob stayed in from his ramblings and we went together down to the cold, oily river to watch the militiamen shoot. There were about forty of them: Yankee farmers, with wool britches stuffed into muddy boots; a couple of merchants in shiny black; a dandy in a tall beaver hat and a frock coat; a smith in a horsehide apron. There was a lot of shouting and hoop-la as they launched the bottles and boxes and logs and kegs that they shot at. We watched them jostling around an open wagon, yelling and laughing, and saw one man near us showing a rifle to another. They had something new. Bob walked down among them for a little while; then when the cannonade began he came back up to where I was sitting by the ferry landing.

"Repeating rifles," he said. He stood beside me and we watched the practice begin. Each man just picked a target and rattled away at it, with smoke rising from the river bank in puffs and clouds, twisted and whipped by the raw spring wind. The river boiled out where the bottles and kegs were floating. Then the dandy tried to organize them, with himself as captain, to fire in volleys. They managed two concerted blasts on command, but the magnificent noise and boil was too

[11]

much for them and soon they were all shooting as fast as they could load.

"Where do you reckon they got those rifles?" Bob asked.

"Massachusetts," I said.

"In a crate marked 'Bibles,' I'll bet."

I took out my cigar case and we each lighted one. The target practice was becoming hysterical. A man would blaze away, shouting with every shot: "See there! See! Look at that!" and all the rest would be firing too and shouting the same thing and knocking each other down at the ammunition boxes and running back to the bank, slipping in the mud and cramming cartridges into the smoking rifles. Some waded out into the icy water, not even noticing that the bullets from the shore were ripping around their ears.

"Cooper," said my friend, "there's going to be trouble."

I laughed. "You finally heard about it, eh?"

"Look at those filthy, stupid animals."

Two ruffians began to curse at each other, down beside the ammunition boxes. They wanted to fight, but everyone else was too gay, so when one jumped on the other the whole crowd grabbed them and dragged them together to the river. They stood up dripping and puffing and shuddering while the mob jeered, then crawled numbly out of the water and went stumbling together up toward the hotel while the militia began launching another fleet of bottles.

"We're in a nest of crazy people," said McVey. "I'd like to knock their heads together. Let's go up to my room, I want to show you something."

He led me across the muddy, frost-crusted slope as the rattle of rifle fire started up again.

The tiny, dirty windows of the hotel let in no more light than a keyhole. McVey lit a lamp and rummaged in the baggage under his table. Then he unfolded on the bed a packet of printed maps: the United States, the West, and one of each of the Western states and territories. We laid out the Kansas and Nebraska maps, one above the other, and examined them a moment in silence. They weren't very detailed.

The map of Kansas showed only eight towns and three forts,

scattered across two thousand square miles of country. The Kansas, Arkansas, and Republican rivers were there, and the two great westward wagon trails were indicated vaguely. Then Bob consulted the map labeled: "Western United States." He put his finger on the junction of the Missouri and the Kansas rivers and said, "Here we are. Look at all there is to the west of us. California. Oregon. More than half the whole country. Out there, they're not fighting about what to do with the niggers. I want to go someplace where there won't be anybody trying to drag me into a fight."

"It's a long way."

"Good. I want plenty of distance between me and Kansas."

"Bob," I said, "it costs money to get out there."

"Not unless you take a stage, or something like that; and I don't plan to travel that way."

"How are you going?"

"Get on that horse of mine and ride."

"To California?"

"To wherever strikes my fancy."

"You can't just ride out there, for God's sake!"

"Why not?"

"You've got to go with someone. You've got to have a guide."

"What do I need a guide for? All you have to do is get on one of these wagon trails and follow it."

"It's wild country. There's Indians out there."

"Cooper, I've got an idea that if I don't bother them they won't bother me."

He was dead serious as he took a calipers from his case of drawing tools and began to make measurements on his maps. Whitaker wasn't on the maps, so he used Ft. Leavenworth, which was due north. He took the distance to Sante Fe and checked the scale. "About seven hundred miles," he said, not at all impressed. Next he checked Ft. Laramie, on the Oregon Trail. "About the same." He took the small-scale map and stretched his calipers across the Rockies, to the great Salt Lake. That was nearly a thousand miles away. Beyond that lay California—fifteen hundred. All these, of course, were distances measured in a straight line upon a map. For a man on horseback, almost anything west of Whitaker was weeks away, and McVey's maps showed nothing of what the country was like. Along the line that marked the Kansas-Nebraska boundary, however, was printed the word "Desert."

"Along those trails," he said, "the wagon trains are thick as fleas. You'd never be far from one. You could kill game for most of your food. Carry a little meal and salt meat and beans."

I didn't know what to say. His ideas were just too wildly unreal to take seriously, and yet he meant it all. Suddenly I realized that if he left I would not have a single friend. He scowled down at his maps, tugging his beard:

"Want to come along?"

"Why don't we talk to some of these wagon outfits?" I said.

"I've talked to them. They want two hundred and fifty dollars for fare to Ft. Laramie." There was nothing I could say to that, either. It was just about as much money as I had left. "If you make up your own party," Bob continued, "a guide runs five dollars a day."

Outside, the rifles were still rattling away as McVey straightened up and stamped his boots heavily. "Root hog, or die," he said. "What are you going to do?"

"I don't know."

"I'm for moving along. The two of us together can probably make better time. I don't know much about horses, and you do. That'd be a help. I'll do the hunting and guarantee meat on the table wherever there's game to be had."

From the corner behind the bed he fetched out a long rifle and brought it to the lamp where I could see it. He'd shown it to me before, an English piece with chased silver work on the lock. As I looked at it, turning it in my hands, he pointed to the window. "You want to stay around here until those fools start a war?"

"Bob, let's talk to someone who knows something about the country."

"Hell, Cooper, how do you think the West got opened up? Men got on their horses and headed out there."

[14]

I didn't answer, and after a moment McVey put his rifle away and sat at his little table, where he began idly sketching upon a sheet of brown paper. He scowled as he drew, clenching and unclenching his jaw so that he seemed to be flexing his coppery whiskers. After all, I knew very little about him. We'd met on the boat playing cards. We'd talked beside the rail at night, first cautiously, then openly, about politics and our Southern homeland. We were the same age and doing the same thing and both of us were educated men. By the time we reached the territory we'd become thick as brothers. Now here we sat, perfect strangers.

"I'll go down to the mission tomorrow," I said to him, "and see if I can get some newer maps."

He grunted and continued drawing. I watched him until I became drowsy.

Bob shook me awake a little later, blew out the lamp, and we went down to supper. This hotel, the only two-story building in Whitaker, was really no larger than a big house back in Georgia. There were eight or ten rooms on the second floor, no bigger than jail cells. Downstairs the dining room and kitchen took up one side and the lobby and saloon ran the length of the other. During our stay there weren't more than six guests in the hotel most of the time, and sometimes we had the place to ourselves. But the hotel dining room was the only place in town to buy a meal, so any traveler who didn't care to camp along the river would eat there, and we saw all the passersby.

This night there was a new face: new to us, that is, but not to some of the regulars. As the stew was handed around they were joshing him. He sat at the foot of the table: a broad, firm-looking man, not tall, with a black beard that outdid Bob's in thickness and curl. His brows were as thick and black as the beard and he was dressed in a shiny black alpaca suit and a dark blue shirt that stuck out partway over his wide, flat hands. His bald head was gleaming white down to a sharp line just above his brows. The hooked nose and round cheeks that stuck out of his thick whiskers were brick red from sun, so that his eyes seemed pale and his shiny scalp looked like a soft, helpless, indecent opening in his black and

[15]

bristly shell. He ate using his big hands very fastidiously, and he had the serious, matter-of-fact manner of a poor school teacher. A tall, thin man in a stovepipe hat gave a wink down the table, leaned out and called to the big man: "Ned, I hear that yellow horse of yours is for sale."

All the others paused and listened. They didn't exactly stop eating, but the clatter and murmur almost died away as they waited his answer. He looked up from his plate and stared curiously at the man who had asked the question. There was a hoarse rumble as he cleared his throat, and then he said, very politely, "Why no. Where'd you hear that?"

"Oh, that's just what I hear. Nothing to it, eh?"

The man looked perplexed. "Just what you hear? What do you mean 'you hear'? Hear from who?"

"I just heard it."

The big man looked intensely interested and puzzled. "I'm not selling that horse. Not for a minute. You don't remember who told you?"

The man in the stovepipe grinned and shook his head. "Nope."

"Must have been someone else they were talking about," said the black beard. That idea seemed to relieve him. He nodded his head very firmly and returned to his supper, but Stovepipe, who again threw a wink at the rest of us, wouldn't leave it at that.

"No," he insisted. "It was you. They said you were going to sell that yellow gelding of yours. What is it you call him?"

The room was practically silent, but we kept on eating, slowly, and some of the others exchanged quick smiles. I didn't understand the joke that was going on, but I was interested in the bearded man. I wondered if he were really as simple and earnest as he appeared. If it was a pose, it was wonderfully well done. He laid down his fork, swallowed, and wiped his mouth on the back of his sleeve. Then he shook his head. "I'm not selling him. I wouldn't think of it. Money can't buy a horse like that one. I've never had a better horse." Then, as an afterthought, he said, "I call him King."

[16]

"King?" said Stovepipe. "King? Isn't that a dog's name, Ned?" Someone down the table sniggered.

"A dog's name? Why, not necessarily."

"Lots of dogs are called King."

The bearded man regarded Stovepipe curiously for a moment. Then he shook his head and returned to eating. "You talk like a fool," he said.

The room went dead still except for his fork and his knife scraping on his plate and the slight kissing sound of his lips as he ate. The man in the hat laid down his fork and sat up stiffly. "Watch your mouth," he said hotly. The bearded man looked up from his plate, but he went on chomping away and he didn't put down his knife or fork. For the space of a minute he looked at Stovepipe. We waited. He didn't say a word. He chewed and stared. I thought I couldn't live until he'd finished that mouthful, swallowed it, and said what was coming. But he swallowed and looked down at his plate and went on eating. When he got another mouthful he looked up at Stovepipe and again he stared for the time it took him to chew and swallow. I watched him as if I were hypnotized, and I think every man at the table did the same. He went on with his supper. He saw nothing to say or do. A few others picked up their spoons and fell to and after a minute a muffled conversation began at the far end of the room. Soon we were all eating except the man in the hat. Then even he started eating again.

After supper there were always four or five of us who stayed at table drinking coffee until we'd emptied all the pots, while the rest went about their business or crossed the hotel for whisky or cards. McVey and I were among the coffee drinkers, and the bearded man made another that night. The man across from me, a watery-eyed wagon driver with tobacco stains circling his mouth, said to him: "You working with them people camped downriver, Ned?"

"If they get up their party," he said placidly. "Good people. Quakers."

"Where you bound?"

"The mountains," he answered, and he said the word "mountains" as if it tasted good.

"Santa Fe Trail?"

The big, bearded man smiled and shook his head. "I don't think so. I think we'll try a little something new."

"What's that?"

"Up the Smoky Hill River."

The driver looked at him patiently for a moment, and then he said: "Can't do it, Ned."

"I wouldn't be so sure."

"Too dry. Scant grass and scant game."

"I know that country," said the bearded man pleasantly, and the driver shrugged and left it at that. I had listened to all this because the bearded man, Ned, interested me, even though I didn't know what they were talking about. The Santa Fe Trail, I knew, followed the Arkansas River westward and then led into New Mexico and southern California —but I had no idea what mountains the man was talking about.

The big man suddenly said, to the table at large, as if it had just then come to him: "Where does John York get the idea my horse is for sale?"

The driver said, "Pay him no mind, Ned. John's full of himself these days, what with being wheel horse in the militia."

Ned waggled his beard. "I might have known he'd be in on that." He shook his head. "I'll be glad to put all this hurrahing and shooting behind me."

I glanced around the table and was relieved to see that no one appeared offended by that.

He went on. "There's none of this marching around and shooting off rifles up there, I can tell you. What few men there are up in the mountains have got enough to do with building and opening the land, without warring among themselves."

McVey said: "Where's that?"

"The great Rocky Mountains," he answered. "The finest unopened land left in the West."

"What's there?" McVey wanted to know.

"Whatever a man could want," said the bearded man, ignoring the driver's chuckle. "Fine farmland, up in the high valleys. Fur-game and table-game as thick as fleas. Timber. Plenty of pure water. There's gold, so I've heard." He sounded like a school teacher.

"Then why is it," asked McVey, "that everybody isn't chasing out there?"

"It's strange. I've asked myself that. But it isn't easy to get at, for one thing, and not many know about it. The Santa Fe Trail runs south of the mountains. The Oregon Road crosses them up north. In between, lies the country I'm talking about. It's something to see, I can tell you."

"Maybe," said the driver, "but if you go up the Smoky Hill River you're liable not to see them mountains ever."

The big man looked at him sternly. "Has it been tried? I ask you that. Has anyone ever tried? There was a first time over every trail, you know."

"I wish you good luck," said the driver.

"It isn't luck that does it. It's getting together people who have some ambition and can pull together and do a thing. After that it's management."

"Just the same, you better not turn down any luck that comes your way. I *still* wish you good luck."

The bearded man set down his cup and stood up. He clapped a soft black hat on his head and, with that gleaming, white scalp covered, he looked absolutely impregnable and impenetrable. "Someday," he said, "you'll be driving freight wagons up that trail."

"Then you can wish *me* luck."

The bearded man huffed himself up and stumped out of the room, the driver chuckling to himself. When the man was gone McVey said: "Who's he?"

"Ned Drum," said the driver. "He's a wagon-master and guide."

"What was that about his horse, at dinner?"

The driver glanced once toward the door. "Drum just got back from a trip," he said. "He's been around trying to raise another party and not having no luck. That fellow that was baiting him was John York. Now, Drum's got a fine traveling horse. That's the yellow gelding York was talking about. Drum's terrible proud of that horse. He wouldn't sell that horse unless he was starving. Not even then, I guess. Anyway, that was what York was getting at."

After a pause, I asked: "What?"

"Well, don't you see? He was saying that Drum ain't going to get anymore trips—because of this last time."

"What about the trip he was just talking about?"

"That's not a trip just yet. He's got a couple of people: these Quakers camped downriver. That ain't enough."

"What happened the last time?" McVey asked.

"Nothing. They left a little early. Fourteen wagons. Got down toward the sandy country and had to turn back. Bad weather, I understand. I don't know, but when a man has to turn back like that it's a black mark on him."

"Could it put him out of business?"

"Anything can put a guide out of business. Sometimes a man can have every kind of trouble and it doesn't bother anybody. Then another man has one turn of bad luck and if someone faults him for it then everyone else starts to do the same. Ned won't have any trouble, though, unless he gets his mind set on this trail he was talking about."

McVey tugged at his beard. "Where are these mountains?" he asked.

"Just go west, friend, and when your wheel horse falls back into your lap, you're in the mountains."

"How far?"

"Nine hundred miles, I'd say. Depends on just where you're going. This way that Drum wants to go would be shorter." He shook his head. "But you can't go that way. Maybe you could, if you got up a pretty big party and had good wagons and good gear and all. Maybe you could. I don't know. I just know that Ned better get it out of his mind, the fix he's in. Nobody wants to risk a thing like that, when nobody's tried it before. Nobody with good sense."

"Then how do trails get started?" I asked.

"I don't know that, friend. I truly don't. Drum has some kind of notion about that, but I don't. Drum thinks. . . . Well, Lord knows what he thinks. But he'd love to be a first-timer. You know, going out there across them plains, the very first of all, and showing the way."

"It's quite a thing to do," I said.

"I reckon so. Just like the first ones out here. Right here where we're setting was one time a place no white man had ever seen. If Drum could do it . . ."

McVey said, "If he could do it he'd be back in business."

"He would, for sure," said the driver. "Well, gentlemen, I give you good night."

When he was gone, McVey and I were left sitting with a litter of cold cups and spilled coffee.

"I like Mr. Drum," I said.

McVey sank his chin into his beard in that thoughtful, stubborn way. "Like the fellow said, he's got himself a big notion."

"Nothing wrong with that."

"Depends on the notion, Cooper. You want to know how new trails get opened up? I'll tell you. They don't. A piece of country isn't filled up that way, with trail-blazers and first-timers. People just drift into it. Look around here. You see any trail-blazers? The West is being settled by trash: men too shiftless or too mean to get along just get pushed west or they drift that way. You heard what he said: nobody wants to be the first unless he has to or he's running away or something."

"Not all of them," I said.

"No? What about you and me?"

"What do you want to low-mouth yourself for?" I demanded.

"I'm not. Cooper, I think I'm better than about ninety-five per cent of the world, but that's nothing to brag about. Hell, no."

"Most people try to be decent, Bob."

"Most people don't try anything." He clapped his hands on the arms of his chair and stood up. "Going to bed?"

[21]

"In a little."

When Bob had gone upstairs I went out into the lobby saloon. As I had hoped, Ned Drum was there. He sat at a table near the front, alone, playing solitaire, his black hat still settled firmly on his head. I watched him from the door. As he turned each card from the deck he looked at it sternly as if there were no telling what fantastic message it might bear. Then, pursing his lips, he'd look over his board. A play. He made the play. He studied the board. He made another play, thought about it, looked for another. No more. He turned the next card. I walked to his table, but he was concentrating so that he didn't even notice me.

"Mr. Drum," I said, "do you mind if I interrupt you?"

"How's that? Why, no. No." He rose. "Have a chair."

I sat down and said, "I was listening to what you said in the dining room, about going to the mountains."

"That so? Yes, I'm getting up a party right now. You interested?"

"Well . . . I don't know. My friend and I have been thinking about moving on."

"Fellow with the bright-color beard? That your partner? Likely looking fellow. You're not settlers, two young fellows together."

"No. We're just ready to leave this part of the country."

"How's that?" he said bluntly.

I gestured weakly and finally said: "All this fighting and all, you know."

He nodded. "May I ask where you come from, Mister . . . ?"

"Cooper. Garvin Cooper. I'm from Georgia. My friend is Robert McVey, from Tennessee." He pursed his lips thoughtfully, and I said: "We're not interested in slavery or Free State, Mr. Drum."

He smiled. "I reckon you do feel lost around here, then."

"It's not just that, you understand. My friend's an engineer. I'm a lawyer. We haven't found much for us here."

"I'd say there's plenty here for a lawyer. No, no. I see what you mean. Kind of a hard go, for a reasonable-minded fellow. You don't need to tell me, Mr. Cooper."

"Would there be anything for us to do, up where you're going?"

"An engineer? Lord, yes. Everything up there is building, building, building. All new. And it'll boom one day soon."

"What about me?"

"Well, I'll tell you, Mr. Cooper. I'd like to see a smart young lawyer be among the first ones in that country. There's settlers now, and soon they'll be setting up government. I'd like to see it done right, from the ground up, just like the building. You're a well-spoken man, and I mark you for a man of good family and good education. Oh, yes! Mr. Cooper. That's how I mark you."

We sat for a moment, I looking down at the table in embarrassment while he gazed serenely at me. "How far is it?" I asked.

"No more than seven hundred miles. Forty days on trail, maybe less."

"What will it cost?"

"Depends on the size of the party. If I get up six or seven people it'll run ... fifty dollars apiece, plus your stores. That would come to another fifty, or less. No more than a hundred, all together." I nodded, silently. "Those wagon trains," he said, "will charge you twice that just from here to Fort Laramie."

"I know."

He let me think about it for a little. Then he said: "It'll be a hard trip, Mr. Cooper. You know, it's never been done before, the way I mean to go. The ones up there now circled down from the regular wagon roads, but there's got to be a straight trail that goes right in there. And somebody's going to make it."

2

THE next day was cold, but the sky had cleared during the night and when the sun came up, the river, which had looked greasy and leaden for weeks, showed a bit of sparkle. McVey came to wake me and while I scrambled into my clothes he jigged about, flapping his arms. Then we tumbled down the stairs to the warmth of the dining room. We were late, and had the room to ourselves. As we sipped at scalding coffee I told him about my talk with Ned Drum.

"You want to go with him?" he asked.

"What do you think?"

He thought for a moment, as if he didn't really know what to say. "Garvin," he sighed at last, "I don't want to get tied up with a bunch of people. I want to go my own way."

"It's just for the trip. We can't go alone."

"Why not?"

"It's too risky. Bob, you just don't know! You've been saying you want to get out of Whitaker. Here's our chance. We've got the money."

"A hundred dollars is almost half of what I've got left."

"Me too, but it's cheaper than we can find any other way."

"I don't know, Cooper. This Drum ... Why's his fee so low?"

"Because he needs to get a party together in a hurry, to save his good name."

"His good name! What kind of man is he?" I shrugged, and he demanded, "What can we lose by trying it alone?"

"Our lives!"

He thought about that for a moment too, and then he gave a chuckle. "I guess so. I guess you're right."

"You want to talk to Drum?"

"I want to get a look at those Quakers, first."

"Bob," I said, "how did you come to leave Tennessee?"

"I wasn't getting along. It was a lot of things. I'm too damned hot, I guess. I'm not big enough a man to have the temper I've got; and when I try to get people to leave me alone they always think I'm picking a fight."

"They're bound to."

He laughed at that.

Bob spent the morning upriver, looking into some job or other. After an hour or so of listening to the gossip in the saloon I went out back to the stables and looked at my horse. Since McVey knew nothing at all about horses I had picked out both our mounts the day we got off the boat in Leavenworth: mine a pretty little sorrel mare and his a rough dun gelding that looked as if it could stand up to the punishment of carrying an inexperienced rider. My mare was putting on fat for lack of work, which was embarrassing, so I saddled up and took her for a canter out the military road. I didn't go far. In those days a man never traveled alone just for pleasure. Whitaker was the farthest east of the Free Soil settlements, with slavery territory all around, and there was no telling what kind of bad tempers you might run into. The landscape itself had a sullen look: the road a muddy strip winding north and south through gray-green hills that bristled with bare trees.

As I was coming back into town I saw that there was a lot of coming and going in front of the hotel, and as I put up my horse I heard the confused shouts of command that meant the militia was gathering down by the ferry slip. It was the first time I'd seen them muster in the morning. In the saloon, I heard the news: Trouble. Like all the news in Whitaker, it was a rumor. The story was that pro-slavery men had massacred a lot of Free Staters down on the Osage River. A man named Hamilton, from Georgia, was behind it, and the number he'd killed was put at ten, twenty, thirty. Most of the loafers at the bar took a grim satisfaction in the news and I was briefly very popular as one who hadn't heard. As soon as each one had given me his version of the atrocity, however, I was of no more use and I went into the dining room to inquire if there was any coffee left.

I sat alone at the long table, warming my hands around the cup, and thought. There was no reason to believe this massacre story. In Whitaker, we breathed rumors with the very air. Still, true or false or half-true, it was stirring people up. I couldn't believe that our wild-eyed militia would be satisfied for long to use those new rifles on kegs and logs of wood. I was not afraid, for I could certainly keep clear of any shooting that started, but what place was this for a man in his right mind? McVey was right about that much. The mountains, then?

The truth was that I had caught a gleam from Ned Drum's vision, and nothing that McVey said dimmed it. I kept thinking: Men sometimes stir themselves and they *do* things, and Ned Drum understands that. What a man does, he has. Suppose McVey didn't want to go along? What difference did that make? I drank down my coffee and went back out through the hotel to the stable yard. The militiamen were forming up on the river bank for a shoot. There was no laughing and shouting, though, and that was a bad sign. The blacksmith was inside his shop, close to the warm forge. He and his young helper were tiring a wagon wheel and as I came in he gave me a brisk nod. We'd talked horses beside his fire one cold afternoon, and he was a sensible, matter-of-fact man. I sat upon an upended keg and watched him work for a moment.

"You know a man named Ned Drum?" I asked.

"Wagon master. I know him."

"Is he a good guide?"

"You thinking of traveling with him?" Smiths are big men

as a rule, but this one was just a little bit of a fellow, covered with burn scars. "Ned's a great hand with horses," he said, "I imagine you two would get along right well. Where you planning to go?"

"Up the Smoky Hill River."

"There's nothing up there."

"We're going to the mountains."

"Is that Ned's idea? To the mountains, eh? Gold? I've heard they're digging gold up there. Mighty hard work, you know—digging gold." He flailed a rivet with his hammer, split it, and swore fervently. The helper picked out another and they grunted and strained to lap the tire again. As he turned the rivet in the forge, the smith said, "Ned's had bad luck, I'll grant you."

"I heard about that last trip."

"That trip's not all. There's been others. Got it, boy? There now." He drove the rivet home with an oath, grunted happily and picked another from the fire. "No, that's not all. Ned's had his share of bad luck and most of somebody else's. Too much, maybe. Mr. Cooper, I'll tell you the truth. Ned's a good guide and a good man, but he wants to be more than that. You know what I mean? Hold it. Ah! All right, boy, you set them other two, and set them good. You take me, Mr. Cooper. I can bend a passable tire and make a mule-shoe and I've done some fancy work that I wasn't ashamed of; but there isn't the makings of a real iron-smith in me." He wiped his hands upon his horsehide apron. "Some smiths can take a piece of iron and knock a curve in it this way and bend it that way and punch it and score it and give you a gate-hinge that's a good hinge and a beautiful thing: a hinge for a church. Not me. I can make a hinge that's just a good hinge and nothing more." I offered him a cigar, but he shook his head. "I get all the smoke and fire I want out of the forge," he said. With the tongs, he gave me a coal for a light.

"And what about Drum?" I said. "He wants to make church hinges?"

"That's right."

"And he isn't good enough?"

"I don't know. But I know that a man who aims high takes more risk than one who doesn't."

"But he stands to win more, too."

"I suppose that's so, but on my oath I can't see it myself."

The boy rolled a second wheel in from the yard and the smith went to help him with the stiff, new-formed iron tire.

"Would you go with him," I asked, "if it were you?"

"No fair, Mr. Cooper, no fair!" he laughed. "Why, man, if you want to keep safe and sure you can go back where you came from. But if you need to go out there—" with a quick motion of his head he indicated the plains and the mountains and the west "—go on; and never mind about Ned Drum, nor me, nor nobody else."

Early that afternoon, McVey came to my room, his cheeks bright with the cold. I was sitting reading a law book with my gloves on, and having a quiet cigar. He threw himself onto my bed.

"Heard about the killing?" he asked.

"Everybody has."

He rolled onto his belly on the bed and propped himself on his elbows with his face in his hands. "Oh, Lordy, Lordy, Lordy, Cooper! What makes men behave like this?"

"Bob, I want to go to the mountains with Drum and his party."

He sat up and regarded me drily. "Do you honest to God think," he asked, "that we couldn't make it alone?" He was asking it as a serious question, in all honesty.

"I do."

"Then let's go with them. Anything to get out of this. But you let me dicker with this fellow."

"I doubt if you'll get very far."

"Don't forget that he needs us, old friend." He got up and flicked his finger at the book I was holding open before me. "Not many lawsuits up there," he said.

"I can do without that for a while."

He regarded me with a smile. "You want to be a first-timer, don't you?"

"I wouldn't mind."

By suppertime, the newspaper had come in from Lawrence, an ill-printed and hysterical little sheet called the *Herald of Freedom,* and we got the details of the killings on the Osage— now entitled "the Marais des Cygnes Massacre." Nine had been shot. Four or five were dead. The militia and the Emigrant Aid Society had called secret meetings.

At supper the table was grim. Wherever you looked you seemed to look into fearful, startled, angry eyes. When Drum stumped into the room the sight of him, simple and solid and calm, was balm on a burn. As soon as the meal was over the three of us went to the saloon and I introduced Bob and told Drum that we were interested in joining him. Drum shook Bob's hand heartily and began to tell all over again about the high valleys of the Rockies and about the trail he was going to open.

As soon as he could get in a word, McVey said, "Mr. Drum, we haven't got much money. We'll give you thirty-five dollars apiece."

Drum scowled in confusion. "How's that? Why, I set the fee to make it reasonable. And all the others are paying the fifty, you see, so it wouldn't be fair."

"We won't say a thing to them."

"That isn't what I mean, Mr. McVey. I can't just charge one man this and the other man that. Thirty-five dollars! Why, if we're forty days on trail that comes to less than a dollar a day."

"It's all we can pay."

Drum waggled his whiskers and shot his cuffs. "Well," he said, "if it's all you can pay . . ."

He tried to reassert himself, but Bob stood firm, smiling, and at last we closed at thirty-five dollars. Then Drum tried to get talking again about his trail, but the haggling had taken his edge off. Besides, Bob wasn't paying much attention. Still, the guide seemed almost compelled to be hearty.

"Mr. Cooper tells me you're an engineer," he said to Bob.

"That's right."

"Well, you'll find a world of work for yourself out there.

[29]

That country up in the mountains is just waiting for men with gumption to come along and make something out of it. A young fellow who knows how to apply himself couldn't ask for a better chance."

"I can apply myself," said Bob drily.

"Good. It's a marvel what can be done by a man who'll work just a little bit harder than the next fellow."

"It takes more than work."

"Oh, yes. He has to have the chance; he has to have the right time and the right place, you might say."

"He has to have some brains, too."

Drum smiled. "You're right about that. You surely are." He nodded emphatically. "And I don't doubt you've got that, Mr. McVey. I don't doubt that for a minute."

"How long until we'll be leaving?" Bob asked.

"That depends. There's five now, counting you two."

"The Quakers and who else?"

"Young man from Baltimore. Hasn't been out here long. He heard about my plans up in Lawrence. The newspaper fellow told him. I guess I'm getting famous." Drum chuckled a little self-consciously at the word "famous." He went on: "I judge him to be of good family. Name's Hopkins. He's interested in developing himself a business in the mountains. Something in the freight line, or trading, as I get it. Fine young man, but he's crippled. He gets around all right, you understand. Just a little hop to his walk. He'll be all right."

McVey laughed, throwing back his head and chortling with delight. "A cripple!" he said. "What a crop!"

Drum gave him a long, silent, disturbed look. "I think," he said, "that you two should meet the others right off. In a small party, it's bad if people don't sort well together. You understand. First thing tomorrow you come to the livery down at the foot of the street. I'll be there."

He stood up, I shook his hand, and he tramped out. McVey looked after him with a grin. "Cooper," he said, "this is going to be a real ring-tailed howler. I need a drink of whisky." He shook his head and went to the bar and returned with two glasses of liquor. We drank and McVey leaned confidentially toward me. "Garvin," he said, "can you tell me what makes people think that building is just a matter of so much work? Did you hear what Drum said? You just need a little extra work and—Boom!—you've got a bridge."

I thought of Bob's drawings: the spans that seemed to leap like deer across the black water.

"It takes more than that," he said. "I've studied seven years now, and I'm just getting on to it. I don't just mean how to make a bridge hold the load. I mean how to make it look like it belongs where it is, doing what it's doing. Does that sound foolish to you? Well for that you have to have more than hard work. God knows what you have to have."

"I think you underestimate Mr. Drum," I said. "He wants to do something special too."

Bob finished off his drink and blew his breath loudly. "Well, I hope he's got more to put into it than hard work."

I went alone to meet Drum the next morning. Bob was asleep when I went to his room, and not very eager to get up. "Go find him," he said, "and bring him up here. I'll be ready by then." I didn't like that, but I said nothing. Bob wasn't taking Drum very seriously, and I had a feeling that Drum would resent it. I suppose that during those first days a lot of my deference to Mr. Drum was an attempt to make it up to him for Bob's treatment—and I did defer to Mr. Drum. In part, however, it was Drum's horse, his yellow gelding. From the first minute I saw the horse that morning, I coveted it. It was a big animal: a hair over seventeen hands and well muscled. I would have marked him down a hunter, except for his yellowish buckskin color. His mane and tail were black and he had sooty stockings on all four legs. On his face, his color faded almost to white. He held his head high in an alert, willing way, and watched us curiously as we looked him over.

"How old?" I asked.

"Going on eight. I've had him for nearly three years. His sire was an Irish hunter, over in Missouri." (Proud of my guess, I was sorry I hadn't said it right away.) "I'm not sure about his dam," Drum continued, "but she must have been

[31]

heavy stock. He's a traveling horse, and I'd say he's the best in the territory."

"Strong," I said.

Drum nodded proudly. He had just curried the gelding and while I waited he cleaned up his feet. A little later, he told me, the farrier was coming to shoe him. He fussed around the stall for a little bit, seeing things right, and then he dusted the hay off his black suit and led me out into the street.

"Where's Mr. McVey?" he asked.

"Had trouble waking up," I laughed. "He'll be ready in a little. Let's go up."

"We might as well find Mr. Hopkins first," he said. "He stays down here at Simpson's."

We found Hopkins on the porch of his lodging house. He wasn't a man you'd miss seeing. "That's him there," said Drum as we came up the street, and I didn't have to ask which one he meant among the three or four on the porch. With his feet on the porch rail and his chair tilted back, Hopkins sat wrapped in a huge great-coat with a fur collar into which his chin was deeply sunk. A tall, gleaming beaver hat was pushed forward on his head, almost to his eyes. From under the brim he regarded the street before him with a petulant, impatient stare. "Mr. Hopkins," called Drum. "Hello there. I've got some news for you. Let's go over to the hotel."

Hopkins, without a word, made a sign with one hand and rose abruptly. As he stalked down the porch to the steps I saw just the trace of a limp in his walk, and I noted that the soul and heel of one of his shoes were built up to a thickness of three inches. When Drum introduced us Hopkins gave me a fleeting touch of his hand and said: "What cheer?" He was taller than I, but most of his size was in his long legs. Around the middle he looked a little pudgy and soft. His head was what you looked at, though. It was large and swept with waves of fine, delicate, reddish-blond hair. Each feature of his broad, pale face seemed set discreetly on its own ground. His nose might have been a nose got up for a contest, it seemed so perfect. His mouth was generous and full, with just a suggestion of girlish sulkiness at the corners. The whole face was

[32]

a study of symmetry and balance. When he spoke, though, you saw that his teeth were dirty and crooked and small— angry, feral teeth. Drum told him that my partner and I were thinking of joining them on the trip to the mountains, and he accepted this information with only a quick bob of his head, as if reports were confirming his private findings. As we walked across to the hotel he said to me: "You're a Southerner?"

"Georgia."

Again he gave that nod and went "Hummmm," but I knew what he meant, and I winced to think what McVey was going to think of *him*.

We found Bob in his room and he called out to us to come in. On the table was Bob's English rifle, which he'd been cleaning and oiling. He had rubbed the dirt off of one tiny pane in his window and he stood squinting out and working on a sketchbook in his hand. He threw the book to the table as we came in and I saw that he was doing a drawing of the riverside and the militiamen at practice. It was just a rough sketch, with the river looking cold and dirty, full of floating targets, while the cluster of riflemen on the shore was seen as a tangle of confused, angular limbs and bodies, with the smoke of the fusillade ripped along above them by the wind. The margin was covered with line drawings of individual men in different poses and aspects; most striking was a gangling, skeletal man grinning with glee as he discharged his rifle wildly into nothing. McVey greeted us, met Hopkins with a genial smile and said, "Cold as a well-digger's ass." With that he plopped down on the edge of his bed.

To my amazement, Hopkins took off his beaver and smiled. "I understand," he said, "that you gentlemen may join us in our trip."

"I thought it was all arranged," said McVey, looking at the guide. Hopkins flushed lightly.

Drum was not at all discomfited. "Everyone must be in agreement," he said stolidly.

McVey looked at Hopkins and said: "Agreeable, friend?"

"You look as if you can pull your weight," said Hopkins. He smiled, then nervously straightened his face, then flushed

[33]

again, and I realized that he was being friendly and didn't know exactly how. "Have you talked to the others?" he asked.

"Going out there now," said Drum. "I thought perhaps we should all talk it over together."

Hopkins continued to speak only to Bob. "The other two," he said, "are a Quaker couple from New England. Joel is fine. Martha, you just have to bear."

"I generally get along right well with the ladies."

"Scarcely a lady," said Hopkins, shaking his head and giving a thin little laugh to show that it was meant in the friendliest way; but the laugh just flashed those ugly, ratlike teeth. "Have you been out here long?" Bob shook his head. "You'll find it strange at first. Everything's wide open—and shifting. But that's the beauty—the advantage. If one can take advantage of the state of things . . . There are fortunes to be made out here. The land is wide open and I don't think there's a man in the territory who realizes what the opportunities are. A man with foresight . . ." He rattled on, and soon was instructing us in the ways of the West. Bob drank it all in with open eyes. Drum fidgeted.

Going to the table, Hopkins began asking Bob about the drawings in the sketchbook. Was Bob an artist? No? They were fine drawings. He held the pad before him. "In the manner of Dürer," he said. "Not much," said Bob—for McVey that was a fairly gentle jibe—and Hopkins quickly laid down the book and began fumbling with his hat and coat to leave. It seemed that every word, every gesture, for him, was a move in a game, and he always had one eye on the scorekeeper. "Come along with us," he said, and then he blushed all over again, slapped his gloves on the table and, with a nod to us, turned and started out.

"Hold on," said Drum, "aren't you going with us out to the Tyrees' camp?"

"All right. Shall we go?" he said—after only the slightest hesitation.

We set out together from the hotel, but Drum marched at a sharp pace and McVey insisted on sauntering. Hopkins kept step with the guide, and I, feeling that our party was so far mixing very poorly, fell in with Bob. As soon as the other two had drawn ahead of us he asked: "What's wrong with that fella?"

"Touchy."

"He certainly is. He doesn't get along very well with that game leg of his, does he?"

"He's keeping up with Drum."

"That's what I mean. He thinks he has to, to show he can."

The wind was sharp and the walking hard. McVey began to hum to himself and I drew my hands and face into my coat and, for the first time since meeting Drum, I seriously faced my own thoughts. There was still time for me to give Whitaker a real try. I could hang my shingle from the hotel window; I could busy myself around the courthouses; I could scout up clients and talk up lawsuits. But there was the militia to think about, too, and the raids and the clownish politicians. After all, I was a brand-new lawyer; maybe a brand-new land was the place for me. It was attractive, all right, this idea of opening up the mountains.

He walked about half a mile along the road downstream from town. There, on the river side, was a grove of runty oaks. In among the trees stood a wagon, and a fire was smoking away in front of a little tent. A pair of big mules were grazing, hobbled, in the short grass along the stream. A man in a brown suit of clothes was crouched by the fire with his back to us. He heard us turn in from the road and straightened to face us: a spare man with square-cut chin whiskers like a preacher's. As we got closer I was surprised to see that he was quite young—no older than I, certainly. That was a feeling I had all the time in Kansas, for you seldom saw a man over forty and the average must have been about twenty-five.

The man in brown called in the direction of the tent, then came to meet us with a peculiar, soft smile which I was later to find as much a feature of Joel Tyree as his whiskers, his sharp little nose or his bulging forehead. He offered his hand to Drum and said, "Good morning, Edward Drum." The

[35]

guide introduced us all and Tyree, in the Quaker custom, addressed us by our full names. As we shook hands, his wife came from the tent. She was dressed in the same brown cotton her husband wore. In fact, it looked as if their clothes had been cut from the same bolt of goods, and they were undoubtedly homemade: hers a long, loose, flowing dress and his a square-cut suit that was too big and had too many empty angles to it. My first reaction to Martha Tyree was that she was very pretty, but she didn't bear up under a closer look. There was a kind of clearness and candor to her face that pleased you, and she and her husband both had a graceful, modulated softness of voice that was very taking. There was a certain unchecked softness about her lines, though, that wasn't pretty at all; and when she laughed, which was often, she whinnied.

The five of us gathered about the Tyrees' fire and Drum told them, very briefly, that Bob and I were interested in coming along and that we understood the rigors of the trip and the conditions of joining. The sharpness of the breeze brought us all huddled together, knee to knee, about the fire. When Drum was finished, we waited for Joel Tyree to speak, but it was the woman who had questions. Once again, the first question was about our origins. I answered for us both, and then she said: "Why are you going to the mountains?"

"We understand there's a little more room out there, in all ways."

"What brought you to Kansas?"

Drum interrupted. "As I understand, Mrs. Tyree, you're trying to find out if these boys are pro-slave. Is that it?"

Instead of answering him, she said to us: "Do you gentlemen know anything about Quakers?"

I started to answer "No," but McVey said loudly: "You're abolitionists, aren't you?"

"We are."

"Why not come right out with it, then? We're not slave owners and I don't care if you free every slave in the country. But I'm not a Free Stater, either."

She curled her lip in disgust. "Free State," said her husband with a laugh. "They're worse than the slavery people." Then he gave me that kind, gentle smile.

His wife continued: "We came out here thinking that the Free State party was a real anti-slave group, but they aren't. They're just anti-black."

"Are you looking for a 'real anti-slave group' up in the mountains?" Bob demanded.

"No," said Tyree. "We're just looking for a place where we can homestead without being a party to what's going on here. We won't live in a slave state, but we won't live under the government that passed Lane's Black Laws, either."

The Black Laws were the Free State ordinances which forbade Negroes to live in the territory. They weren't law, of course, for the Free State legislature wasn't a legitimate body. Still, as far as legislatures went you could take your pick in Kansas in those days. Elections were almost constant and some legislature or other was convening almost every day. But for all I knew at the time, Lane's Black Laws were the law of the land. I hadn't had time to get the governments sorted out, so Tyree impressed me as knowledgeable and high-principled.

"Well," said McVey, "I guess I'm an abolitionist myself, but I don't get all fired up about it."

"Thee should," said Martha Tyree sharply, and McVey looked at her in absolute alarm.

"What do you mean?" he cried in outrage, but his voice rose perilously near a squeak and the proud boy behind that orange beard was fleetingly revealed.

The woman turned to me. "Is thee an abolitionist too, Garvin Cooper?"

"No," I said stoutly, "I'm not." I made the most of the dramatic pause that followed. I drew out my cigar case and selected a cigar. Then I bit the end off it and spit it into the fire. "I used to be," I said. "But if I meant to call myself an abolitionist I'd stay here and fight for abolition. As it is, I don't see how I can."

"All the fight is not here," she said.

"Mrs. Tyree, when men are better men they'll stop doing bad things. That includes owning slaves."

Joel Tyree smiled. "What will make men better?" he asked.

"Time," I said.

He shook his head. "The Word," he said.

"I doubt it."

Drum was visibly shocked, but I could see that I had impressed Willis Hopkins. Martha Tyree sighed and turned upon me a gaze of anxious concern. "Does thee still wish to come with us?" she asked. I nodded. She looked to McVey and he said, "The question is, do you want us unbelievers along?"

"Thee is no unbeliever, Robert McVey. Thee is proud."

"What's wrong with that?"

"Thee must find out for thyself."

"I would like to find out some things, all right," said Bob. "And I'd like to ask a few questions now, instead of answering them. Are you people missionaries?"

Martha hesitated and her husband said: "We could be called missionaries, in a way. We want to homestead, and after that we'll do some good if we can."

"What kind of good have you got in mind?"

"We thought we might be of help here," said Joel, "but we feel that this is not our call. Martha is a school teacher. Out in the mountains, we think we may try to start a school for Indian children."

"That takes money."

"The concern is more important than the money."

"From what I hear, the Indians are getting along all right."

Martha Tyree pleased to take that as a joke. She laughed and said: "We shall see. Will thee come with us, Robert McVey?"

"I think I will."

"Good, good," said Drum. I'd almost forgotten him; now he bent over the fire, rubbing his hands almost in the flames, and said, "As long as the five of you are pretty well set, why don't we talk about our stores and supplies?"

He then ticked off, from a list in his mind, the things we

had to buy. He offered to let us oversee his purchases, but Tyree told him that wouldn't be necessary. We had to have two mules, of course, to alternate with Tyree's team on the wagon. Then we would need four or five pack animals and spare riding horses. There was food to think of, and we left it to Drum to decide how much flour, bacon, sugar and salt, and so forth. He asked us all what firearms we had, and decided we had best add three short dragoon rifles. McVey had his English breech loader. I had a pair of flintlock dueling pistols. The Quakers had a fowling piece.

We wound up, as Drum must have expected, by commissioning him to gather the supplies. Tyree, after closing himself in the tent for several minutes, produced gold twenty-dollar pieces and gave them to Drum, who made a record of the transaction in a tiny pocket notebook. McVey and I agreed to give him some money as soon as we got back to town. We had gold money on us, of course, but we didn't want to reveal just where and how much.

As soon as all the business was settled, Martha Tyree brought a kettle from the wagon and set it in the edge of the fire to boil. Then she fetched a bag of coffee and set her husband to work on the crank of the mill. Sitting there at that fire, on that cold, raw day, and smelling the fresh-ground coffee spilling from the mill, I lost my doubts. Now that McVey had come around, and now that I'd seen him in another light—thanks to Mrs. Tyree—I had the feeling that good things lay ahead for us. These Quakers were people I could talk to. The very fact that I felt free to argue with them made me like them. And, now that we were relaxing, they turned out to be pleasant company.

As the coffee boiled, the Tyrees set up a song. It was "Pretty Polly," a song that was going around the river settlements just then. You heard it everywhere, and in every kind of voice. Martha Tyree had a lovely, clear soprano, but her husband could scarcely carry the tune, so she and I sang the air with Ned Drum singing a fair bass and Bob doing the tenor. We pleased ourselves so much that we did an extra chorus and clapped for ourselves at the end. "This is the weather for 'The Frozen Girl'!" said Martha Tyree, and we took that one, singing it all the way through with one or another of us dropping a line now and then for laughing at the foolish words of it. Then she taught us a song she called "The Quaker's Wooing," a pretty air that we picked right up and plentiful refrain lines that McVey embroidered gorgeously with his tenor. Drum suggested "Where O Where is Old Elijah," and gave a fine, booming bass to the performance. By then the coffee was ready and we were all glowing and laughing. I decided I had never heard anything finer than the Tyrees' "thee" and "thou."

We left the Tyrees at work around their camp and the four of us hiked back into town. Hopkins stopped off at his lodging-house and Drum went in with him to get his money, while Bob and I waited in the cold street.

"I think we're doing the right thing," I said, stamping my feet.

"It isn't too much money," he said, "and it'll be worth it just to see what becomes of this bunch. What an outfit! I look at it this way, Cooper: if everything goes along all right, that's fine; if anything goes wrong, I'm still my own man. But I don't know about Drum."

"You ought to see the horse he's got: a real goer."

McVey nodded. "That's what he'd like to be himself."

Drum walked down to the hotel with us and up to my room, where Bob and I got out our money. Mine was in a belt around my waist, under my clothes, and his was in a sort of holster strapped to his leg above his boot. We each gave him thirty-five dollars gold. He put it into his pocket so nervously and shamefacedly that I said to him, "Mr. Drum, I'd like you to have a look at our horses and tell me what you think of them." He agreed happily, so we left Bob in his room and went out back to the hotel stables. He admired my sorrel and swelled me immensely by saying: "You're a good judge of horse flesh, Mr. Cooper, I can tell. You must come from among horsemen."

"I've spent quite a bit of time with them," I said, slapping my mare's neck.

[40]

"I've known men to spend their lives with horses and never get the feel for them. That's what it is—the feel. Some have it and some haven't. What do you call her?"

"I haven't really given her a name. I don't guess I've ever named a horse." The truth was that I'd never even owned a horse until two months before that time.

"Now's your chance," he said. "You should name her."

"Well, let's see. I'm going to have to go a long way depending on her. I think I'll call her Hoecake." I smiled at the mare and rubbed her muzzle. "You hear that? You're Hoecake."

I looked at Drum. He seemed startled. "Hoecake?" he said. "What do you mean 'Hoecake'?"

"Hoecake," I said. "You know: it's a meal cake cooked at an open fire."

"I know what a hoecake is, but that's a funny name."

I thought it best not to try an explanation. I just said, "I sort of like it."

"Well, if you like it. Hoecake. I never heard of that for a name."

He examined Bob's gelding carefully. It certainly wasn't a horse that would strike the eye, but Drum agreed that he seemed strong and unexcitable, which was important for an inexperienced rider. There's nothing more tiring to a horse than carrying an inexpert horseman on a long trip. This one looked as if he could stand up to the punishment.

"Mr. Cooper," Drum said, running his fingers down the horse's foreleg, "I want to speak frankly with you. I'm a little worried about Mr. McVey. I don't think he takes this undertaking very seriously."

"It's just his way of talking."

"No. It's not his talk that I mean."

"What is it?"

"All of us," said Drum, "will have to buckle down together, and Mr. McVey strikes me as being . . . touchy, you might say. Prideful."

"He's a proud man, all right."

"Have you known him long, Mr. Cooper?"

"About a month."

"Out there," said Drum, with a jerk of his head to indicate the trip ahead, "someone has to be in charge. It doesn't do if someone lets that rub him the wrong way." He hesitated. "It ought to be pretty well settled in advance."

"You want me to say something to Bob?"

"Oh, no, Mr. Cooper. I'd just as soon you didn't, really. But you've got a level head on you, I can tell, and I wanted to mention the matter. That's all." Squatting beside the horse, he took off his hat and rubbed his shiny scalp. "We have to pull together," he said.

"I wouldn't worry," I said.

Drum said that he wanted to go down to the livery and see what kind of job the farrier had done on his own horse, and I went with him just for another look at that buckskin.

When we walked into the livery the first thing we saw was a big hand-drawn sign tacked to the stall where Drum's horse stood. It said: "For Sale."

"What's that?" he said.

"Somebody put up a sign on your horse."

"It says 'For Sale'!" He walked slowly up to the poster and peered incredulously at it. "That horse isn't for sale!" he cried. "Who put that up?" He looked sternly around the barn. "Hey, there!" he called, but there was no one in sight. "Hey!" he shouted again. A Negro swipe came in from the corral door and peered at us. "What's the idea of this?" Drum demanded.

"Yessuh?" inquired the Negro.

"What's the idea of this sign on my horse?"

"What sign is that, suh?"

"This sign right here. It says 'For Sale'! That horse isn't for sale."

"I don't know," said the Negro. He was suspicious. "The owner is over to lunch, Cap'n. You better talk to him."

"You're in charge here. Do you let people come in and put up signs on other people's horses?"

"I been out to the corral, Cap'n. Mr. Davis is the owner. You best talk to him."

[42]

"Well, you take that sign down."

The Negro did as he was told and stood holding the sign in his hand as if it embarrassed him. For a moment he seemed to think of giving it to Drum, but he wound up holding it discreetly behind his back. "Most likely," he said, "somebody got the sign on the wrong stall."

"They certainly did." Drum stalked into the stall and anxiously examined his horse, while the big gelding placidly nibbled at his shoulder. He looked over the shoes and admitted that they looked pretty good. That mollified him somewhat. The Negro returned to his work and Drum and I walked out into the street.

"Cooper," he said, "this is a strange thing. The other night at supper a fellow started saying he had heard my horse was for sale. Fellow named John York. I told him it wasn't, but he seemed to have the notion stuck in his head. He kept carrying on about it." I did not remind Drum, since he apparently didn't remember, that I had heard all that. "How do you think an idea like that gets around?" he asked very seriously.

"I don't know."

"I don't like it."

"It doesn't seem anything to worry about," I said. "Someone just made a mistake."

"It looks funny to me."

Drum was getting the idea that somebody, somehow, was after his horse. I couldn't very well put him right on it, so I kept quiet; but I had the uneasy feeling that he was afraid.

"We'll be gone soon," I said.

"Funny things going on," he murmured. "I'll be glad to get away from this town." He stopped and looked up the street toward the river road winding west. "Out there," he said, "you know what's happening. You know what to do, and you buckle down and do it. That's why I asked you about Mr. McVey. I want him to understand ... All of you. What we're doing amounts to something, and we must go at it in the right spirit. It will be a great thing for us: a thing that will be told about us after we're gone."

[43]

3

UNDER Drum's direction, we began getting ready for the start
of our trip. Drum asked me to help him buy the stock and he
and I rode up and down the valley for two days to locate
some good horses. We bought six rough Western ponies that
could be used under either pack or saddle, but there wasn't a
decent team of mules to be had. The Tyrees' camp was moved
upriver past the town to a site that offered better grazing and
we picketed all our stock with them. McVey left the hotel and
went out to help the Tyrees care for the animals and prepare
the wagon for its rough trail. He and Tyree borrowed a forge
and bought some iron to make angle braces for the wagon
frame. The camp became a busy place, with the clatter and
clang of ironwork. Martha Tyree helped Drum with getting
together foodstuffs and camping gear, making up bedrolls and
stitching a canvas cover for the wagon. There was harness
to be examined and mended and pack saddles to be built. The
tent and our bedrolls were to go in the wagon, along with
most of the food, and the hard goods and our personal belongings went on the pack horses. Drum got two sturdy kegs for
water barrels and spent all one day sealing and caulking them.
Hopkins was at the camp most of the time, but he didn't do
much. Any little chore seemed to pose a test of strength or
skill, and you could see him shy from anything that held the

chance of failure—even a petty, unimportant task like sawing lumber square or punching holes in harness straps.

I was not with them the first few days. I was riding from sunup to sunset in search of a good mule team. Downstream I traveled as far as Kolb's Crossing, which was known as a stronghold of slavery sentiment. I found them just as jittery as the Free Staters of Whitaker, but a good deal more belligerent. There were a lot of Missourians there, camping in filthy shacks along the river bank. I'd seen their kind before, on the boat up from St. Louis, but these at Kolb's Crossing were even dirtier and rougher. They had their "militia" too, and it was even wilder than Whitaker's. They weren't very well armed. I didn't see but one repeating rifle among them and there were a lot of flintlocks. They didn't spend much ammunition in target practice, either, so I judged that they hadn't much to spend.

I found my mules, at last, in an emigrant camp outside Westport. The owner wanted to trade for oxen, but I talked him into taking cash. They were a sound team, and well fed, but fifteen years old at least. I wouldn't have bought them as a permanent possession, but for a short-term investment they seemed all right. It stood to reason that where we were going they'd bring an even higher price than I'd had to pay. We sealed the bargain with a drink of whisky, the owner and I, sitting on the tongue of his wagon with his three children viewing me narrowly from behind a wheel. He was an Ohioan: a leathery, sour fellow with few words. He laughed too much at my jokes, though, and I saw that he was trying to make friends with me for some reason—to play the good fellow. Finally, after the second drink, he came out with it.

"Pretty much Free Staters around Whitaker, I hear."

"That's right."

"I hear they got a regular army up there."

"I wouldn't call it an army," I laughed. He laughed too, and tipped the jug.

"The Free Staters are pretty mad about that shooting down on the Osage, ain't they?"

"I wouldn't be surprised," I said.

"I wouldn't neither. I wouldn't blame 'em a bit. What they gonna do?"

"What can they do?"

He laughed nervously, as if I'd made a grim joke. "Yeah, I reckon that's about it," he said. He was frightened. He handed me the jug. "I hear they got a list of all the fellas that was in on the shooting."

"Is that so?"

"I don't know. That's just what I hear." He laughed again. "Well, you tell 'em," he said, "that we're right on their side, will you?"

"Are you?"

"Well, we ain't really in, one side or the other, but we haven't got no slaves."

I stood up. "You're in it," I said. "If you stay around here, you're on one side or the other. My advice is for you to clear out; go on upriver."

"Then it's true about them militia?"

"What is?"

"I don't know. I just heard."

"What did you hear?"

"Well, I heard you fellows up at Whitaker was fixing to run the Missouri men out of Kolb's Crossing, and clear all the slavery people out of the valley."

"Where'd you hear that?"

"It's just around. Is it true?"

"Don't ask me. Just clear out; that's my advice. Thanks for the liquor."

I put my mules on a leadline and towed them at a fast trot toward Whitaker.

During the ride up the river, my alarm cooled off a little. I had time to remember the rumors and counter-rumors that had been about me since St. Louis, and also I just couldn't imagine those militiamen starting anything as ambitious as an armed revolt. The cold, drab street of Whitaker was reassuring, too. It was not the site of a revolution. People were going about their business just as they did every other day.

[46]

The town was not big enough to hide preparations for an armed foray by forty men. Just the same, before taking the mules out to the camp I stopped by the hotel to see what I could hear in the saloon. What I heard relieved me considerably. The rumor was that the Missouri men were organizing an attack on the Free State capital at Topeka, complete with cannon. On the other hand, there was news that General Smith had brought dragoons down from Ft. Leavenworth and was bivouacked near Lecompton.

At the camp, I found McVey and Hopkins helping the Tyrees mount the wagon-cover. Martha put the kettle on for me and Joel had a look at the new team, agreeing with me that they'd do the job. I unsaddled Hoecake and as I began to wipe her down Bob came over, with Willis Hopkins limping close behind him.

"Where'd you find them?" he asked.

"Downriver. Damn near to Westport. Have you heard anything about a raid on the slavery settlements?"

"Like what?"

I told them what information the emigrant Ohioan had given me.

"There's plenty of talk like that around," said Bob. "They're all full of fire and vinegar." He squatted on his heels in the grass. "Willis has turned up something you ought to hear, Garvin."

Hopkins edged up to my horse and gave her a gingerly pat on the rump. "Indians," he said, as if the idea amused him.

"What about them?"

"Well, it seems we're heading right into a nest of them."

"Where'd you hear that?"

"In Lawrence. I know the editor of the *Herald*. I went up to tell him about our trip. He's going to publish our plan as soon as we're well started, you know."

"No, I didn't know," I said, "but what about these Indians?"

"The Cheyenne tribe inhabits the headwaters of the Kaw. He says that General Smith has been chivvying them, and they're hostile."

"I never heard them called hostile."

[47]

McVey asked: "What do you think?"

"Have you told Drum?"

"We shouldn't have to tell him. He should know."

"Have you asked him about it?"

"Not yet. He's in town—him and our new traveler."

"All kinds of news," I said. "Who's the new traveler?"

"A boy that Drum decided to take under his wing. A runaway apprentice."

"What?" I was scandalized, which amused Hopkins.

"He's all right," said McVey. "He's got a lot of sense. He'll be some use to us. He's a wheelwright."

"We can't just take in a runaway apprentice."

"Talk to Drum about it. After we finish talking to him about these Indians."

"Do the Tyrees know?" I asked, and Bob nodded. "What do they say?"

"They're Christians. They're not afraid of anything."

I smiled at him. "You were all set to go out there alone."

"And remember what you told me? You can get honest-to-God dead fooling with Indians."

"Let's not fall down dead just yet."

"All right, Garvin. Go get scalped," he said, suddenly laughing. "You want to be a pioneer. Go get your hair lifted."

Drum returned to camp just before dinnertime, and I met James Pierce, our runaway, and heard, from him and from Drum, his story. His master had hit him with a wagon-spoke, which amounted—so said both Drum and the Quakers—to an attempt on his life. Therefore, he was free to go, since even though his articles weren't legally broken the attack was sufficient grounds to break them. You couldn't doubt for an instant that what the boy said was true. And it was true, too, that getting his bond broken would take court proceedings lasting weeks and maybe months—and the nearest court of competent jurisdiction was in Leavenworth.

He was a big boy, at least six and a half feet tall and skinny as a spider. He said that he was seventeen. He looked like a rooster with no feathers, but if I have ever seen a man without guile it was that boy. When he spoke, you knew that

[48]

what he said was true and that he meant it. It wasn't that he gave an impression of honesty, it was something far more solid: a sense of literal fact. In the time I knew Jim I never saw any of the ordinary boy's fantasy and melodrama about him. I suppose that was why he seemed so mature for his years.

He had come to the Tyrees with an offer to work his way with us and when they had explained that we were all working *and* paying, he had admitted that he didn't have the money. The Quakers had then asked Drum and McVey and Hopkins to let him join us for whatever he could pay. It turned out to be twenty dollars—in paper.

McVey waited until after supper to bring up the subject of the Indians, and this time he didn't let Hopkins tell the story. As we sat together in a ring about the fire, licking our fingers, he said: "Drum, how long is it since you've been up where we're going?"

"Well, now, that's hard to say, Mr. McVey. Some parts of it, I was up there last fall. Then, we'll be going through other country that I haven't seen in six or seven years."

"I take it the Indians were peaceful when you were up there."

"Still are."

"I hear they're kind of touchy these days."

"Where do you hear that?"

Willis explained, very coldly, about his friend the editor. Drum smiled tolerantly.

"Everybody seems to have the idea that the Indians are painted wildmen," he said, "and it just isn't so."

"People get killed by them," said McVey.

"Oh, yes. And people get killed by white men, too, Mr. McVey. Don't forget that. I know the Cheyenne. I know them well." He settled himself on his heels and gazed into the fire. "There's about three places up there we might meet Cheyenne. There's camps sometimes on Rush Creek and up around Wild Horse Springs and then up on the Arikaree. As a matter of fact, there's been one band camped on Rush Creek

[49]

all winter under a chief that I used to know: man named Bear Walks Around."

Martha Tyree asked: "Will we go there?"

"We may pass within fifty miles of there, I'd say."

"How do you know things haven't changed in seven years, Drum?" McVey demanded in a voice of exasperation.

"It's my business to know," Drum replied mildly, never taking his eyes off the trembling flames. "A long time ago," he said, "this chief, Bear Walks Around, killed a man of his tribe at a camp up on the Platte. I was there with a train of wagons under Joe Stallman, and the Indians were camped just below us. I was a young fellow myself. Bear Walks Around killed his man with a cavalry sword, not twenty foot from one of our wagons. It was a quarrel over a woman." Drum slowly shook his head in wonderment and pain. "He came to Stallman, because he thought of a wagon master as a kind of chief. He said that his people would be coming for him soon, and he wanted Joe to tell them where he was. He rode along the river a ways until he found a patch of willows. Then he built a little wickiup of branches and he took off his clothes and sat down in the wickiup to wait, with his sword on his knees. They came to us: men from one of the soldier bands that enforce the laws. We told them where he was and I got on my horse and rode along behind them along with another young fellow like me, who had to see. When they found him we held off a little ways and watched.

"They came on him at a gallop, and he never moved. He watched them. One of them killed his horse, first thing, and still he never moved. He just sat there naked in his little hut. They pulled it down over his head and they broke his saber in two and his bow and all of them together threw him down and whipped him with bow strings. He covered his face, but he didn't fight nor try to run. They beat him until he bled and left him. They even pulled his moccasins off and slashed them.

"When they were gone we rode down to where he was lying in the mud by the river bank. He wasn't hurt bad. He stood up and looked around at his smashed gear and his dead horse, and he waded into the river and washed away the blood and the dirt. He didn't want any help from us. I asked him if he wanted to ride double behind me, back to the camp. He said no. He wasn't going back. He couldn't. They had turned him out. 'For good?' I asked him. He said no, that they'd take him back someday. 'And what'll you do until then?' I says. 'I'll follow after them,' he says. We were about of an age, you understand, and he was more man already than I hope to be. 'They'll let me ride with them again,' he says, 'when the stink is off of me.' And he found his knife in the wreck of his gear, and he went over and started to skinning his horse. Peeling a horse is a job, you know, even with a good knife, and his was made from a piece of kettle handle. I helped him, and when we were done I gave him my horn-handle knife. He thanked me and he lifted the green, bloody hide onto his back that was all covered with welts from the whipping he'd had, and he limped off up the bank." Drum took off his hat and ran his hand across his white scalp. "That's how I come to know this chief," he said. "But there's more to the story.

"The Cheyenne hate murder more than you can understand. When one Cheyenne kills another, it curses the whole tribe. They say that the murderer has a smell that will kill crops, and they mean it. They turn him out. They won't kill him, you see. That would just be more murder, but they won't have him with them. Sometimes he goes away and lives with another tribe, like the Arapaho or the Sioux, but most often he and his wife and his children tag along behind their band, camping within a few miles of the main camp and getting along as best they can. If he does that, sooner or later they let him back in. They can't really harden their hearts against a brother. It isn't in them.

"Bear Walks Around followed after his band—him and his family—and one day, after four or five years, the soldiers came out to his tepee. It was soldiers from the same group that had beaten him before, up on the Platte. One of them brought Bear Walks Around a horse. It was his own horse, to replace the one he had shot that day. And one of the chiefs sent a saber, for the one that had been broken. And the next

[51]

day he took down his lodge and moved it into the camp with the rest of the band. It was all forgotten. The stink was off of him."

Joel Tyree, listening with a soft smile, murmured: "Christians."

McVey snorted. "What do they have to be Christians for?" he asked.

Drum went on. "There's no Christians among them, Mr. Tyree, as far as I know." He added, thoughtfully: "With all respect to you and your wife. Well, sir, Bear Walks Around was a hot-headed man, and he knew it and all the others knew it. He was ever in and out of quarrels. This was about the time that I was with the Army, and I was dealing a lot with the Cheyenne, in and out of their camps. He was a great warrior, but he had a bad name for his temper. He knew it, and he tried to behave, but he didn't have an easy time." Drum smiled and looked up at McVey, on the other side of the fire. "So they made him a chief," he said.

"Why was that?" asked Martha.

"Because a Cheyenne chief *has* to keep his temper. He has to be the first in charity and the last in anger. That's why. A Cheyenne chief, by custom, has to take four insults from any man before he can quarrel. The first four times, he must give a soft answer. The fifth time he can answer back."

I said: "You don't change a man by changing his title."

"They changed him," said Drum.

"Did they?" asked Martha.

"Yes, they did. I've seen him many times since, and I've been in council with him. He's as soft-spoken as you, Mr. Tyree, and generous to a fault. Of course, I've seen him when he had to bite his lip to hold in a harsh word—I mean, actually bite his lip. But that's the more credit to him."

Hopkins said: "The power of public opinion."

"There are men," said Joel Tyree, "that I would like to see made chiefs."

"Mr. Drum," I asked, "do you speak their language?"

"I used to talk Cheyenne pretty well. I imagine I can still get along at it."

[52]

McVey, who had been brooding silently over the story of Bear Walks Around, leaned toward the fire, and said, "That's how they feel about one Indian killing another Indian. What about whites?"

"No man blames you for killing your enemy in war," Drum answered.

"*No* man?" said Tyree with his sad smile.

"Do you?"

"Yes, I do. I don't mean I set myself up to judge; but, for myself, I would not do it."

Drum was thunderstruck. "You mean," he said, "no matter *what?* Self-defense?"

"Even then."

"You'd rather die than kill?"

"That's right."

"Does all your set hold to that? All Quakers?"

"We try to. The light of the Lord is within every man, Ned Drum. To strike him, is to strike that light."

Drum was fascinated. "Mr. Tyree," he said, "it isn't for me to say, but I don't think that even the Good Lord asks all that much: to let yourself be killed."

Martha said: " 'Thou shalt not kill.' The Commandment has no 'ifs' or 'buts' to it. It is only man's law that has 'ifs' and 'buts.' "

"It would be a cruel law that lacked them," I said.

"Man's law," she said, "is a frail thing beside God's."

The rest of us found no answer to that. What can you say to piety? Only Drum knew. He nodded his head slowly into his black beard. "Amen," he said.

The next day, as James Pierce went to work on the wagon along with Tyree, you had only to watch him for a few minutes to know that he was a thorough, clever workman. His long-fingered hands, like a pair of steel tools themselves, gripped wood or iron or leather with a knowing, forthright touch.

The horses and mules were my job. During the morning I tested them all in harness and under saddle and got to know

[53]

them a little. We still lacked two saddle horses. Hopkins had been getting about on one of the pack horses and he had asked me to help him buy a saddle mount for the trip. We had to have another for James Pierce, so after lunch I rode into town with the two of them to look over the offerings in the livery. The boy was mortified at the idea of our spending money on him, but he felt a little better when I explained that we would sell the horse in the mountains and make a profit.

"What part of the country do you come from, Jim?" I asked.

"Ohio State, sir."

"You needn't call me sir. What brought you out here?"

"I come with this Mr. Gaunt, that I was apprenticed to. He's with a wagon train bound for California."

"Why didn't you head back for home?"

He pursed his lips thoughtfully, like an old man. It was hard not to smile. "Well, sir," he said, "it just never come into my mind."

"Want to see the wild Indians?" I asked with a smile.

"No," he said judiciously. "I think I can learn a lot out here, from men like Mr. Drum."

"Want to be a guide?"

"No sir. I just want to learn how to get along on my own, the way he does. I respect a man who can do that."

At the stable, I selected an old bay mare for Pierce, making sure she was built tall enough to keep his feet from dragging. He was awesomely pleased. With Hopkins, I had a problem. Since it was his money, I couldn't just tell him what to buy. Besides, he was very sensitive about my helping him at all. He was no horseman, but if I picked a plain-out rocking chair for him he was sure to be wounded. On the other hand, it would be a needless cause of trouble for everyone if he got a mount he couldn't handle. I stood with him beside the corral and said: "See one you like the looks of?" and he pointed one out. It was wind-broken. The next he chose was just what I had expected: the raciest colt in the corral. I looked it over with a great show of concern and led it around. I could tell just by holding the bridle that it was not a gentle mount.

I gave the lead-line to the stableman and said to Hopkins, taking care that the owner didn't hear: "Sore feet. Wouldn't get twenty miles."

By this method, I worked down through his choices to a mount that was in good condition and which I judged would give him no trouble: a ten-year-old gray gelding with feet like snowshoes. From the fetlocks up, it was a fairly stylish looking horse. After adding two stout cavalry saddles to the bill, we left Pierce with the horses and Hopkins and I went to find McVey, who was to ride back out with us. The weather was improving. That sharp wind off the plains had died, and in front of some of the houses along the street there were flowers. The ground, too, had lost the crumbly feeling of cold. The sun was shining and a lot of people had come out to let it draw the cold from them.

"What's this about putting our trip in the newspaper?" I asked.

"Oh, I just happened to mention to Ned that I knew the editor and he asked me if I thought the paper would be interested in our story. As a matter of fact, I had already thought of it myself and I'd even mentioned it to them. Of course, they look on it from the point of view of developing and opening the western sections of the territory."

"Of course. How do you look on it?"

"They're going to pay me for the article. I'm writing it now. They'll hold it until we're a week or so along on the trail. That way no one will be tempted to try to beat us."

"I didn't know we were racing."

"Everything's a race out here," he said. "We're working against time. It won't be long before everything's taken. Fortunately, there are many who don't know they're in a race."

"Like me."

"The Lawrence paper has even asked me to send them some dispatches from the mountains. They're particularly interested in news of the gold fields. I was told that a party set out just last week up the Arkansas, heading for gold country in the Rockies. Pike's Peak."

"Is there gold there? For certain?"

"So I'm told. You know, it's a funny thing about gold rushes. The people who get rich in them are mostly those who can take their minds *off* the gold and sell picks and shovels to those who can't."

"That what you plan to do?"

"Among other possibilities. There's all the opportunity a man could ask right now—particularly because no one seems to realize how much opportunity there is."

"Except you?"

He lifted his eyebrows and twisted his mouth in a most self-satisfied way. "We shall see," he said.

As we crossed the street we saw a crowd of men coming up from the head of the street, by the ferry landing, and at first I thought it was the militia on drill. It was just a crowd of men, though, a couple of them carrying rifles.

We found McVey at the smithy and then the three of us went to the hardware for a keg of nails. As we came out of the store that same crowd of men, we saw, had stopped in front of the hotel. They were stalking about, or standing in little groups, and we could hear their talk like the growling of a pack of hounds. We stopped to watch and as we stood there other men came running up to the mob and joined it. One of them came past us from down the street: a fat man in a tight suit, puffing as he trotted and holding his felt hat clamped to his head with one hand. In the other hand he held a pistol.

"What's that?" asked Hopkins.

"Trouble," I said. "Let's go."

McVey said, "Let's find out what's going on."

I hefted the keg onto my shoulder and started across to the livery. Whatever was happening was none of our affair. Hopkins started to follow me, but Bob jammed his hands deep into the pockets of his coat and strode off toward the hotel. "Bob!" I cried, and in my fright and excitement my voice cracked. The first thing I thought of was that with his hands down in his pockets like that he looked as if he were armed. Hopkins, of course, spun around and trotted after him. I cursed, set the nail keg on the ground and started after them.

With my eyes on Bob's stubborn shoulders, I didn't see what happened. He stopped, and Willis came up beside him. The crowd in front of the hotel was gone: disappeared as if it had melted in the soft spring sun. One man remained. He was bent over in the middle of the street loading a revolver. He was having trouble with it and he bit his lip in frustration and excitement: a tall man with graying chin whiskers and a checkered vest. There was the sound of a shot and I realized that there had been others that I had heard but not really heard. The man in the checkered vest dropped his pistol and straightened up. Then he turned and ran off down the street. He began to stagger before he got very far, but he made it to the corner of the printing shop and disappeared. Hopkins, McVey, and I were alone in the street.

What the others did, I don't know. I ran back to my keg of nails, snatched it up and ran into the hardware store. The proprietor was standing by the door, as pale as his shirt. "Close the door!" I shouted. "Close the door!" He stared at me, so I closed the door myself. "Get the doctor!" was my next command. For the next few seconds I ran blindly around the store, still carrying my nails. The storekeeper got a rifle out of his storeroom and took up a defensive position just inside his door. Finally I calmed down a bit and stood behind the counter watching him. "What are they doing?" I asked.

"Who?"

"Whoever it is."

"Is it the Missouri men?" he asked.

"I don't know. I saw one man get shot."

Just then there was a rattle of gunfire, perhaps seven or eight shots, and next a horse thundered down the street past us. I didn't see who was riding it. Standing his rifle against the wall, the storekeeper began barricading his door with crates and barrels. The tiny store, and being where I couldn't see or get any idea of what was happening, began to work on my nerves. "Have you got a back door?" I asked.

"You going?" he said. He was frightened too, and I saw him for the first time: a stumpy man with a fringe of dirty-gray hair, puffing and straining at a crate too big for him to handle, his knuckles white as he gripped it, looking squarely at me, being honest, saying: "You going?"

"No," I said. "We'd better close it up."

"My God! I forgot about it. Here." He thrust his rifle into my hands and ran out through the back of the store. I heard the door slam and a barrel being rolled across the floor. I walked to the wall beside the door and peeped out. I could see the houses opposite and the door of the livery, but nothing else. There was not a human being in sight. Not even a corpse. The storekeeper came back and together we stood guard for five or ten minutes. Then we heard footsteps outside and a man in a beaver hat strolled casually past the door, glancing in at us curiously and sauntering on down toward the hotel as carefree as a preacher on a Sunday walk. We looked at each other and the storekeeper chuckled. When we heard no shots or yells or horses, he put down the rifle and commenced clearing the doorway. I helped him, and then he cautiously opened the door and we leaned out. There were people in the same pose at every door along the street and at most of the windows. A few were walking toward the hotel and every few seconds another brave one started out. I nodded to my host and stepped out into the street. My first impulse was to go and find out what had happened, but I realized I had better find Hopkins and McVey.

I wandered around for a bit on the edges of the throng that now milled in front of the hotel and eventually Hopkins found me. He came striding briskly across the street, grinning.

"Did you see it?" he asked.

"See what?"

"The shooting."

"The man in the street?"

"No, no!" he protested. He sounded as if that were the poorest shooting ever arranged. "Four men went up on the hotel porch and fired a volley through the windows. God knows how many they got. Then they rode off."

"Nobody stopped them?"

"No!" he chuckled. "You should have seen them! They were *magnificent,* Garvin. Cool as could be. They just marched up and fired and then jumped on their horses. Another one was holding the horses by the corner there, and they all rode off in different directions."

I glanced nervously at the men knotted around us. I didn't know what had happened, but I knew that the men who'd shot up the hotel were not likely to be the heroes of Whitaker.

"Where were you?" I asked.

"I stood in there." He pointed at a recess between the hardware store and the adjoining building. There was just about room for a man to stand sideways. He beamed and slapped his gloves against his thigh.

A hatless young man with drooping mustaches had climbed to the top of the hotel steps and begun to shout for attention. There was too much hubbub to get what he was saying, but I gathered that he wanted to go after "them" right now, to trail them down. The crowd-noise dropped a little as a few turned to listen to him, and over it I heard a voice I knew. It was McVey's voice, even though it couldn't be.

"That's right!" he shouted. "Let's have some killing!"

I looked wildly around for Bob, and so did a lot of other men.

"What we need is a little bloodshed!" he yelled hoarsely. "A little throat-cutting! Let's have ourselves a *real* play-party!"

He was backed against a store front across from the hotel. He had his fists clenched and his head down like a charging bull, and the sun struck sparks in his red beard.

"Come on, you militia!" he shouted. "Come on, you great defenders of Whitaker! Get out your repeating rifles and get on your horses and go kill somebody. What are you waiting for?"

Thank God the clamor that he stirred up drowned him out, for all but those right around him. As I pushed my way toward him he went on howling, railing at the whole mob, and some of them were beginning to scowl and mutter at him. I took his arm and he said: "Hell, Cooper, where've you

[59]

been? Come on and get in on the big murder and barn-burning."

"Come on with me," I said.

I dragged him as quickly as I could through the throng. He let himself be led, but he kept on railing, now half to himself. "Now here's a fine body of men!" he rasped. "Ready to do and die!"

"Be quiet and let's get out of here," I begged.

"What's the matter, Garvin? A little horseplay got you nervous?"

"What's into you?" I pleaded. "Quit it, Bob."

"You heard them. We're going to go off and start us a war. Hell! You don't want to miss that, do you?"

I let go of him and ran into the livery. James Pierce came running out to meet me shouting, "What happened?"

"I'll tell you later. Get those horses together and saddle them."

"They're ready."

Later, I found that as soon as he had realized something was wrong Pierce had saddled our horses and made ready to go. He was a good, level-headed boy. Hopkins had gone ahead of me into the stable and the three of us mounted. I led McVey's horse. He was standing in the street, shaking his head.

"We're going to miss the sport," he said.

"Mount up," I said, then I turned and rode at a sharp trot up the road—away from the milling, shouting crowd in front of the hotel—and circled the backs of the buildings to pick up the river road two hundred yards below the ferry. There I slowed to wait for the rest. Hopkins was not far behind me, bouncing along, and the other two caught up. McVey sat stiffly in his saddle, staring straight ahead. He was spent. Whatever rage, whatever despair had set him off, it had been vented now. When I saw his eyes I thought it better not to look into them, so I put my heels to my mare and led them at a good clip out to the camp.

As they saw us galloping up, the others dropped their work

and came together to meet us by the campfire. Drum held my horse as I dismounted.

"What happened?" he said calmly.

"There's been some shooting," I said. "I don't know just what it was about."

McVey rode up and sprang from his horse. "A picnic!" he cried. "Big Kansas picnic and shooting match! They're all going to kill each other, damn their souls!"

"We don't know who it was," I said, "but at least one man was shot in the street in front of the hotel. Then some other men fired into the hotel and ran for it."

Hopkins came up rather glumly, no longer delighted with having witnessed a real, honest gunfight. He eyed McVey from the side of his handsome face.

"Politics!" said Drum sternly. "Politics. They've stirred each other up and now the shooting is started again."

"Does thee know how many were hurt?" asked Joel.

"No." I told, once again, all that I had seen and what Willis had reported. I noticed that no one except Martha Tyree seemed to have noticed Bob's first outburst. He was standing, breathing deeply, looking back toward the town, and she was watching him with a kind of curious, pitying look. Drum turned to Hopkins.

"Do you think they were Missouri men, those that shot into the hotel?"

Hopkins got himself together and looked knowing. "That's what they looked like to me," he said firmly.

"Did they say anything that you heard?"

"No."

Drum shook his head and marched over to the fire. "If this is the start of real trouble," he said, "the best thing we can do is leave and travel fast. We're almost ready anyway, but I'd hate to run off without all the things we need if it isn't serious. I'd like to find out." He stared thoughtfully down the road toward town.

"I'll go back," I said, "and see what I can find out." The memory of my moment of panic in the hardware store was sharp.

"No, I think I'd better ride in," he said. "I have people I can talk to, who'll probably know what it was all about. Just in case it looks bad, why don't the rest of you get things in order so we can start packing."

Pierce fetched Drum's horse and saddled it. Before he mounted, Drum took off his coat and handed it to me. "I want everyone to see I'm unarmed," he said.

"Mr. Drum," I said, "I left the nails in the hardware store. You could pick them up."

We watched him ride off down the road alone. All but one of us did. As I turned back to the campfire I saw that Martha was still watching Bob with that same sorrowful face.

"Martha," I said, "what will you need help with?"

She took her eyes off McVey and shook her head. She went to the fire and silently began to get together her cooking gear. I called Pierce. "Get the horses together," I said, "and water them but don't let them take too much. Then come help us with the packs." Bob and Joel began stacking beside the wagon the things it was to carry. With Hopkins, I set to work dividing the rest of our stores into pack loads according to my memory of Drum's plan. The Tyrees struck their tent and rolled it. When Pierce had finished his work he asked me, "Should we harness a team?"

"Not yet. Let's wait until Drum comes back."

It took us an hour to break camp and get everything ready to pack. We then sat around the wagon and waited. We didn't have much to say. When Drum returned he didn't have the nails; he had enough to carry without them. As soon as we saw his horse, laden with sacks and tied parcels, we knew what the answer was. We lined up like mourners at the coffin as he rode in.

"The Missouri men," he said. He swung down from his horse and started unloading. He looked around the camp and nodded. "We'll straighten things out later," he said. "Here's some of our necessaries. I couldn't carry much. I think I've got the straight of what happened."

He started around, checking the pack loads I had made up, and we trooped after him to hear what he had found out. "A

[62]

bunch of Missouri men came to the edge of town and asked to talk to the sheriff and the town officers. A bunch of them went down there. These men had some kind of grievance. It seems there was somebody or other they wanted arrested here in town. Something about a land dispute. Anyway, that's what they said. About half a dozen of them left their horses at the landing and walked up to the hotel with the sheriff and some other fellows. They set in to quarreling and just as they got to the hotel somebody passed an insult or something and a man named Perkins drew a gun. That was the man you saw in front of the hotel. He shot and hurt somebody. Most of them ran, but Perkins stood in the street and loaded his pistol. While he was loading someone shot him from the hotel window. He ran around behind the print shop, where some of his friends were lying low, and in a minute he died."

The man in the checkered vest, biting his lip in vexation, was dead. Drum went on. "When the men down at the landing heard that Perkins was dead, they started carrying on and in a minute some of them rode into town. They came on the hotel from the side and while one of them held the horses the rest ran up and shot into the windows. Then they all rode out."

Drum completed his inspection and turned to face us. He pulled at his beard. "One man was killed outright in the hotel and another is like to die. A bunch of those militiamen got together and they've gone down the river towards Kolb's Crossing. Nobody knows what they mean to do, it seems, but there was about twenty-five of them, with repeating rifles. People are clearing out of town as fast as they can. They're boarding up their windows and locking their doors and hiding their goods. It looks bad. I think we'd best go."

The job of breaking the camp was nothing compared to loading the packs and the wagon. We grunted and strained and sweated, each of us intent on his own thoughts, and finally got it done. Tyree hitched his team and he and his wife climbed up on the wagon box. The rest of us mounted. Drum swung his beautiful horse around in front of the mules. He rode like a sack of meal, but any man would have looked like

[63]

a leader on that horse. "Just follow me," he said to Tyree. "James Pierce, you ride back behind the wagon and sing out if anything bounces out. Keep the pack horses in line and don't hurry them. Mr. Cooper, will you keep an eye on them and see that the packs don't trouble them? They may not be balanced very well." Then he took the buckskin horse out onto the road and turned it west.

4

THE first hours on the trail we didn't talk. We were all worked up, of course, and we were having a hard time realizing that we were really going, that we were riding for the mountains. It would be a little while before we settled down to putting one foot after another, to the tedious, painful business of riding a horse for seven hundred miles and God knows how many days. I kept myself busy with keeping a close watch on the packs. It was a good thing I felt the need to do it, for twice in the first two or three miles I had to call a halt while we readjusted a pack.

We turned off the river road after about an hour and headed southward into a maze of little, rolling, black-dirt knolls, with patches of woods folded into the creases. We kept to the high ground, where the footing was firmer, and from the crests you could see nothing ahead but more miles of flowing hills, greening with brand-new grass. As we began to sense the vastness ahead of us, we relaxed. We camped early, as soon as the shadows began to deepen in the bottoms, and Drum and I looked over the horses and found them all taking their loads well. I was proud of my work with the harness. Everything seemed to fit just fine, with no signs of chafing or strain.

We made our stop in a hollow, beside a mucky, slow-running creek. It was a pleasant spot and out of the night wind—

and our fire wouldn't be seen very far away. We ate heartily on beans and fat meat and johnny-cake, and we all spread our bedrolls as soon as the stock was bedded down and the camp cleared up. We were tired. The way Willis Hopkins was walking I guessed that his splay-foot gelding was punishing his behind pretty cruelly. I took out my cigar case and the thought came to me that I had only five cigars in it and about forty more in a bag on the wagon. I had been meaning to get a box of a hundred before we left, but it had slipped my mind. I had been meaning to get them just that morning. I would have remembered, if it hadn't been for the shooting. I thought of that and I could see the man in the checkered vest, his grayish whiskers stiff and straight, as he fussed with the pistol. If he had not had that trouble, would he have gotten away? What had it been that killed him? A cap that wouldn't fit? A little piece of paper folded the wrong way?

As we watched the fire die, Hopkins said wryly: "Now no one will know."

"Know what?" Martha asked sharply. She had been absent-minded all evening.

"About our project," said Hopkins. "The *Herald* won't get my article now."

"No great loss to the world," I said.

Hopkins grinned. "Why, Garvin," he said, "I want to make you famous."

Drum came from helping Joel with the Tyrees' tent and loomed over the fire. "We'll pass just south of Lawrence," he said. "You could ride up there and see the newspaper fellow and still catch up to us."

"It doesn't matter," Hopkins said thoughtfully. "It may be very definitely for the best."

"How's that?"

"I have another idea. I'm going to keep a journal of this trip, if no one minds."

"What for?" McVey wanted to know.

"I have an idea. I know someone who'd be interested in it, I think."

"Who's that?"

[66]

Hopkins hesitated a second and said: "The editor of the *New York Post.*"

"Is that a fact?" said Drum.

"Yes. My father knew him quite well."

"And you think that he might ... well, put it in his paper about this trip?"

"If it were written up the right way."

Drum rubbed his hands together and beamed around at us. "Well, now," he said, "that would be something, wouldn't it?" He chuckled. "I never imagined you might do anything like that, Mr. Hopkins. An article in the New York press!" McVey chuckled as Drum went on. "Well, I don't see anything wrong with that," he declared. "It isn't every day that a completely new country is opened up. It isn't every day that a new route is tried. It's an important thing, when you come down to it. No reason why it shouldn't be in the New York papers, that I can see."

I had my doubts, but I didn't see any reason to speak them. He was proud as could be. Besides, I had other things on my mind.

McVey had laid out his bed next to mine. When everyone was settling for sleep, and the fire was a bed of hot ashes, he moved over and sat down on my blanket beside me. For a little bit he just stared at the embers.

"I guess I could have got you and Hopkins hurt today," he said. "I forgot about you."

I shrugged. I waited and then said: "What got into you, Bob?"

He only shook his head. Then he reconsidered and made an effort to explain. "When I saw them all getting set to go crazy, I just decided to go crazy along with them."

"But you didn't mean what you were saying. They did."

"What can you do?" he asked the ashes. "What, for hell's sake, can you do?" He faced me. "Did you feel it, Garvin? Did those men look to you the way they looked to me? Or is it just me? There was a man lying dead in the hotel door. He was honest-to-God dead. Gone forever. Another one dead behind the print shop. And here were these fools getting ready

[67]

to make speeches and have a parade and kill more. I felt like giving up."

"It's none of ours," I said. "Forget it."

"We'll carry it with us," he said. "All the way, wherever we go."

He slapped at a mosquito buzzing around his ear. "Here," I said, "take a cigar. That'll keep the bugs away." He took an ember for a light and when he tossed it back into the fire a flash of sparks danced up and one of the horses whickered sleepily. "Bob," I said, "I couldn't kill a man. I wouldn't. I guess I feel the same way the Quakers do."

"That's what you say here and now," he answered. "You know what Martha said to me this evening, when I was pouring water for her? She said: 'Forgive them; for they know not what they do.' She was talking about me cursing them. She said that it's a sin to despair. Do you believe that?"

"I'm a lawyer, not a preacher."

He thrust his booted feet toward the fire and lay back on one elbow beside me. "I started to kill my father once," he said. "I could have done it, too. It was about a year ago. That's when I knew I had to leave before much longer." He gazed into the embers, but the fire was too low to show me anything of his face except the glitter of his beard.

After a little I asked: "A fight?"

He shook his head. "My dad's a good man, but he's a fool. I figured that out when I was little. He just hasn't got good sense. I don't mean he's a fool, because that isn't the word. He's stupid. He's thick." He hesitated, feeling for words.

"He's a lawyer, and he's been in politics all his life. He got onto General Jackson's coattails and for a while there he did pretty good. For a while he talked about running for Congress, but nobody would have voted for him. He just got elected to the state legislature twice, running as a Jackson man, and that was the highest he went. Then he had different state jobs that he was appointed to. About the time I was born Jackson lost hold of things and Dad was out in the cold. He practiced some law and about five years ago he got appointed county judge.

[68]

"Last year, when I was studying in Nashville, I began to make some good connections. I was all set, Cooper. I was going into an engineering company that builds bridges and dams. I was all ready. I wrote my dad about it and he came down from home and went up to see the people I was going to work for. He wanted to help me."

McVey's cigar lit up his face as he puffed fiercely for a moment. "Cooper, that fool went in there and blew himself up about what a big man he was in government, and he told them that if they treated me right he'd see they got plenty of state business. Old man Donaldson must have come near having a stroke. He was a fire-eating Presbyterian to begin with. Anyway, the next time I went around there Donaldson told me they couldn't use me. He said he knew I was all right but he couldn't afford to hire me after what my father had said. It would look too bad for him if it ever got out. He had my father sized up right. He knew the old man would go around telling everybody how he'd used his influence on Donaldson and Sons. So I was out. And I guess Donaldson spread the news around.

"I went up home to have it out with him. I just wanted to tell him what I thought of him. Well, he was sorry and he carried on and cussed old Donaldson, and then he started telling me how he was going to fix me up. He was going to see different people. I told him I didn't want him to. He said he was duty-bound to do it. I told him not to do any more harm than he already had. But he got on his high horse and told me I didn't know a thing about politics and he would take care of everything. Cooper, I begged him not to do it. He was set on it, though. We sat up in his office until midnight, while he went on about it. I tried everything. I couldn't think of what would put a stop to him. We had some liquor and smoked some pipes and the room got pretty smoky, so he opened a window. We were on the third floor of the courthouse, with a flagstone yard underneath the window. He leaned out that window, still carrying on about the people he would use his influence on, and I was standing right beside

[69]

him. He's no bigger than you, Cooper, and he was leaning halfway out already.

"He just did close that window in time. With the liquor all around, everyone would have thought he was drunk and fell out. He's known to be a drunk and a simpleton. Some of the things he's done!"

"Did he do what he said?" I asked.

"I guess so. I went back to Nashville and finished up school and then I went to work for a carpenter to get some experience with lumber. He wrote me a lot of letters about the things he had fixed up. Before long, every builder in Tennessee knew what he was up to and knew that everyone had heard about it. Any man that hired me would have been in jail for swindle within a week, I guess. The trouble was, my dad didn't have any influence, any more than he had good sense."

"So you left."

"Not because of the jobs. I was determined to get work on my own worth, and I could have done it. I told the whole story to a couple of big builders that knew me, and they told me to wait a few months. Donaldson promised to help me all he could if I could make my father shut his mouth. So I wrote him that I had a good job. I made up the name of the company. I told him everything was fine, that he could stop now. And I guess he did. No, that wasn't why I left. I left because he came down to Nashville once to see me, and I went up home two or three times, and every time I saw him all I could think of was how near I had come to putting him out that window. I would have done it, Cooper, if I'd had another minute."

He tossed the end of his cigar into the last, cooling coals of the fire. It was growing chilly. He sat up and drew his knees under his chin. We watched the embers. Bob's discarded cigar-end began to smoke on the coals and the ends curled and suddenly it flared up in a brief, fragile yellow flame that illumined the motionless, blanket-wrapped figures all around us and the wheels of the wagon and Bob's rough young face above his fierce beard. The darkness snuffed out that flame in an instant, and we were in blackness. I heard Bob rise and stamp his boots.

"Cold night," he said softly.

"We'd better turn in. There's a long day tomorrow."

"And plenty more after it," he said. "Good night."

I folded myself into my blankets and after a little bit I curled up with my knees against my chest. I thought about what Bob had told me, and then I began to think of my own father.

My father liked me, and he took it hard when I went away to the West. I remember still how he and I walked together up from the barn after I'd told him I was leaving.

"Is it the horse?" he said thoughtfully.

"Sir?"

"Is it the horse you want that's got you down on me?"

"No sir. I'm not that crazy for a horse."

"But you're down on me all the same, eh?"

"I didn't mean that. I just think I should go my own way."

"There's plenty here for you."

"I'm twenty-two years old," I said.

"By God! Don't you think I know how old you are?"

"I don't see what good I am to anyone around here."

He stopped and looked at me. "What good do you want to be, Garvin? What's your ambition? What do you aim for?"

"Someday I'd like to be a judge."

"Fine. I can make you a judge—down there." He raised his hand and pointed toward the town four miles away. He was telling the truth. He *could* make me a judge down there, given a little time to work on it.

"That's not what I had in mind," I said.

"I'm glad of that," he said, "but it might be a start. What court do you want to sit on, then?"

"I want to go as high as I can."

"Good. Good. You can do it." He lowered his eyes and began to pick bits of cotton lint from his suit front. We did our ginning right there on the place, and the dusty, grayish lint crept into everything: clothing, books, food, furniture. "Garvin," he said, "you're hardheaded, but I think you're right-headed, too. You can get cases. You're my son, but I don't mind saying that I think you're a smart lawyer because you're a smart man. You can get cases, but you'll have to go down to town and dig for them and ask for them."

"I know that."

"You think that people don't hire you because people don't like your ideas and your convictions. That makes you feel pretty big. The truth is, people make allowances for you, whether you know it or not. For one thing, you're my son; for another, your notions aren't quite as loud and fierce as you seem to think. The trouble is that you have the idea that anyone who doesn't agree with you about politics and religion and slavery is probably a thief and a rapist and God knows what. People feel it when you look down on them."

"I don't look down on people. I just don't see where anybody gets the nerve to take things for granted the way most do. But all this isn't why I'm leaving. I just feel like I have to go, if I'm ever to get started in law practice."

"Why?"

"I just don't feel like a lawyer here. In Brighton, it's like you said. I'm your son, and that's about all I am. Everyone I might work for or meet in court is somebody that knows you and me or is related to us or does business with us. It just is all wrong."

"I don't see why."

"I want to practice where I don't know all the feuds and scandals and where I'm not mixed up with the people; where it's just me and the law and a set of facts."

"You want law with the people sifted out. Is that it?"

"I'm learning. I want *law*. I want to learn it, pure, so that someday I can be a good judge."

"Well, you may be right. I could help you set up an office in Milledgeville."

I shook my head. "Maybe I'll come back," I said. "In a way I feel bad about leaving. But first I want to go out there to the West and get in on what's happening."

"Tell me something, son," he said. He was a little embarrassed. "Why Kansas?" I didn't answer, and he said: "You want to fight slavery. Well—that's what you feel you have to do. Why not fight it here, in your home? I'd think you'd rather root the evil out of your own yard than some place you've never even seen." He pronounced "the *evil*" very fastidiously.

"You'd break my back," I said, and he smiled.

"No, Garvin, I wouldn't do that. I know you think you have the right of it, and maybe you do. Come along, and let's tell your mother about this."

Aside from all these high-flown issues, of course, there were other, simpler reasons for my wanting to leave. For one thing, I was lonely. My father was about the only one in Brighton, Georgia, with whom I could hold a connected, intelligible conversation, and with him it was always savagely competitive. I was exhausted all the time from thrashing things out with him, for he made our every exchange into an assault on the ultimate values of life. For still another reason, I knew that he had more than he could do to take care of my mother and my two young sisters and to keep the land together, even with the help of my brother, a taciturn and self-contained man four years older than I, who had a deep love for hard, grinding work. It was the winter of 1857-58, and sometime during the last few months all the money had disappeared, and I don't mean only ours. I don't know where money goes when it disappears, but it all cleared out of our part of the country. No one had money to buy our cotton, and cotton is an inedible vegetable. We couldn't sell slaves, for no one had money to buy them, and slaves eat. We couldn't even set the slaves free to get out of feeding them, for by that time manumission was practically a legal impossibility; there had already been too much trouble from pinched farmers turning loose their dullest, weakest Negroes to lower their costs. We had seven hungry slaves, and a barnful of mildewing cotton.

My father led me up to the house and into the hot kitchen, calling for my mother. I stood by the door like a wooden soldier while he chafed his hands over the cook-fire. When my mother came in he said to her: "Mattie, we've got something to talk about. Garvin wants to go out to Kansas and set up on his own." That was his way; everything had to be talked about.

My mother was not at all upset by this announcement. She was a big, round, easy-going woman whose interest was always in details. Men she regarded as foreign bodies, living in a world which she did not question. This made something of a mockery of my father's strict practice of taking her into his confidence for all decisions, but at the same time it assured that he would always have his way. By the same division, she left the two boys to my father and reserved to herself my two pale, sickly little sisters. We all loved her, but I can scarcely remember her at all, as a person. Instead, she is an image symbolizing gentleness, grief, trust, and human kindness.

Still, I had expected the word "Kansas" to give her a turn. Kansas was an exotic name in those days, a name in newspaper stories about strife and hardship. As a matter of fact, I could not have told you that day whether it was mountains or prairies or fields of daisies.

The three of us sat at the kitchen table and my mother asked, only: "Have you made inquiries?"

"What does he need to inquire?" said my father.

"Well, he can't just set up law practice without any introductions, can he?"

"If he can't, he's out of luck. Who's to introduce him?"

I interrupted. "I may not even practice law, right away. I may wait a while."

"And do what in the meantime?" my father asked.

"I'm thinking I may get some land. All you have to do is stake off your claim and build on it. In one year it's yours."

"Are you going to farm?"

"I'll probably have to, at first."

He groaned. "You'll have your fill of that in a hurry. Farm if you want, but don't plant cotton. What do they grow out there?"

"I don't know. I'll have to find out. Of course, there's gold, too."

"Gold?" said my father sharply. "Have you got any notion what goes into digging gold?"

"Plenty of people have hit it," I said.

"You don't just pick it off the ground. When I first came to Georgia there were plenty of people hitting gold, too, up around Dahlonega, but they worked for it and for every one that found it a hundred went broke. There's two things wrong with gold-hunting, boy. You don't know where the gold is, and if you did you'd have a year's digging to reach it."

"I'm not saying that gold is what I'm after. It's just one possibility."

My brother came in about then, covered with lint, and when he found out what was going on he slapped my arm and then he and my father fell to arguing about what was the best way to travel to Kansas. My mother had wandered off, bemused, to look into my clothing supply. That was when it came to me that I was actually going. Father settled the argument about travel by giving me the horse, the one he'd earlier asked me about. It was a fine bay gelding with white stockings. He'd taken it in payment of a debt and had been planning to sell it. He didn't approve of keeping fancy horses. He advised me to ride it to Mobile and sell it for my ship passage up the Mississippi. I could take a coasting schooner to New Orleans and catch a packet boat there for the trip upriver to St. Louis. There I could change ships for the Missouri River. He got out maps that showed me where I'd be going—except that there was no Kansas on the maps, just a big region marked: Indian Territories. They were fifteen years old and, although we didn't realize it, they might as well have been fifty. "As I make it," he said, "Kansas runs about like this," and he drew a huge rectangle taking in most of the Rocky Mountains. Have you any notion just where you're going in Kansas?"

"The capital is in Leavenworth," I said.

"Here's a *Fort* Leavenworth, on the river."

"I'll look around after I get out there."

"What will you be looking for?"

"A place to settle."

"Well, how'll you judge it? Are you looking for a busy town or a pretty town or no town at all or what?"

"I'll take everything into consideration," I answered.

"If you can do that, my boy, you're a better man than I am . . . But try." He folded the maps and looked at me. "It's the kind of thing I would have done at your age," he said, but he did not say it as if he were proud or touched or amused. He sounded very sad and lost.

That night I went out to have a look at my horse. He was clean and healthy, with good feet. Willing, but not too well trained. I wanted to be very sure of my mount before I set out, for I had no intention of going to Mobile and selling the horse for passage to New Orleans and there taking packet for St. Louis and so forth. I had a good horse under me and I meant to ride to the West. I wasn't going to arrive out there on foot, coming from a steamship with a valise in my hand.

It was four days later that I actually set out, and it was a fine leave-taking. My father had little to say. He took me aside and told me to remember that the place to go when you're in trouble is home. My mother seemed to have the idea that there was a carpeted office in a marble building awaiting me just west of Birmingham. She had some suggestions about how to meet the right people in a strange town. My brother slapped me on the arm half a dozen times, slapped my horse, and cuffed a couple of pickaninnies. Then he lit up a pipe and watched me ride off. My two little sisters wept. The Negroes stood by the gate and waved, my horse ambled calmly out past them and I was gone from my home and my people.

The horse was not quite all my fortune. My father had added three hundred and fifty dollars in gold, a dozen sterling spoons and a pair of fine pistols. My mother's gift was a carving knife with a china handle. I still have it. My brother gave me a cigar case of soft calfskin and my two little sisters each made me a handkerchief with my initials worked in the corner. That was the sum of my goods. That, and some books. I had decided I could comfortably carry only three: one in each saddle bag and another in my coat. When it came to choosing the three books, though, I couldn't think what I wanted to carry. I was an educated man, with a law degree and some knowledge of the scope and direction of civilization; but with civilization to choose from on the shelves of my father's study, there seemed no part of it which was particularly my share. Well, I had a profession, so I chose Cardwell's *Common Law* for the right saddle-bag. It was a heavy book. To balance it on the left I took Aristotle: the *Ethics, Poetics,* and *Metaphysics,* in heavy board covers. For my pocket, after much thought, I decided to follow consensus, and I chose a limp leather volume of Shakespeare containing *The Winter's Tale, The Tempest,* and *King Lear.*

I changed my travel plans, of course. I had only to ride as far as Montgomery, Alabama, to see that my father's idea about the boats was very sound. I went to Mobile, sold the bay, sailed to New Orleans and took a side-wheeler up to St. Louis. There I caught the Missouri steamer on which I met Bob McVey.

Now I lay alone in the prairie night. The last ember had faded. There were strange night noises all around, but there were very ordinary noises, too: Drum's soft snoring, the stamping and blowing of the horses, the gurgle of the creek. I thought about the miles ahead. Drum was all right. If we got out of the settled part of the territory without running into trouble, it would just be a matter of sticking at it, one day after another, until the trip was done. So many miles a day until all the miles were gone. There would be hardships, but I would bear them well and so would Bob and James Pierce and probably the Tyrees and Willis Hopkins. We would make it. Then I thought: What a thing to have done! This prairie, for hundreds of miles, without a track or a road, without a town. We will have done it. Many will have gone the easy way, taking the roads and traveling with the wagon trains. We will have come alone across an unmarked way, with only ourselves to trust.

5

WE MADE an early start the next day, with Drum calling us
up in the first light. He took the trouble of reorganizing the
supplies a little to get things just the way he wanted them.
It was a clear day, the first really warm day of the season,
and we set out in good spirits, still heading south. Drum was
taking us to the Overland Trail, the main wagon route westward. He had already explained that we would stay with it
for the first ninety miles or so. We came upon the road about
mid-morning: a set of wheel-ruts. There was actually one
main pair of ruts, and on either side a lot of meandering
marks. With all the prairie to spread out on, the wagons never
felt much inclination to stick square in the road. To the west,
the trail wound over grassy, rolling land that rippled away
like ocean swells to the horizon. It was a pretty sight, with
some kind of purple wild-flower blossoming in splashes on
the sheltered hillsides, but all that up and down would keep
Tyree jumping on the reins of the wagon.

Martha Tyree, sitting the swaying wagon box beside her
husband, began to sing in her clear soprano. "Where O
Where is Old Elijah?" she sang, and Drum, riding up ahead,
turned in his saddle to boom out: "Where O Where is Old
Elijah?" Then I sang: "Where O Where is Old Elijah?" and
all altogether we answered: " 'Way over in the Promised
Land." Then the refrain: "By and by we will go and see

him." We sang it for a mile, Martha giving us the verses one after another, Drum taking it and then me, and everyone together on the last line and the refrain: " 'Way over in the Promised Land." After that one, we sang another and another, until our throats grew tired. Drum, his golden horse pacing along out front, looked as near to gay as he could come.

All that day, we rode the rolling grassland westward. The little, scrubby bushes that bordered the occasional wandering creeks were about the nearest thing to a tree that we saw. We all got grandly wet splashing through the creek fords, but they were no more than trickles for the most part. We stopped in the early afternoon for johnny-cake and coffee and Drum gave each of us a handful of dried apples.

A little later we came to the fork of the trails, where the Santa Fe freight wagons turned off to the south and the emigrant trains to California and Oregon angled north. Tyree pulled his team to a halt and his wife called to us to "Come look!" so we all rode up beside the wagon. There next to the rutted trail, just beyond the fork, a post had been driven into the ground with a sign at the top of it. The letters were weathered and faded, but still legible. It said: "The Road to Oregon." I stood in my stirrups and looked all around. There was no other mark of mankind on the whole of creation, except the lonely road and the bleached sign.

"Who put it there?" I asked.

Drum shook his head. "I couldn't tell you. This fork used to be further on up, but wagons keep cutting the corner and that moves the fork back." He smiled at us. "Seems they just can't wait," he said.

We made our second camp not far from there. We were much more at ease and the sensation of being on our way seemed to make everyone feel a little warmer toward the others. "How far have we come?" Hopkins asked at the campfire.

Drum thought about it and said, "Something over thirty miles."

"Then we must have made over twenty today."

"That's right."

"A good pace," Willis said knowingly.

"Fair. We'll have better days, though, once we get onto the high prairie, out of these hills."

"Where does that begin?"

"Oh, another hundred and fifty miles out."

We thought about that. "A week's travel," I observed.

"With luck," said Drum.

James Pierce said: "Mr. Drum, where is it that the Indians are?"

"There's Indians all through here. Pawnees and Kaws. We may see some of them before long."

"What'll we do?"

"We'll say good morning and keep a close eye on our movables. Settlement Indians, Jim. Thievish."

"What's a settlement Indian?"

"Lazy fellows that stay around near the white men, stealing and drinking whisky."

McVey said, "You know, we haven't got a drop of liquor with us."

"Do we need any?" asked Drum.

"It's a help."

"I can't say I ever saw anyone helped by it, Mr. McVey."

Bob laughed in very good humor. "You should see me, then, when I've got a little drop of help in me," he said. I smiled, and Drum wrinkled his nose very piously.

"We've a good-sized creek to cross tomorrow," he said. "We all need our sleep."

We reached Wakarusa Creek at mid-morning. It was another fair day, and we had been pushing right along as fast as the wagon could move, singing a verse now and then, all of us very cheerfully businesslike now that we had a few miles behind us and had seen that they were nothing to be afraid of. Even Hopkins loosened up to the extent of joking with me when I yelled at him for jostling the pack-line leader. We first saw the creek as a line of lush growth cutting the prairie ahead, and as the trail curved Drum explained that the ford was lower down. He rode beside the wagon as we crossed a gently sloping meadow and angled in toward the stream. Joel Tyree suddenly gave a yelp and reined in his team. He stood up on the box and stared ahead. I went up to see what it was and Drum said to me, "A nasty one here."

The "ford" looked to me like no ford at all. On the near side it was a sharp drop of about twenty feet into dark, oily water. The other side was easier.

"Are we going to cross here?" I asked.

"It's the best there is, Mr. Cooper. Bigger wagons than this one cross it every day." Drum turned and called to Pierce. "Oh, Jim," he said, "you help Mr. Tyree chain the rear wheels. Now, gentlemen, there's work for all of us."

Drum climbed onto the box and set the brakes as hard as he could. Regular wagon brakes were still a new-fangled thing in those days, and no one really trusted them. In addition to the regular shoe-type brakes, we had a rig called "wheel buckets," that Jim Pierce and Drum had fixed up. This was a pair of big wooden chocks, looking something like sugar scoops, that hung on chains in front of the front wheels. The chains were fixed under the box by pins so that the driver could yank on a cord, pull the pins, and drop the chocks in front of the wheels. Now, on top of all that fixings, Pierce and Tyree chained the back wheels so they couldn't turn.

While they worked at that, Drum and the rest of us picketed our horses and he unloaded a block-and-tackle made up on two double-sheave pulleys. As he straightened out the tackle I said: "Are we going to lift it across?"

"Just about."

Dragging the blocks, he walked down toward the ford with the rest of us following. In the grass just where the descent began to get steep, there was a post the size of a telegraph pole driven into the ground so that it angled slightly uphill. A notch had been cut into the pole about three feet from the ground and ropes used by thousands of emigrants had worn the notch smooth. Drum made a rope collar and hitched one end of the block and tackle to the post.

We got the wagon up to the post and fastened the other

end of the tackle to the rear axle. Then we unchained the wheels, but we left the brakes set. Joel stood on the box clucking to his mules as cheerfully as he could and ready, I saw, to jump. His wife and I brought up the second team, got them into harness and made fast to the hauling end of the block and tackle. We took up the slack, then Tyree sprang down and he and Drum quickly unhitched the front team. Now the wagon, weighing about two tons, was hanging over the ford like a bucket over a well, held by the second team.

Tyree drove the first team, with trailing traces, down into the ford. They plunged in up to their collars, but found footing and scrambled across. While he was doing that, Drum, with Pierce's help, was feverishly rigging lines to the wagon doubletree. Then the boy tumbled down the slope, paying out line behind him, and into the water. He came up gasping and grunting, and waded out to Tyree on the far side. There they made the two lines fast to the traces of the team.

"Everyone clear!" Drum shouted. "Now, Mr. Cooper, let's ease off a bit."

I was up in the meadow with the second team, and I had my back to the ford. I started backing them very slowly and the tackle groaned. It was all I could do to keep from turning around to watch that wagon smashed to flinders, but Drum called: "Little more! Easy, now! Little more!"

Backing inch by inch, we let the wagon down until it was practically standing on its head, just out of the water. The bank was that steep at the bottom: or so it looked. Then Tyree, on the far side, started very, very gently to haul on his team so as to lift the front end. The joints of the wagon popped and the braces screamed, and my two mules sank on their haunches as the whole weight of the wagon was suspended between the two teams. It was just as if you stretched a string between your two hands with a bucket hung in the middle—only my team had the advantage of the block and tackle, and the sunken post.

"Back them, Mr. Cooper!" Drum commanded. By then we had no more than twenty feet of line left between my team and the head block. I backed them, clucking to them and pleading

softly: "So-o-o now, mule! Do it easy! Handsome, now!"
and I could hear Tyree over on the other bank encouraging
his team.

There was a soft splash, and Drum called: "Ready, Tyree!"
and "Ease off some more, up top!" I gave another five feet,
and then Drum yelled: "On the far side: Hit 'em!" and
Tyree called to his mules just as both of mine tumbled to
their knees. Drum had slipped the knot on the axle, and my
team had fallen lurching against the sudden slack. But I didn't
know that, and I gave a shriek and jumped clear, thinking
that the two kicking mules were about to be dragged right
over me by the falling wagon. I tumbled down the slope and
fetched up with a thump on a bed of pebbles. Each pebble left
its own bruise and I sat up feeling as if I'd been rolled in a
dice cup.

"What's the matter, Cooper?" said McVey. "Fine dive,
but you missed the water."

I saw that everything was all right, the wagon standing
in shallow water, safe, and the whole party grinning at me.

"Bob," I said as I rose, "here's the spot for your very next
bridge."

We hauled the wagon, creaking and clanking, up onto high
ground and Tyree began to re-hitch his team while the rest
of us went back to finish the crossing and Martha did what
she could to straighten out our goods, all tumbled and tossed
in the descent. We were all feeling loose-limbed and silly from
the letdown and we talked and laughed a mile a minute. The
loose animals were easy to handle. Hopkins and McVey
herded them down and into the water with whoops and yells
and they splashed across. The pack train wasn't so easy. The
heavy-laden horses didn't like the steep footing, so Pierce
and I unhitched them and led them over one at a time, sliding
and balking and shying from the water. Before we were done
a light rain began. In all the excitement we hadn't noticed
when the sun went behind a cloud. When the last pack horse
was across I went back for Hoecake and when she slipped
on the way down I hadn't strength enough in my legs to keep
my seat and went right over backwards as she sat down and

[83]

slid sedately into the water. I was so wrung out I just lay there laughing weakly while McVey gibed at me from the far side.

We assembled at the wagon, all unhurt and with our gear intact, but feeling like the last waltz of the ball. Martha looked up into the rain, her hair lying like wet weeds, and said wistfully: "I was hoping to get my clothes dry; but not now."

It was getting chilly, and the rest of us nodded bleakly.

"There now," cried Drum, "we're over and no harm done. That wasn't so bad, was it?"

"It'll do," said McVey.

"There's worse ahead," said Drum. "That ford has a hard bed. It's the quicksand streams that make you want to quit."

He walked to his horse and mounted. The rest of us hesitated just a moment before starting to our places, and we must have looked pretty sorry, for he laughed and said: "We needn't kill the mules. I guess they can use a rest, and so can we. Besides, we wouldn't get far in what's left of today. Let's make camp right here."

As we prepared to camp, Drum called brightly to Willis: "Eight miles today, Mr. Hopkins."

None of us slept that night, unless Drum did. The rain wasn't hard; it was just a steady drizzle that turned toward morning into a clammy, dripping mist. We needed no one to turn us out. As soon as there was enough light for us to see what we were doing we got up and into fresh, but not quite dry, clothing. We stamped around chattering teeth at each other, aching in every bone, while Joel and Drum made a little fire beside the wagon out of some twigs and leaves that Drum had dried by keeping them in his bedroll all night. Then we huddled together and gulped down coffee and fat meat while Drum tried to be jolly with us.

"Spring rains," he said, "never last for long out here. We'll all feel better once we're in the saddle."

As miserable as I felt, I wondered about those others who weren't so used to riding. Pierce remained solemn as ever, but Hopkins had a very pinched look about him.

"Now's the time," said Drum as we mounted up, "when

[84]

we really need a song. Anyone can sing on a fair day. Mrs. Tyree, will you lead us?"

So, as the wagon lurched along in the muddy ruts, Martha bravely struck up "The Quaker's Wooing," and we all joined in. It really did make us feel better, but, looking back, it seems a little pathetic.

The mist and the chill continued all that day, and as the trail turned first to stew and then to soup, the mules began to make heavy going of it even though we turned out of the ruts and tried to keep to unused ground. We stopped for a cold lunch and to swap teams on the wagon, and in the afternoon we passed through a settled stretch of country where we saw, through a gray curtain of fog, snug little cabins of sod and new timber with smoke at the chimneys and light at the windows. We made camp just outside a little village of five or six cabins, and lay down in our damp, musty blankets trying not to think of the warm beds and hot suppers that the settlers were enjoying. We were just too exhausted by then *not* to sleep.

In the morning the mist was gone, but the sky was steely and the breeze was cold. Drum had rolled out before any of us and gone to the nearest cabin for some dry kindling, so when we woke up there was a crackling little fire where we could warm our boots. Martha fixed us a whopping hot breakfast and we felt a little more like pioneering.

We were back in the main valley of the Kansas, and for the next couple of days we saw lots of small farms and homesteads and a number of settlements. Instead of going into Topeka and taking the ferry across the Kansas, Drum decided that we would continue upstream to a place called Unionville where the river was broad and shallow and could be forded. We crossed a couple more creeks, but nothing like the Wakarusa, and pulled into Unionville early one evening just at the start of a fresh thundershower. In the morning it was still raining and the river was running high, so we talked it over and decided to go ahead and spend the ferry fare. Our crossing took two trips, and the work of handling the skittish livestock on and across and off the flat-bottomed ferry, with the thunder rumbling and the boatmen shouting and cursing, left us all pretty tired when we finally got collected on the north bank.

The prairie just above the ferry landing was a vast marshalling yard for emigrant trains, where they reorganized and formed up for the Overland Trail, and it seemed we would never get out of that morass of criss-crossing ruts and tracks, all gluey mud without a blade of grass. I think that if the rain had not let up just before evening, so that we could at least have a fire, we would all have given up and sunk like drowning men into the mud.

The discomfort and the hard work had shut each one back into himself, in a way. No one was much concerned with what the others were doing, or what they were thinking. The Tyrees clung pretty close together, of course; but then, they were set off from the rest of us right from the beginning by that tent of theirs. It probably wasn't much more comfortable than our bedrolls, for it was soaked right through after the second night, but it put them apart; at night when they went into it and tied the flap, closing us outside, there was always a little bit of uneasiness until they had settled down. That night above the Kansas, as McVey helped me bed down the horses he said: "It's the wagon that makes all the work. Hell, Cooper, you and me on horseback could be making twice the speed."

"For God's sake!" I moaned, wrestling a sodden pack to the ground, "we're not even out of the settlements. I'm glad to have company. Alone I'd have quit by now."

"Alone we could stop at these homesteads and get put up in a bed at night." He heaved a saddle and muttered: "Him and his goddamned spring rains!" The horse butted at him nervously and he gave it an irritable slap to shove it away. The horse was already on edge and at the blow it tossed its head, slipped the lead-line and galloped away tossing a bucket of mud at every step.

"You can go get that one," I said.

He stared in exasperation after the runaway as it turned and headed at a trot up the trail ahead. "Does it matter what

I do when I get him?" he asked, and trudged off to saddle his horse.

Supper was ready by the time Bob returned. He came back at a trot, whistling, with the horse on a hand line. The rest of us were just squatting at the fire when he rode in and called to us: "Wagon train up ahead." He picketed the pack horse with the rest, unsaddled his mount, and stalked jauntily up to the fire. "Thirty or forty wagons parked up there," he said.

"Emigrants?" Drum asked.

"They say they're going to Oregon. They've really got those wagons fixed up, you know." Martha helped him to beans and johnny-cake and he found a semi-dry spot to squat. "Lot of them," he said, "sleep in the wagons. Just like home. I had a look at one of them. High and dry."

"Where they from?" I asked.

"Different places—mostly down along the Mississippi: Memphis, Natchez, New Orleans. Young people, mostly. Couple of fine little gals. Quite a few of them."

McVey hummed softly to himself as he put away his beans.

Drum said: "Well, there's some stars coming out. That's a good sign. Maybe it'll be clear tomorrow." We all looked up and, sure enough, three or four wan stars shone in the darkening sky.

"Those people up ahead," said McVey, "really know how to do their pioneering. Lot of them have regular cook stoves set up by the wagons. Pictures. China cups and saucers. Comforters and quilts on the beds. Some of them just put a mattress right in the tail of the wagon. Right snug."

Martha said: "I'd like to know how they got those china cups and saucers across Wakarusa Creek in one piece."

"They've got plenty of quilts and feather beds to pack stuff in," Bob said. He finished his beans and sipped at his coffee. "They're even carrying guitars and banjos and fiddles. Tell me they have music and dancing every night that the weather's good."

Martha glanced up at the sky. "They'll not dance tonight, then."

[87]

"Oh, they might," he said, and he folded his arms across his knees. He looked into the fire for a moment and suddenly began to sing:

> "Back your donkey up Sourwood Mountain,
>   Hey! Diddle-um-tee rink-tum-day!
> So many pretty girls I can't count 'em,
>   Hey! Diddle-um-tee do-wa-day!"

"What do you call that song?" asked Martha.

"Damned if I know. It's an old one."

"Are there more verses?"

"I guess, but that's the only one I know. Hey! Diddle-um-tee rink-tum-day! How about a little more coffee?"

"Martha," I said, "why don't you lead 'Pretty Polly'?"

"That's the way," said Drum. "There's a song we all know."

So we sang "Pretty Polly" and a couple more. Martha really had a pretty voice, if she just hadn't made all the songs —even the funny ones—sound so rare and serious and wistful. When we stopped we all sat still and McVey cocked his head as the sharp sound of fiddle-scraping came to us from the night up ahead. It was a long way off, but you could hear the fiddle plainly, and a little bit of the jingle of a banjo.

"Play party," said McVey.

"How about 'The Quaker's Wooing'?" I said.

Bob stood up. "I'm going for a ride," he said. "There's one of those little gals I'd like to dance a step with." And he turned and went, humming his song, toward the hobbled horses.

"Well," said Drum, "Who'll take the tenor?"

"I'll try it," Hopkins answered.

"Mrs. Tyree?" And Martha turned back to the fire and began, "The Quaker's Wooing." We were singing as Bob saddled, mounted, and rode out.

We didn't turn in quite as early that night as we were used to. We sang, and had some more coffee, and looked up at the stars, and talked about the weather.

[88]

"You know," said Drum abruptly after a silence, "this Mr. McVey is a strange sort of fellow. You never can tell what he's liable to do. I wonder what got into his head to go riding off to that camp alone in the middle of the night?"

"He wants to dance," said Hopkins.

"Well, there's nothing wrong with that. One party calls on another all the time, sort of visiting. That's expected. But he acted almost like he was invited and we weren't."

"That could be, couldn't it?" said Martha.

"I don't hardly see how."

She laughed. "Thee is a mother hen, Ned Drum," she said. "It's late now. Good night," and she went alone to the tent. Joel joined her very shortly, Pierce crawled into his blankets, and Hopkins and I pulled off our boots. Drum fussed about the fire, now and then glancing up toward the road ahead at some sound.

"Going to bed?" I asked.

"I don't know," he answered, very perplexed. "This is a strange thing, Mr. Cooper. You don't reckon Mr. McVey is in any trouble, do you? Got lost in the dark?"

Hopkins chuckled. "I imagine he knows his way around in the dark."

"It's right late," Drum declared. "Maybe I should ride a ways up the trail and see about him."

"I wouldn't," I said, and I crept into my clammy blankets.

"Well," he said, "I don't hear any more of that music. They certainly aren't dancing *now*."

No one answered him, and with a little more muttering he finally got to bed.

I was wakened in the chill just before dawn by Drum. I lifted myself stiffly to my elbows and looked around the camp. Everyone else was still asleep. The wagon, dripping with dew, the huddled blanket rolls, the sea of mud around us and the stolid, sleeping horses and mules, looked very grim and pitiful in the weak, gray light.

"Mr. Cooper," said Drum, squatting beside me and whispering hoarsely, "I'm worried about Mr. McVey."

[89]

I looked at the bedroll next to mine. It was still empty.

"He's all right, Ned," I said.

"But he's been gone all night."

"He's up at that wagon-train camp."

"All night?" Drum said incredulously. "What would he do there all night?"

I couldn't help laughing, sleepily. "Ned, he went up there to see some girl."

He stared at me and then muttered something I didn't catch. When I asked him he said: "Nothing. I'm just afraid he may have got lost trying to come back here after dark."

"If he did, he won't go far, and he'll turn up now that he's got light."

Drum's stage whisper had waked Jim Pierce, who crawled out of his blankets, tugged into his boots and began to poke the warm ashes of last night's fire. Drum sighed and went to stir Hopkins while I got up.

Pierce and I went to look after the stock and when we got back to the wagon Drum had the kettle on. Martha shortly came from the tent, her face still puffy with sleep, and as she began mixing meal for johnny-cake Drum kept looking nervously from her to Bob's empty bedroll to me to the trail ahead. As we gathered about the fire for breakfast I watched Martha with interest. She noticed as soon as we were together that Bob was missing, and she glanced once, quickly, at his neat, unused blankets. Then she began eating. Drum cleared his throat and said: "I'm a little worried about Mr. McVey. He may have got lost."

No one said anything at all, and he waggled his beard unhappily. "It's a serious thing," he said. "He could wander all over creation and never find us."

"If he's not back in an hour or so," I said, "we can start worrying."

Drum stood up and looked angrily around the horizon, as if Bob might be in sight. "What kind of a way is this to do?" he cried.

"Let it be, Ned Drum," said Martha serenely.

"But what can he have in his mind, to stay out like this?"

"Let it be," she repeated.

Very unhappily, Drum finished his breakfast. Then we broke camp with no more said about Bob—although Ned kept looking peevishly up the road now and then. I rolled Bob's bedroll and stowed it in the wagon. As Drum was saddling his horse I went over to him and said, quietly: "We'll overtake that wagon train soon. If he's not with them we'll know something's wrong." He started to exclaim about it all over again, but I didn't listen. We were just getting under way when Bob appeared up on the trail, topping the rise that had separated us from the emigrant camp at a canter. Drum trotted out to meet him, but the rest of us just went on with the order of march.

"Mr. McVey!" Drum cried excitedly, "there you are! You've given us a bad turn, you know!"

Bob pulled in his dun horse and smiled at Drum. "I overslept," he said cheerily. "Am I too late for breakfast?"

"Breakfast!" cried Drum. He was sitting his horse square in the middle of the trail, so Joel had no choice but to rein in his team and we came to a stop with the two of them facing each other in front of us. "Breakfast!" Drum repeated. "Well I think you *are* too late for breakfast, and mighty near too late for dinner. Overslept!"

"I'll do without breakfast," said McVey, and he swung his horse around to clear the road. He waited a moment, but Drum still sat staring at him. Bob, whose face was turning red now, finally said: "Well?"

"It beats tar out of me," said Drum. "We didn't have any notion where you were. You could have been lost or drowned or Lord knows what."

"I told you I was going visiting, Drum."

"You didn't say you meant to stay the night."

"What the devil is that to you?"

"I'm responsible! That's what it is to me!"

Bob stared at him narrowly. Only the flush on his face showed how unsettled he was. "I'll tend to my affairs," he said, "and you attend to yours." With that he turned the dun about and trotted back to the rear of the wagon. Drum turned

[91]

about in the saddle to follow Bob with his eyes. Then he straightened up, glanced once at Joel, shook his head, and put his golden horse into a walk.

During the whole business, I had kept looking out of the corner of my eye at Martha Tyree. She had sat throughout looking down at her hands, folded primly in her lap.

Within an hour we overtook the last wagon of the emigrant train ahead. We got a good view of them as we topped a rise : their white, ship's-sail tops rocking along in clumsy row. In all, their line of march was strung for nearly a mile along the trail, counting the riders out ahead searching out holes in the trail and the herd of loose oxen plodding at the rear. We were an hour passing them, and there was a lot of waving and calling-out between us. Bob was right. They were mostly young people : red-necked men trudging beside their ox teams, swinging their long whips; scrubbed-looking young farm-wives with their pale faces hidden way back in deep poke bonnets; a few knobbly children. The drivers would nod solemnly to us or call out to ask where we came from. The women waved and bobbed their bonnets. The little ones stared or fluttered their hands.

It was the girls that I looked at. Whenever I spied a pretty one I'd steal a look at Bob to see if he'd give himself away, but it was useless; he seemed to know just about everybody in the train. For him they laughed or waved their hats or winked and shouted a joke. It must have been quite a dance. I had to settle on one little black-haired girl who sat holding with both hands to the cover hoops of one wagon as she rode on a pile of bedding just inside the tail gate. When Bob came in sight she let go with both hands (that was worth her life, the way those big wagons lurched and rolled) and waved, shouting : "Hey, there ! Rattlin' Hound !" and he rode in by her wagon to touch his hat, grinning, and exchange a word with her as he leaned from his saddle.

When he got a little further on, just passing the leading wagons, I rode up beside Bob and asked him : "What does that mean : 'Rattlin' Hound'?"

"I showed her a dance called Rattling Hound. It's a kind of a shuffle we 'do back home."

"I'll bet," I said, grinning.

He threw back his head and gave a whoop, and then he laughed with me.

6

IT was not long after that that we saw our first Indians. We were once more traveling west, now staying always close to the Kansas on the north bank. Although the weather continued gray and windy, the rain let up, and it was pleasant country we were traveling. The river bottom was well forested with oaks and buttonwood, all in fine new leaf. Settlement was sparse and the trail was very rough, for we had left the Overland Trail the same day we passed the wagon train.

The first good grass that we found in the river bottom, Drum called a halt to rest and graze the stock. The sun came out a little that day and we were able to spread our blankets and get some of the damp out of them. It turned into a two-day stop, for Drum reckoned up and found that the next day was a Sunday and, as he said: "It's good to have a regular day of rest, and Sunday is the right day for it." That day, as on all the Sundays after, there were devotions led by Drum before breakfast. This began with a lengthy prayer during which Drum stood with his hands folded before him and his eyes squeezed tightly shut. His prayers were pretty much the same: entreaties for the Almighty to watch over us and guide us—tinged with pride as he explained what a bold and dangerous and grand thing we were doing. He likened us often to the children of Israel in their long wander-ings. Then he would read Scripture, usually a whole chapter from the Old Testament. He leaned toward the feats of kings and war leaders and one of his favorites was in Exodus. I remember how he glowed as he chanted: "And the Lord went before by day in a pillar of cloud, to lead them the way; and by night in a pillar of fire, to give them light; to go by day and night."

After the reading there would always be another prayer. Sometimes he asked Joel Tyree to deliver the second prayer, and once he asked me. I told him I knew no prayers. The whole service took about half an hour, usually, and although I am not a church-going man I found it no bother, except that Drum was not a very good reader. But Hopkins always sulked during the devotions and McVey's eyes would slowly glaze over with distraction. Rest, contemplation, and meditation were not in Bob. Whenever he was silent for half an hour you could almost see him building bridges in his head. James Pierce was Drum's only real congregation for these times of worship. The Tyrees, I could tell, had only professional tolerance for his efforts. They held their own little meeting later on, with earnest talk between the two of them, broken from time to time by moments of shared meditation. Drum often sat with them, but their religion was not his kind. He was more businesslike.

The remainder of our day of rest we usually spent doing minor jobs of repair, reading, talking, singing, and napping under the wagon. I usually read my Aristotle for a couple of hours every Sunday, and I found that Hopkins also read Greek. He was, it developed, a Yale graduate, and although he did not find the College of William and Mary very impressive, he thought better of me the minute he saw the book in my hand. We even managed to have a couple of polite arguments about philosophy. He was far better read than I, and knew it, but I was his match in Aristotle and, being a lawyer, could quote by memory from the *Politics,* which set him down sharply. He argued anxiously, and a point won or lost was always terribly important to him. If I felt like baiting him I would try to bring the talk around to our trip, our companions and then, subtly, to horsemanship. I found that it galled him dreadfully that he was such a poor rider, even though there was no reason he should be a good one. Everyone in the party, except him, had at some time or another remarked on my way with a horse, and I'm afraid I occasionally bludgeoned Hopkins with my reputation. It was easy to do, for the little, biting envies he had for each of us were painful to see. Willis was clever and quick-thinking. He could read Greek much better and faster than I, and quote from authors I had only heard of; yet the things that mattered to him were the things he was weak on. He envied me my horsemanship, Drum his knowledge of the plains, Tyree his easy craftsmanship, McVey his fluent sketches, and Pierce his trade. He seemed determined to meet each one of us on the other's best ground.

It was the evening of that first Sabbath that the Indians turned up: three Kaw braves coming up from the river afoot, bundled in soggy blankets. Compared to the civilized Delawares and Shawnees back around Whitaker, these were real wild men—thin, watchful, silent, with their heads all shaved except for a roach down the middle and with their faces streaked in white and red paint. They squatted just outside our fire circle and stared.

"Just go right on eating," said Drum. It wasn't easy, with a pair of dark eyes following each mouthful from the plate to your lips. After a bit Drum made up three little packets of flour with a strip of fat meat in each and gave them to the three Indians. Silently, they ate the flour and sucked the meat. When they'd got all the fat off they sat contentedly chewing the rinds. They made no effort to talk to us, except by signs of eating, pointing at objects, and the like, and Drum said he didn't know their language. About the time we bedded down the three of them rose and melted into the night.

For the next week, as we followed the Kansas westward, the Kaws were almost always with us. Usually it was one or two braves, some of them mounted on poor, starveling ponies but most of them afoot; and once we entertained a whole family: three braves, four squaws, and six thin children.

Sometimes a group would ride along near us during the day, but more often they came into our camp at nightfall. They were no bother, although if they got too close you found their blankets a little high for civilized noses. If you paid no attention they would edge closer and closer into the camp and soon be curiously fingering knives, firearms, clothing, pots, or whatever else was handy. When that happened, Drum always warned them off by shouting and waving his arms, but he was careful to make little gifts from time to time—usually flour and meat. One evening a gawky brave refused to be warned off, however, as he was dipping his fingers into the meal bag to help himself. When Drum waved at him he just scowled and stuffed another handful into his mouth. When Drum came closer he rose and dropped his blanket—standing naked in the firelight except for a loin cloth and a beaded belt—and drew his knife. But Drum grabbed him by the top-knot and began thumping his skull with his knuckles, and the Indian howled, twisted away, and ran—leaving his blanket and the knife he had dropped without even trying to use. These Drum courteously sent to him by one of his companions.

"Don't you try that," he warned us. "I can tell when it's safe. That young fellow was just putting on an act. An older man, one with a reputation to think of, might have put that knife right into me."

The weather got steadily better, and once the sun took hold it really began to bear down. The streams were still pretty high from the rains, though. We forded the Big Blue and ferried Republican River where it came down through rough, grassless, flinty hills that seemed, when the sun hit them right, to be strewn with jewels. Beyond Fort Riley we saw no more isolated settlements. The river valley opened out, the river itself became clear and sandy, and the trees on either side thinned out to scattered clumps of cottonwood. Then we noticed that the trail had ended. Somewhere, it had just melted into the ground without our noticing. The rolling, sandy valley was easy traveling, though, and in patches along the river there were blossoming vines that looked a little like honeysuckle. The Indians' visits stopped.

We forded the Solomon River on the third of June, the first really hot day of the trip. Square in the middle we mired the wagon in a sand bar. We double-hitched the two teams and while Martha handled the reins standing up to her waist in water beside the wagon all the rest of us got down and put our shoulders to the spokes. The mules couldn't really hit a good pull, with the water washing the sand under their feet as they heaved, and the harder we struggled the deeper the wagon sank. When the water was lapping the floor boards, and the wheels were in the sand almost to the hubs, we gave up and began unloading. We had to go a quarter of a mile downstream to find cottonwoods of any size, and when we had felled and trimmed enough of them for a fair-sized raft we had to drag them overland with a team because the current was too strong for us to float them up. By then it was dark, and we lay down on the bank to sleep, blistered, bruised, and exhausted and with no cover but our saddle pads. Drum and Joel spent the night on the wagon, to give warning in case the current threatened it, and took turns sleeping and watching.

It was a moonless night, but there were stars so bright and seeming so close that they would almost dazzle you if you turned on your back. Hopkins and Pierce collapsed into sleep like dead men. McVey and I cut a little brush, laid it out and covered it to make a bed for Martha. Then we lay down nearby. I was so racked and shattered with that day's work that it seemed I couldn't pull myself together for sleep. As I lay there, breathing deep and with my head swimming, I heard Bob say: "Sleep well, Martha."

After a long time, when there was nothing but the rush of the water and the calls of the night birds, she said, very softly, "Does thee miss thy feather bed tonight, Robert McVey?"

"Damned if I don't," he said. "Does thee miss thy tent?"

"Is thee a Quaker now, with the Plain Talk?" That was what they called their "thee" and "thou"—Plain Talk.

[98]

"I'm a friend to all," he said, "and a helper in time of need."

After another silence, she said softly: "In the tent, the stars are shut off."

"So is the rain."

"Yes," she sighed. The branches creaked as she shifted. "Could thee see the stars from thy feather bed?"

"A few."

"Does thee care for anyone, Robert McVey?"

"A woman?"

"Not that. Anyone. Your people, or friends. Does thee care for anyone?"

"What makes you ask that?"

"Thee does not care for us. Thee shuts us out, or turns away from us. And thee turns away from all—the way thee cursed the men the day of the fight in Whitaker."

"What about that? I was a little hot, that day."

"Other days thee is cold. Does thee hate all men? Does thee look down?"

"Not all," he said.

The branches creaked again. "Do they disappoint thee so?"

There was another long silence, and at last he said: "I guess they do, Martha."

"I am sorry."

"Don't be sorry for me!" he said, a little louder than before.

She went: "Sh-h-h," and for a moment they were both silent. "We would be thy friends," she said. "All of us. There is no need to turn away from us and shut us out. No one judges thee or blames thee. Thee need not hide thyself from us."

I heard his very soft laugh, and the sound of his movement. Something scraped on the ground. I held my breath and could make out the whisper of his stocking feet. "Martha," he said, his voice sounding a little nearer to me, "I told you not to feel sorry for me. Do you feel sorry for yourself?"

"No, Robert," she breathed. "No, no. Go thee to bed. Dream of feather beds."

[99]

"The hell with that feather bed. It's far gone now, and her with it."

"Get thee to bed!" she whispered urgently.

His feet went whispering across the ground again, and he crept quietly back into his blankets. I uncoiled slowly and let out my breath with a deathly sigh.

In the morning we built our raft on the near shore and towed it out to the wagon. We ran a line to the far side and fastened the raft to it with a running hitch. Then we loaded it and poled laboriously across. It took the whole morning to unload the wagon: six trips with the raft. By then we were all near breaking and the two suns—one in the sky and another flashing, shattered one in the water—had seared our faces and hands. We had lunch and then rested in the scant shade of the scrubby brush along the bank. Drum, who usually kept us hopping right along, said nothing to hurry us. For once, he was as beaten as the rest of us. I was glad for the exhaustion that stretched us all mute and gasping, each to himself.

I was afraid that Bob might not be willing to leave things where they were with Martha; and I was not even sure about the woman, for that matter. As long as they were both laid out in stupor, they were safe. It was some consolation that Martha, by daylight, was now quite a sight. Her hair drooped in frizzy hanks and her nose and cheeks and brows were burned an angry, puffy scarlet.

I began to worry, as I thought about it, about Pierce and Hopkins. Had they gone so quickly to sleep? Had they slept so soundly? I watched their faces. I felt that Pierce, if he knew anything, would surely give himself away. About Hopkins I was not so sure.

When we'd got our breath back we hitched a team and drove them out to the mired wagon. With the lot of us heaving at the wheels, they hauled it free and Joel drove up and parked beside our stacked goods.

"We'd better go over our things," said Drum, "and check what we need. Tomorrow we'll reach Salina. That's the last chance we'll have to buy supplies."

"What's beyond that?" I asked.

"Nothing. The plains. Four hundred miles, more or less."

We had all flopped wearily down in a row in the shade of the wagon.

"You mean," said Bob, "four hundred miles like this?"

"That's about the size of it," said Drum. "It gets a little flatter, and we won't see many trees. We'll be cooking over grass fires, pretty soon, unless we find buffalo chips."

"What's that?"

"Buffalo droppings, dried in the sun. Burns good."

"Are we out of the Indian country?" asked Pierce.

"Just coming to it, Jim. Plains Indians, not these trail beggers you saw back there."

McVey said: "Pretty country." He was looking out ahead, up the broad, flat valley. We all turned and looked. There was nothing to see, at first. Just treeless flatland rising gently away, rocky and brown, sparsely covered with spiky grass.

"Looks bare to me," said Joel.

"Strong country," said Bob.

Drum said: "That's right, Mr. McVey. Strong country. That's just what it is. That's well put."

As your eyes took it in, you realized how far you were seeing, how much of one piece the world had become. The horizon, sharp and clean as a knife's edge, made your eyes hurt. The river wandered, broad and gleaming, out into the green-brown vastness and was lost somewhere between us and the sky.

Joel Tyree was a good man to travel with. He was a hard worker, and skillful with his hands. He was so quiet that you tended to forget his presence. With the little bee I now had in my bonnet, I began to pay more attention to him. In fact, I rode beside the wagon for quite a ways the next day just to talk to him. I was pleased, and a little surprised, to find him a quietly humorous man, once he loosened a little. What I mean to say is, things pleased him. Almost *any* things.

He nodded to indicate the prairie ahead. "I have been

thinking what Robert McVey said about this land," he said.

" 'Strong country.' That is a thing he *would* say. He's right. He is a very seeing man, Robert."

"Yes, he is," I observed.

"Does thee know him well?"

"I think so."

"He is a good man, I think. He is too short with himself, perhaps, but he must be a strong man. I think he will reach the place he is going."

"Don't you expect to, yourself?"

"I do not always know just where I am going, I'm afraid. That's because I like to be with others like me, and yet I've left them."

"Oh, now!" said Martha, "at meeting thee is ever disputing and disputing. Thee only misses that."

He smiled and nodded. "I like talk," he said, "but I cannot talk on many things." He pursed his lips and leaned out over the rumps of his mules, chirping to them as he guided them across a rough spot. "Now I know," he said, with the most childlike delight, "about Robert McVey. Robert is an Old Testament man!"

I laughed. "A prophet?" I asked. "Jeremiah?"

"He would have been a warrior," said Joel. "The young David, perhaps."

I thought of Uriah's wife. "The next town is the last one," I said. "After Salina, nothing."

"I want to see it," he said. Then that smile of bland pleasure, and: "Curiosity is a kind of pride!"

"If there were no sin," said Martha, "Joel would invent it, just so he might think about its clever ways."

"It is clever," he said, "because we are so clever. Always nosing out the hidden, tedious ways around God. It is strange."

"If you like that," I said, "you'd make a good lawyer."

He shook his head. "I would always defend the guilty," he said.

I wondered.

"What made you come out here?" I asked.

"This land is new," he said. "We are young and free, and that gives us the opportunity to come here and bring with us whatever we can."

"Religion, you mean."

"I am not so proud as to claim that," he smiled. Then, as if it were no change of subject at all, he said: "Robert McVey does not trust our guide, Ned Drum. I think it is because he does not want to, because he does not trust himself to trust any man, because he is afraid to. Does thee know him well enough to tell if I am wrong?"

I took a moment to digest that complicated idea, and said, "I don't think you're altogether right. Bob's not a fool."

"No, no," he agreed, still smiling lightly out over the reins in his hands. "He is no fool. I think that it would help if someone talked to him. Does thee think that he would mind if Martha tried to do it?"

I looked over at the woman. She was looking at her husband with a very serious, judicious expression. Then she turned her eyes, questioningly, upon me.

"Not at all," I said. "But I think it would be a waste of time."

"Time can be well wasted," said Joel. "We have much of it, too."

Late that day we had our first sight of the river we had been hearing so much about: the Smoky Hill. It is formed when the Kansas splits into two streams. One fork comes down from the northwest and is called the Saline River. The other bends up from the south; that's the Smoky Hill. We forded the Saline easily, the river bed firm underfoot and the water no higher than your knee.

When we had pulled up onto the bank I noticed McVey leaning from his saddle as he studied something on the ground. I rode over and he pointed to the sand under his horse's hooves. In the space of about a square yard, there were eight or ten parallel ripples of the kind formed in the bed of a stream.

"That river's been high," he said.

"It sure has."

I swung from my saddle and paced off the distance to the water. It was eight yards. Drum saw us fooling about and came over to see what we were doing. Bob showed him the ripples and made some comment like: "Look how high this water has come." Drum sat for an instant and stared dubiously down at the sand. Then he frowned and shook his head.

"A rain pool," he said.

"You wouldn't have ripples in a rain pool," said Bob. "The current makes these ripples."

"If the river was ever that high," said Drum, "it would have taken a long time to fall, and the rain would have washed away those ripples by now."

"Maybe there hasn't been any rain."

Drum stared at him in astonishment. "Of course there's been rain," he said.

At that, McVey got hot. "What do you mean, 'Of course?' How do you know there's been rain?"

"There's bound to have been rain."

"Why?"

"That's a funny idea," Drum complained. "No rain! I don't know where you'd get that idea. Besides, if the river was ever this high, then how come those ripples are just in one place?"

"The rest were leveled by the wind," said McVey quickly. "These are in a little hollow here."

"Just the kind of hollow where you'd get a rain pool."

There they had come full circle, and I laughed out loud at both of them. Drum looked at me irritably. "I don't know where you fellows get the idea that it doesn't rain out here," he said, and he turned his yellow gelding and rode with great dignity to his place at the head of the march. McVey looked down at me.

"What's wrong with that man?" he demanded.

"My God!" I said. "What a thing to argue about!" and we forgot the whole business.

We camped that night on the bank of a little stream that came into the river a few miles further down.

"Salina's just upstream," said Drum, "but there's no need taking the wagon down there. We'll ride down for our supplies. We're going to leave the Smoky Hill for a little ways now. It makes a big bend down to the south, almost a loop, and then straightens out to the west. We'll go up this creek here and then pick up the river again further out. We'll cut off a day's travel or more." He turned his head to look at the prairie, rising westward. "This is the jumping-off place," he said. "We'll go over our gear and our stock as careful as we can. Mr. Cooper, I'd appreciate it if you'd have a look at the horses and the mules. Mr. Tyree, you and Jim had best inspect the wagon and see how it's standing up. Mr. Hopkins and Mrs. Tyree and I will go over the food and the rest of the gear." He paused, looking at Bob. "Now let's see, Mr. McVey, if there isn't something you can do." Bob instantly turned crimson, but Drum seemed not to notice. He went rambling on, looking vacantly around the camp. "There must be something," he said. "I guess you could lend a hand to... No! I've got just the thing. You might as well go over the firearms. Make sure everything is clean and oiled and in working order. All right?"

"Fine," said McVey brightly. "Then can I shoot something?"

Drum laughed. "Not much to shoot just yet, I'm afraid. But you'll get your chance. From here on we'll depend on killing game for our meat. Are you a good shot, Mr. McVey?"

"I'm fair."

"Maybe we'll give you the job, then," Drum chuckled. He was in high good humor. He bustled around unloading the wagon, clambering in and out like a boy and beaming on his helpers, Martha and Willis, while the rest of us began the chores he had set for us.

There wasn't much daylight left in that day, so we made a start on getting things in order, had an early supper and went eagerly to bed. On the trail we usually didn't stop moving as long as there was light enough to make out the ground in front of our mules, and by the time we had made camp, fixed and eaten our supper and bedded down the stock, it was late—particularly since Drum regularly called us up at dawn.

As we stretched out in our blankets McVey said to me: "You know, Garvin, there's one thing the same about every woman. They all want a chance to make some man over."

"That's about right."

"Poor Martha's out of luck," he said. "Most women can remake their husbands; but Joel's already perfect." He chuckled happily and bade me good night.

We all worked pretty steadily through the morning, but it was restful just to be out of the saddle. I was off by myself, with the livestock, and that was restful too. When I came in for lunch Drum said to me: "Well, Mr. Cooper, how do they look?"

"Good enough, for the most part. That bay mare in the pack string has the beginnings of a quarter crack. Maybe we ought to let her travel light for a couple of weeks. She might still be some use."

"Does it look bad?"

"No, but it will. She needs a month on soft pasture."

"What's a quarter crack?" asked Willis.

"A crack in the hoof, around at the side. As it opens up under pressure, the horse goes lame."

"We can leave her," said Tyree. "No need to make her suffer needlessly. Couldn't we trade her down in this town?"

"Not likely," said Drum. "There isn't much to Salina. We won't find a livery, anyway. We'll drive her along, if you think it wise, Mr. Cooper. We may have need of her."

I pointed out to the west with my spoon. "If it's rocky out there, she won't get far."

"It is a shame to take her," said Martha.

"Funny thing about horses," I said. "There's no sense to the way they're put together. Here you've got a thousand pounds, more or less, of horse. Big bones and heavy muscles.

And the whole business is set up on four little feet half the size of a man's. Poor planning."

Drum frowned. "I wouldn't scarcely call it *that*," he said.

"It's true," I said. "A horse's feet are a poor job of work."

"*We* think so," smiled Joel. "That's only because we ask more of them than God meant them to give. They belong on the grass. We take them onto stone and clay and hard roads."

"Maybe," I said, "but it has always bothered me. Spindly legs, exposed tendons, brittle hooves. It looks slipshod."

Hopkins laughed. "Who do you blame?" he asked.

"The horses," I answered. "It's just like them to be weakest where they ought to be strongest."

"I thought you were crazy about horses," said McVey.

"They fascinate me," I said, "many ways. But I face facts: they're vicious and stupid."

Martha, who had been quietly eating her beans, cried out in protest. "Garvin! Thee is unfair! They are poor beasts, and we make use of them. We cannot blame them for what they are."

"Besides," said Drum firmly, "I've seen horses as smart as any dog, and I've never seen a vicious horse that wasn't made that way in training."

I shook my head. "I can't see the horse's side of it, I guess, but I don't see why I should. We try to make something out of the world, and the world doesn't care and doesn't help. We just have to beat it into the shape we want it—horses included."

McVey listened with interest to what I said and nodded thoughtfully, but Martha dismissed me with a wave of her hand. "Thee is only being perverse," she said.

"Every place that man has gone and broken new ground," said Drum, "the horse has gone with him and been his best helper. All the great people of the bygone ages depended on the horse."

"If there'd been no horses," I said, "we would have used camels, or lions or elephants. Anything. We had to have something to pull and carry for us, so we made do with the horse."

[107]

Drum chewed over my heresy for a moment. Joel Tyree looked up at me. "Thee is a cynic," he said lightly.

"Just because I don't love horses? I don't love any animals, and I don't see how anyone can, to tell the truth."

"You've never been alone," Drum said, "on the prairie, in hostile Indian land, with no food and scant water, and your life depending on a horse."

"I hope I never am."

"You may be," he said solemnly, "very soon."

"And if I get out alive it'll be my doing, not the horse's. Men broke and trained the horse. Men saddled and shod him. I ride him and control him by my will and my skill."

"Even with no danger at all," Drum insisted, "a horse can be a lot of company alone out there."

"Not half as much as the poorest man alive would be."

"I can't understand you, Mr. Cooper. I hate to hear you talk like this. All you say may be true. I don't grant it is, but it may be. Just the same, shouldn't a man have some faith in the animal that he may have to depend on someday? Isn't it best for his peace of mind?"

"It would be, but the truth is there for anyone who looks: You hear about how loyal and smart and affectionate horses are, and it just isn't so. It may be sad, but it's true."

"I'd hate to have to feel that way."

"Garvin's right," said McVey softly. "It's best to face the facts."

Drum shook his head. He pointed to where our stock was grazing down by the creek. "If I didn't have my faith in that yellow horse of mine," he said, "half my nerve would be gone."

"Keep thy faith," said Martha.

"He's right, Garvin," said Hopkins. "We do great things only by deceiving ourselves into faith. Skeptics like you and me will never storm the battlements. But we have to admit that there are battlements that need storming."

"I stick with Cooper," said Bob. "I'd rather count on myself. Then I know the limits."

Martha said to me: "Tell me this. If thee really feels this

way, why is thee such a horseman? Why is thee so fond of them and kind to them?"

"It's not fondness," I said. "I just know how you have to treat a horse to get the best from him."

"Thee said that horses fascinate thee. Why?"

I thought about the question seriously for a moment. "I suppose I want to have power over them," I said.

"Shame!" she cried. "So thee does them down in an argument. And they are mute."

I smiled at her. "I never heard of a horse saddling a man," I said.

"Mr. Cooper," said Jim Pierce, who had been silent so far, although listening closely, "I think you're wrong. A horse can be right fond of a man."

We were all a little surprised. The boy rarely spoke in our campfire talks, and never to enter an argument on anyone's side. He seemed very upset about this. He looked at me and then around at the others, who were all smiling at him.

"It isn't something that you have to believe, either," he said. "It's a fact."

Martha leaned over and put out her hand to touch his arm. "Thee is right, Jim," she said with a smile. "Thee speaks from thy heart. Thee is right."

7

WE went down to Salina that afternoon, Martha riding side-wise in front of Joel, to renew our supplies of meal, salt, flour, fat and sugar—and for a last look at the world of man. The town was as close as you could come to no town at all: three log huts with sod roofs, a corral containing a mule and three pitiful Indian ponies, and a sort of pavilion of split timber where the traders laid out their goods whenever Indians came in to trade. The head man, a red-whiskered and merry little Scotsman, let us use the pavilion so that we could tie up our horses and assemble our supplies in the shade. Drum asked the man what he had heard of the Plains Indians.

"You do not hear *of* them," he chuckled in a thick burr. "You see them or you don't, and in between they may be on the moon."

"Have they been trading lately?"

"There was five Kiowas in here three days ago. The last before that was two weeks: a big bunch of Cheyennes."

"What band?" asked Drum.

"I dinna know them all that well, man."

"Do you remember any of their names?"

"Ah, one of their names sounds like another to me," he laughed. We were loading our supplies on the two pack horses we had brought with us, while he sprawled on one of the big trading tables, puffing a short pipe. "You've a long way to go," he said.

"It's shorter than it might be," smiled Drum.

"Aye. If you follow the river south," he said, "and then keep on going south when the river turns west, you'll hit the Santa Fe Trail about forty miles from here. Why don't you take it?"

Drum continued counting out little bags of salt. He managed to be polite. "Because that's not what we're out to do," he said.

"Aye, I know. You're going straight across." He sat up on the edge of the table and dangled his short legs onto the bench below. "The rains have been good around here," he said, "but all the while that river has kept falling. All the spring it's been getting lower. Now, to me that means there's been no rain out on the prairie."

McVey leaned forward with interest, but he waited for what Drum would say. So did the rest of us.

"Those Cheyennes that came in here," said Drum, "rode all the way down from the headwaters of this river. *They* found water, and so will we."

The Scotsman shrugged and smiled. "Who knows what keeps an Indian alive out there? It's my belief they can eat dirt and get fat on it."

McVey said: "How far down is the river?"

"Oh, along here it's dropped about two feet since December."

Bob looked quizzically at Drum, who did not deign to notice him. He wrapped his bundle of salt and turned to fit it onto the packload. Then Pierce helped him put a hitch across the load.

"Before you leave," said the Scot, "I wish you'd join me in a drink. Just one minute." He hopped down from the table and hurried into his cabin. He was back in a moment with a brown bottle clutched in his hand. He drew the cork tenderly and set the bottle on the table. "I keep it hid," he said, "because of the Indians. Have a drink, Mr. Drum, with my good wishes."

[111]

Drum hesitated only briefly, then he made the trader a smile, took up the bottle and held it briefly to his lips. "Thank you," he said. The trader passed it to McVey, who tipped the bottle high and drank deep. He gasped and smacked his lips and said: "That's good whisky."

"Aye," said the Scot.

I was next, then Hopkins. Joel declined with his bland smile, but Pierce gulped a husky swallow. The trader drank last, and lovingly. Then he looked down at the bottle in his hand, replaced the cork and gave it a ceremonious tap with his palm. For a moment we stood in silence, each with his eyes upon that bottle so that we must have looked as if we were in silent prayer. Then the trader smiled up at us and said, "It isn't often I have company. My two friends are up at Fort Riley for supplies. They'll be sorry they missed you. We make a rule never to drink whisky unless there's other white men stopping here to drink with us. That way we're not likely to drink more than we ought. Not many come this way. I wish you good luck."

When we had all mounted and were riding back out to our camp, he walked out after us a little way to wave a farewell. He was a decent, friendly fellow, and this felt very much like a real leave-taking.

Back at the camp, we put everything in shape for an early start. At least an hour of daylight was left to us after our supper, and we sang a couple of our favorite songs while we watched the sun slip down the last stretch of western sky.

"We've made a good start," said Drum, "and I think we are ready for what's ahead. Before we set out now, I'd like to tell you again that what we are doing is a big thing. That fellow back there wished us luck, and I think there's many another would do the same, if he knew what we're up to. That's a fact. We must pull together, and have good spirit. To do that we have to remember what our aim is, and that it's a good one. It's easy to forget that every step your horse takes is part of the whole trip. Try to remember, and the steps will seem easier."

McVey sniffed audibly, and for an instant I despised him for it. Why couldn't he leave Drum alone?

We separated to spend the last light of that day in our different ways. Hopkins sat beside the wagon writing in a notebook. I asked him if that were his journal of the trip and he said it was, but made it plain that he wanted no help. Drum went out to the hobbled horses and started currying his yellow gelding. Joel and Martha sat beside the cook-fire talking softly. Jim Pierce found something to put his hands to: whittling a pot-hook from a cottonwood stick. McVey took out his drawing board, that he hadn't used since Whitaker, and sat down on the spit of land where the creek joined the river, sketching.

I read Cardwell for a while. At least, I sat in the red glow of the falling sun with the book open on my knees. I couldn't keep my mind on law. The anger I had felt when Bob scoffed at Drum kept hold of me, nagging at my mind and tripping my thoughts, until I had to stop and admit that I was not really angry—I was simply a little afraid. Now that we stood on the threshold of the unknown I was seeing my companions in a different light. Not that I knew them any better—far from it. Rather, I realized how little I knew them, and how deeply I had committed myself to the hands of a crowd of strangers whose strengths and weaknesses could be my life or my death. I closed my book and went to the Tyrees, beside the fire, almost as if by being near them I might make them more solid and more real. They smiled and made room for me; I guess my feelings must have been all over my face.

"This time tomorrow," said Joel, "we will be making our own trail."

"Ned Drum's trail," his wife corrected.

Joel nodded. "This means a great lot to him."

"To us, too," I said, "now that we're in it with him."

Martha looked down toward the river. In the failing light we could make out the form of Bob, squatting with his drawing board on his knees, his head bent. The sun, in its last red decline, struck the water of the creek at his feet and

[113]

made of it a gleaming trough of blood, silhouetting him against flashing crimson.

"I know," she said, "why Robert McVey scoffs and gibes at Ned Drum: it is because he envies him his dream."

"Envy?" I said. "Bob has his own plans."

"His building? His bridges?" She shook her head slowly. "I think that all these buildings are something that he has seized upon to be his dream. I think it is not real."

"He hasn't had a chance yet."

"He takes a strange way to find his chance," she mused.

"Everyone has his own way. He wants to be left alone."

"I know," she nodded. "Perhaps he wants no one to look too closely at this vision of his, and see it empty."

"No," I said flatly. "Bob knows what he wants to do, and he wants to do it well, and he wants the chance."

"The bridges that he draws," she said, "are but a sign that he carries. And I think he does not know what the sign really stands for."

"Maybe you're the one who doesn't know."

She continued, unperturbed. "He wants to understand Ned Drum, and share Ned's courage. I wish I could help him understand."

"He has plenty of courage," I insisted. "And, speaking of visions and dreams, why don't you respect Bob's, the way you respect Drum's? That's what he has, you know. Bob has some kind of ambition and vision—whatever it is, and black as it is. Why not leave it alone?"

"You are very fond of him, aren't you?"

"I respect him because he wants to think for himself."

Willis Hopkins, who had stopped his writing as the light failed, plopped down beside me with his notebook clutched tightly under his arm and said: "Who's that?"

"We were talking of Robert McVey," said Martha.

"Well, it isn't 'thinking' that Bob wants to do; it's something else." Hopkins looked at me. "What happened to him that day we left?" he asked.

I shrugged. "He just ran out of patience."

"He certainly did. I hope he never runs out of patience with me. He looked dangerous."

"To himself," I said.

"What did he do?" asked Martha.

"He started making fun of an angry mob," said Hopkins, "at the top of his voice."

She lowered her head and sighed. "Poor man," she said.

"Save your pity," I said.

"By all means," Hopkins agreed. "I think that Bob may be stronger than any of us."

The sun was nearly down. Against the paling reflection in the water we could see McVey rise, with a sudden uncoiling motion, and turn to come up toward us. He strode up, slapping his drawing board against his thigh, and gave us a tolerant, amused smile. "You're a gloomy crowd," he said. "What are you worried about? Drum's in charge. All is safe and sure." He shook his head. "As long as we're in this," he said, "let's be cheerful about it. Let's have a song."

We were rolled out of our beds the next morning with a wild hurrah. There was a whoop and a clatter and I sat up in my blankets to see Bob, in his underwear and his shirt, frantically pulling on his boots. "Look there!" he shouted, pointing up the creek. I turned just in time to see the white rumps of three bounding deer as they leaped off into the dawn. McVey snatched up his rifle and went romping after them at full speed. The rest of us crawled hurriedly out of our bedrolls and began to dress, and in a moment Joel Tyree stuck his head out of the tent and asked what was going on.

When we told him he said: "Lord! We thought it was the Indians."

By the time we had breakfast started McVey was back, empty-handed and chagrined. We all jeered good-naturedly at him as he got into his pants.

"It won't do you any good to be a dead shot," said Drum, "if you can't get close enough for a hit, Mr. McVey."

"There's no cover," said Bob.

"Not a bit. You have to use a little guile on them."

[115]

"Funny looking deer. What do you call them?"

"Not exactly a deer," said Drum. "They're pronghorns. You've heard of them as antelope, most likely."

"Good eating?"

"Fine eating," Drum chuckled, "once they're in the pot. Not much good running around up on the prairie, though."

"I'll put one in the pot," said McVey, "the next time they come nosing around camp."

"You're going to make us wait, are you?"

"Come on," said McVey, rising. "Get your rifle and let's go. I'll bring one down just as quick as you will."

"Later, Mr. McVey. They're probably close along the water up there. I'll show you how to get one. You don't need to wait until they come to camp." He reached his cup to Martha and she poured the coffee still bubbling. Drum laughed. "I learned about shooting in camp, I remember, when I was along with Bill Reed, twenty-five years ago, on the Missouri. We were camped with our flatboat beached, trading with the Mandans. Woke up one night and found a herd of buffalo stomping and snuffling around. Quick as a flash I loaded my rifle and shot the nearest one to me, and the others went off running. Reed comes up and says: 'Drum, what do you think you've done?' 'Fetched us some meat,' I says. 'You've broke camp,' he says. I says, 'How's that?' 'Well,' Reed says, 'It's easier to move camp than to move that buffalo.' I hadn't thought of that. You see, there was four of us to eat, and about a ton of buffalo, I guess. It was summer. We moved, all right."

Tyree chuckled. "That's when you were new out here?"

"There wasn't any 'out here' back then. That was 1833. All this part of the country was thought to be a big desert. No one knew. Then someone had the gumption to come out here and look, and it opened up. Easy as that."

"How do you know it was so easy?" said McVey.

"Oh, I don't mean it was easy. It was hard, I know; but it was done and here we are. There's just a few more places yet to be opened, and that will be that. It won't be long."

"I guess it won't," said Tyree.

"No. There's one or two trips like ours left to be made."

"Last chance," said McVey drily.

"For a fellow like me," said Drum, "that's about it."

"Why didn't you come out here back in 1833, Drum?" asked Bob.

"I don't know," said Drum. "I don't know." He didn't mean just 1833. He was thinking of all the past twenty-five years.

"No gumption?" said Bob.

Drum gave a sheepish short of chuckle. "Didn't think of it," he said.

"Thee must have started very young," said Joel.

"Yes. I was fourteen, when I come out here, and twenty when I first hired as a guide. That was in '32. I took a party of surveyors up the Missouri, working for the government. I was guide, and the youngest man in the party. Twenty years old."

"That's more than I had done," I said, "when I was twenty. Two years ago. I was just finishing school."

"Different sort of a thing," said Drum. "After all, Mr. Cooper, you're a professional man." He sighed. "Different sort of a thing altogether."

"Mr. Drum," asked Pierce, "don't you think a man can learn just as much from getting out and working as he can from studying?"

"Oh, I guess he can, Jim. But, I swear, I don't know what I've learned. I expect Mr. Cooper knows just as much as I do."

McVey grunted. "I hope you've learned the way across this prairie," he said.

Drum said, "That's the one thing I do know, Mr. McVey. If I don't know that, I don't know anything."

"Is that right?" Bob said, smiling.

"Absolutely," Drum replied.

We followed the creek all that day, up a rocky, sandy hillside grown with coarse grass and scrubby brush. Along the water-course things were green, but twenty yards out to either side the weeds grew brittle and brown, crackling underfoot. The rise of the land was gentle, but it was enough to make the mules' work pretty hard. Along with the rocky ground, it kept us to a pitiful pace. By the noon halt we had not covered more than six or seven miles. It wasn't long after lunch that Drum signaled a halt and called Bob up to the head of the party. He pointed to the ground beside the creek and showed us the tracks and the fresh droppings of the antelope that McVey had chased that morning.

"Bring that rifle of yours," he said to McVey, "and we'll go ahead on foot and see if we can't catch sight of them. They'll be browsing along the water, most likely. You too, Mr. Cooper, if you'd like."

The three of us dismounted, left our horses with the wagon and pushed on ahead. It was not like strolling in the park, and Drum went like a scared horse. When we had gained about a mile on the struggling wagon, he slowed up and cautioned us to silence as he began scanning the slope ahead for sight of the pronghorns. I was about to fall, and McVey, with his heavy rifle, was blowing like a whale. We got a chance to catch our breath when Drum stopped long enough to cut a slender sapling from a clump of stunted cottonwoods that we passed. He trimmed it with his clasp-knife to make a light staff about six feet long and then was off again, using it like a walking-stick. Just about the time Bob and I began to reel and stumble, Drum spied the antelope: five of them grazing together along the creekside so far away that I had to look for quite a while to see them at all. Their coats of tawny brown washed with white blended perfectly with the scrubby prairie, but when they moved you could see them. McVey and I were panting like hounds, but Drum showed no sign of wear at all.

"Are you loaded, Mr. McVey? Cock your rifle."

"Drum," Bob gasped, "if you think anybody can hit those things from here, let's see *you* do it."

"I'm going to bring them down to us," said Drum. "But get cocked first. They can hear that hammer click half a mile away. And be still. They can see an ant on a woodpile, if he's moving." Drum crept, very slowly and carefully and

with no sudden movement, into the cover of a sandy bank
overgrown with green-brown reeds. As we settled ourselves
into the hot, dry sand, he rolled on his back, drew his blue
bandanna handkerchief from his pocket and began to tie it
to the end of his cottonwood staff. "Get comfortable," he
said, "because we'll have to lie still for a little. And when
you shoot, Mr. McVey, pick one of the does. The bucks make
poor eating."

Then Drum slowly lifted his makeshift blue flag as high
as his arms could raise it. He held it still for a moment, then
he wig-wagged it gently from side to side. I peered through
the reeds to see what effect this had on the pronghorns. The
buck stopped grazing and stood frozen with his eyes on the
fluttering handkerchief as Drum continued to wave. One by
one, the does, as they noticed their lord and master on the
alert, raised their heads too, and stood motionless to watch.
They remained like that for what must have been two or
three minutes, while Drum kept wig-wagging. Then the buck
gave a shake of his head and trotted a few yards down
toward us. There he stopped and played statue again, while
the does wavered. Another minute passed, and I began to
feel the itch of little grains of sand under my clothes, on my
sweaty skin. The buck lowered his head like a charging bull
and swayed his stumpy horns from side to side. Then he
trotted toward us, and this time the does followed. McVey
muttered: "Damned stupid things," and Drum shushed him
quietly, as he pumped away with his flag. The whole bunch
came to a halt, and then one doe, seeming to have enough
of this male foot-fiddling, came out at an officious trot,
stopped, gave us a searching, no-nonsense look, and then
came on again. The others trooped after her.

The next time they stopped, the doe out front was less
than a hundred yards from us. A long shot, but not impos-
sible. McVey carefully drew his rifle up to the ready, but
Drum shook his head. Ned's face was getting a strained look.
He'd been wiggling that flag for ten minutes now, and his
arms must have been near dropping off, but he kept it up.
The antelope were close enough for us to make out their

eyes, shining with angry curiosity, and to see their nostrils flare as they tested the wind, but the breeze was blowing crosswise to us and they couldn't get our scent. They tossed their heads and pawed the ground and peered at the flag that continued to wig-wag, wig-wag, left-to-right, so infuriatingly. The old doe couldn't stand it. She raised her head and minced forward, stopped and came again. Now she was close enough for us to see her velvet rust-and-white sides rise and fall as she breathed. The tendons of her forelegs tensed and trembled as she hesitated, then came on. The buck had stopped and was watching her, while the other three does were strung out between them. "Now," said Drum softly, and McVey stood up with the rifle at his shoulder.

The doe spun, throwing an explosion of sand and flashing her black-and-white rump toward us, and in the same instant Bob's rifle cracked. She hit in the rocks, her fore-legs folding under her, and Bob broke the rifle to reload. He sprang to the top of the bank for a shot at the others, bounding wildly away up the prairie with the frantic white hindparts like dancing birds, but he missed and by the time he had reloaded they were out of range and almost out of sight. The first doe was writhing in the brush, her head raised and straining and her hind legs scrambling in the stones, but her forelegs still folded. Bob ran up toward her and shot her in the head from ten feet. Then she was still except for the jerking of her hind legs and one last shudder of her neck. Drum and I walked up beside Bob. She was bigger than she had looked out there on the prairie, and not quite so pretty. Her velvet coat was marked with scars and mangy-looking spots, and one of her ears was ragged, as if it had been chewed in a fight.

"Good sized doe, Mr. McVey," said Drum. "And that was a nice shot. You didn't need to get up, though. You could have shot from cover and had her standing."

"Why not give her a chance?" said Bob.

"This is meat hunting. For a while there I was afraid the

[120]

wagon might come up and scare them before we got a shot. Well, let's skin her out."

She was safely still, and her eyes were glazing. Bob's first shot had broken her spine just above the shoulder, a perfect kill. Drum seized one foreleg, rolled her over and put his knife into the front of her belly, just in the arch of her ribs.

"It's a shame to kill them," said Bob.

"Oh, I wouldn't feel that way about it, Mr. McVey. After all, it's to feed ourselves."

"Yeah. That's what I mean."

Drum, opening the carcass, stuck his knife into the ground beside him and began to draw the hot guts. "How's that?" he said, perplexed.

"Here she was, out here doing her way, whatever it is they do, and now she's dead so we can stuff our bellies."

"We have to live, don't we?"

"What's so important about us, Drum?"

"That's a funny question."

"Can you answer it?"

Drum took up his knife and slashed the white hide up one hind leg. "Answer it?" he said. "I don't see any reason to *ask* it."

Bob squatted with his rifle across his knees. "Is that the truth?" he asked.

"Why, yes. Of course. Mankind is ... is the masters of this world, Mr. McVey."

McVey hooted. "Where do you get that?"

"It's *so*," Drum insisted flatly. "Of course, we have to use some sense, and we shouldn't be cruel or wasteful. God put meat in the world for us to eat, not to waste."

"Suppose we just left these deer running free. Would that be waste?"

"I guess it would, in a way."

"So it's God's will for us to kill them?"

"I think so."

"Because we're better than them?"

"Well," frowned Drum, "I don't know about 'better.' It's just that we're *men,* and God gave Adam dominion over the

birds and the beasts and the fishes. That's Scripture." He
had peeled the two hindquarters out of their hide. He plunged
the blade of his knife deep into the flesh and began sawing
at the hip joint, twisting the leg at the same time to unseat
the bone. He worked fast, with blood to his elbows, while
the tendons popped and the knife chewed into gristle.

McVey laughed. "Drum," he said, "what makes man different from the animals?"

"How's that? Why, *everything!*"

"Just one thing. Man is the only one that wars on his own
kind, or holds his own kind as slaves."

Drum looked up from his bloody work. He stared at Bob.
"Is that really all the difference you can see?" he asked.

"Well, what else is there?"

"Mr. McVey, all I can say is that you must have mighty
little pride in yourself, to believe like that."

"How many of the buffalo did you kill, Drum?"

"I killed a lot, Mr. McVey. But I never killed one for his
hide and left the meat on the prairie to rot, I can tell you
that."

From far off down the creek came the sound of the wagon:
a crashing rattle as it lurched over some rock or hollow.
Drum seized the skin of the antelope in both his thick hands
and ripped it off the ribs. "Just in time," he said. "We'll be
done by the time they get here."

8

WE continued to follow the little creek all the rest of that day and part of the next. During the next morning we came to the top of the land's rise and before us a huge grassy table-land spread out to the west. The creek became a muddy gully and then a dry one. We had filled our water barrels that morning. Now Drum called a halt while he laid down the discipline for the next leg of our trip. He was very stern about the necessity of doing just as he told us. We would be on a compass course for two days, without water. He brought out his maps and showed us just what we were going to do. If we held to a due west heading, we should hit the Smoky Hill just where it came around from its southern loop and straightened out westward. The trouble was that we would be coming on it from an acute angle, almost parallel to it, and if we steered a little too far north we might actually *get* parallel to it and miss our connection.

Drum's navigational equipment included a good Army-style spirit compass, and three small needle compasses. He had a brass telescope, too, and an octant. He put great store by that octant, but I think it was mostly for the purpose of impressing us. I couldn't see much use in knowing our lati-tude but not our longitude, and we carried no chronometer. Besides, his maps were clearly inadequate. One was a large scale chart with absolutely no detail of the region we were in and the other was a hand-drawn map, done very prettily in violet and black inks, which showed no parallels and no scale, only estimated distances. I'd found in Fort Leavenworth, however, that there just weren't any maps of the territory that would satisfy a navigator. I put much more faith in Drum's experience and good sense than in his maps. But again, perhaps they were just another part of his professional apparatus—window dressing.

With his large compass on the saddle before him, Drum was to set our course. Joel Tyree, driving the wagon, was to steer on him. Whenever there was a halt, Drum would not move left or right until the wagon had come to a full stop, and if he were to veer for any unexpected reason then Tyree was immediately to stop the team and not start again until Drum had taken a new reading from the wagon.

As for the rest of us, each rider had specific duties. To begin with, Bob was to ride just ahead of the team to examine the footing and warn Tyree of gullies or other bad going. James Pierce was to ride behind the wagon, leading the first horse of the pack-train and at the same time keeping an eye on the wagon from the rear. My responsibility would be the pack animals and spare saddle horses and the second team of mules: keeping them in line, seeing that they were traveling comfortably and watching for strains or minor injuries that might mean a horse should be relieved of his load for a day or two. Willis Hopkins was sent to the very rear of the party to keep the loose animals moving, watch for lost gear and generally keep an eye on things. Drum cautioned him to let none of the animals get behind him. He must have everything in the train in his view.

The long climb up to the high prairie had done one thing: it had brought us just that much closer to the sun. It blazed squarely into our faces all afternoon. Down on the river we had all sunburned and we had made fun of each other's peeling faces. But the sun down there had just been heat; this one was fire. First my nose and cheeks burned, then my neck and hands, my ears and chin, and the lids of my eyes. It was more than I could do to go on facing the west. I had to stop from time to time and put my back to the sun while I pretending to check over the horses as they came past me. Poor Willis choked along through a boil of dust at the tail of the parade, but at least it must have cut the sun's light a little bit. Martha hid in her poke bonnet. McVey and Tyree and Drum had some protection in their beards, and I swore to grow one just as quick as I could manage it.

We stopped just about the time the sun went down and riding became bearable. I suggested to Drum that we should try traveling at night and resting by day.

"We can do that," said Drum, "but it's hard on the animals. They don't seem to rest very well in the sun."

"I don't think I could either," said Martha. She spanked her flowing skirt and dust flew. "It's caking on me," she said.

Drum didn't make the fire until Martha had everything ready for cooking. All the fuel we had was dry grass and an armful of sticks that McVey, on Drum's directions, had scavenged one at the time during the day from little clumps of brush we passed. We had planned to finish off McVey's antelope doe, which had made us a juicy supper the night before and a farm-hand's breakfast that morning, but during the day the flies had got to it and it had begun to smell, so Joel took what was left out onto the prairie and threw it away. Then we made our supper on meal cakes and beans and water (there would be no coffee until we reached water again) and Drum passed around a double-handful of dried apples for each of us.

"Best to eat them," he warned. "They keep you from binding up, if you'll excuse me, and prevent the scurvy."

They also bloated us, and the rumbling of our bellies that night must have kept the mules awake—that night, and many other nights.

Our fuel was barely enough to parch our meal cakes, and we ate in the dark. With no camp fire to gather around, we just huddled about the wagon, laying out our bedrolls by touch and peering uncertainly to identify each other. I groped my way to a shape in the darkness that I took for

McVey, but it was Hopkins, so he and I sat against a wheel and chatted hoarsely. I told him about the argument between McVey and Drum over the antelope killed the day before, and he chuckled.

"They're both self-righteous," he said. "Each one in his way. Not that there's anything wrong with that. I'm self-righteous myself."

"Bob's too belligerent," I said.

"Bob's just Bob. As a matter of fact, that's his whole trouble. He works at being himself, like no one I've ever seen. He reminds me of my mother." I laughed at that, which seemed to please Willis. "It's true," he said. "My mother is a hostess. If she was ever anything else, you'd never know it. You see, she *was* a hostess for a while, in Baltimore. I mean, she had the social position of a hostess, and the money. Now she has neither, but she still thinks of herself as a hostess and she doesn't know how to stop."

"Is everybody's money gone?" I asked. "We used to have a little, too, and it disappeared."

"Not everyone's. As a matter of fact, I know a lot of people who have money and always will. But money is easier lost than gained. We'd still have money, if my father hadn't died."

"I'm sorry."

"Don't be sorry for him. It was his way of escaping."

I remained silent for a moment. "This yours?" I asked.

"Yes. Partly I came out here to get away, but mostly I came to get some money of my own. My two dutiful brothers are taking care of mother, and bearing the burden of my father's honorable debts." He snickered.

"So you're going to win a fortune," I said, "and return in triumph."

"No," he replied thoughtfully, "I don't imagine I'll ever go back. But I would like the fortune."

There were others talking, like us, all around the dark camp. I could make out Martha's voice, and it came to me that the voice answering hers was not Joel's but Bob's. I

[126]

tried to listen, but Willis said: "You know, the construction of our teeth indicates that we are meat-eaters by nature."

"What?"

"The antelope. You know. Bob's question about Divine purpose. Our teeth indicate that Drum's right. We are naturally carnivores."

I caught just one word from Martha—"kindness."

"It's just as you said about horses, Garvin," Hopkins continued. "No horse ever saddled a man. No antelope ever ate a man, but plenty of men ate antelopes. To me, that is enough to prove that it's a natural arrangement."

From the darkness Martha's voice came: ". . . asks nothing and gives all." McVey's murmered reply was too low for me to catch, except that he sounded a bit impatient.

Hopkins went on, at length, about man's place in the world, while I kept straining at the darkness to hear Martha and Bob. Joel was not with them or, if he was, he was remaining silent. I kept catching words, mostly Martha's, that told me nothing at all. What I heard seemed safely unspecific, like a sermon.

We had hoped that once we got up onto the tableland we would make better speed, but we soon found that the prairie was not nearly as flat as it looked. The whole grassy expanse was cut and scored by hundreds of little dry gullies, some no more than creases and others fifteen or twenty feet across and five or six feet deep. The worst of it was that they all ran north and south, directly across our path. There was no hope of setting a fast pace while trying to follow Drum's compass course across that kind of ground with a loaded wagon, a string of pack horses and half a dozen loose animals. When we hit a deep one we would have to stop, unless the banks were gentle enough to drive across, and ride up and down until we found a "ford," then cross and bring the wagon all the way back to our course before continuing westward. Once or twice Joel had to drive the wagon into one of those washes, wheel it around at the bottom and follow along it to another spot where he could get out.

We made seven or eight miles, nonetheless, before our noontime stop the next day. We were all very discouraged by the slow going, the dust, dry throats, and the prospect of the sun in our faces the rest of the day.

Drum sat in the shade of the wagon, slowing sipping his cup of water, and fanned himself with his hat. He looked down into a little gully we'd just crossed and said: "Lots of these washes out here are generally dry. They only have water right after a storm."

"When do we get water?" asked McVey.

"Tomorrow sometime, we'll hit the river. Then everybody can have a good wash."

Joel said, "I think the gullies may fill up today." He pointed to the north. A black bank of cloud lay near the horizon there, with tufts of it puffed up into gray columns.

"That's rain, all right," said Drum. With a smile of delight he turned to Bob. "There's your rain, Mr. McVey."

"My rain?"

"You were talking the other day about rain being so scarce out here. Well, there it is." He looked again at the dark clouds, and beamed.

He was wrong, however. It did not rain. We had our fat meat and bread and wearily mounted up. As we took our positions Martha cried: "Look!" and pointed toward the storm. At first we saw nothing, except that the cloud bank seemed now to fill a little more of the sky. Then a vivid yellow tongue of lightning licked the ground. It was so far away we didn't even hear the thunder, but the bolt seemed as clear and bright as sunlight.

"Glory," said James Pierce.

We set out, and as we rumbled along we kept eyeing that storm, impatient for it to get between us and sun, and for rain that would wash the dust off of us. As it boiled nearer, though, we could see no rain beneath it. We began to hear the thunder: an echoing, rumbling, crashing barrage that grew louder and sharper as we rode until at last the pack horses began to flinch at every peal of it. Hopkins' splay-footed horse didn't even blink, I was proud to see, but

[128]

McVey's showed some uneasiness and finally even the mules started to shake their ears and rattle the bits. The black pall reached toward us, spreading wider and higher until half the sky was covered, but still we were in blistering sunlight. We could see the lightning, bolt after bolt of it and every shot so bright and yellow that it was a little eerie. Since there were no trees or hills to draw it, it just struck at random on the prairie. And still there was no rain. I rode past the wagon and spurred my horse up beside Drum's buckskin.

"The stock's getting nervous," I said. As a matter of fact, I was nervous myself. I've always been afraid of lightning and this was the strangest storm I'd ever seen. "I think we'd better stop," I said, "and hold them until this is over."

"Good idea," he said. He turned and raised his hand for a halt. When Tyree had stopped the wagon Drum and I rode back to them. "Mr. Tyree," he said, "I think you'd better set your brake and then get down by your mules' heads and hold them. They might bolt if the lightning hit nearby."

Joel nodded and sprang down. I rode back and told James to dismount and hold his horse and the lead pack-horse, then I had Hopkins do the same with the last one. McVey and I took charge of the loose stock. Every flash of lightning gave a crack of thunder that made your ears ring. We brought the animals up by the wagon as well as we could, and I tied Hoecake's reins to a wheel spoke. The rest of them were beginning to snort and jostle each other, but she was cool and alert. I was beginning to think she was an even better horse than I'd known. When she was tied I took the bridles of the spare mules, one in each hand, and tried to sooth them a little by talking to them. McVey had three horses by the reins and I told him to shorten his grip on them. I looked around at the others. Tyree and his wife had the team firmly in hand. Pierce was murmuring calmly to the head pack-horse, Hopkins was grimly holding at the rear, and Drum had come back to take the middle of the pack line. At each crack of thunder every horse's head would go up just a little higher.

"Bob," I called, "remember to face them. Don't turn your

[129]

back on an excited horse. He'll do anything to get away. Keep his head down."

Just about the time I said that, the two mules climbed the air, taking me with them, and a stunning crash of thunder seemed to shake the ground. The odor of ozone tingled in my nostrils. I'd no sooner got my wits together than there was another and I'd have sworn that the bolt hit me just behind the right ear. The mules plunged and bucked, but I leaned back and put my weight on their bridles, pleading: "Steady, now! Easy. Easy there!"

The lightning seemed to strike in volleys and every flash seemed aimed at us. I could hear horses whinnying and stamping and Martha Tyree praying at the top of her voice: "God of the heavens and the thundercloud, we are in Thy hands. Thy will be done. We are in Thy hands." Her prayers helped me, at least, for I was so amazed by them that it took my mind off my fright. She went on and on, in a perfectly level voice, telling the Almighty that she was ready. I heard Drum, too, saying firmly every few minutes: "There was a blazer! Look at it rip!"

It passed. In all, we couldn't have been under the storm for more than ten minutes. The clouds rolled on and the flashes and the crackling thunder moved with them. When Martha stopped praying I decided it was safe to take a look around. We'd come through all right. Hoecake was still safely tied, and as far as I could see none of our animals had got loose or done any damage. The stock was in a wild state of fright, though, and the people weren't much better. Drum walked among the horses, soothing them with his voice. Tyree crooned to his mules. Martha came around the wagon, a little pale, and asked me, "Is everyone all right?"

"I think so."

She rolled her eyes up to the sky and said, "That was the Lord, God of the Heavens. He was kind to us. His Mercy is everlasting."

"Amen," said Drum.

Hopkins laughed. It was not really a laugh. It was a giggle of relief and exhilaration. At the sound, I giggled too. I couldn't help it, but she was hurt and started to turn away with a sad face.

"Martha Tyree," I said, "your prayers helped us."

"I wasn't praying *for* us," she said, "I was praying God's praise."

"It helped me, all the same."

"Then I'm glad," she said. "You know, it seemed to calm the mules, too."

We decided to rest a bit and give the animals time to get over their fright, so we gathered by the wagon and talked excitedly of the storm. Each of us had to tell just how scared he had been and to tell which bolt had been the closest. We scouted out around the wagon and finally found a place where the grass was blackened and smouldering about a hundred feet away. That was the closest, and each of us had his idea of just which bolt it had been. We stamped out a few little tongues of flame and examined the spot closely. There was one place where it looked as if a giant moldboard plow had turned a furrow a yard wide for twenty feet.

We were very dry, so we had a drink all around, then we mounted, Drum consulted his compass, and we started out. With the horses still jittery, we went slowly. I was proud of Hoecake. The excitement just seemed to put an edge on her spirits. As we got under way I spurred her out from the rest and into a gallop. We ran a wide half circle around the wagon, flying, and then I slowed her, took a short rein and brought her chin back, and she did a couple of high capers as prettily as a circus horse. With that, we fell back into our place. We got a cheer from the others. For the first time everyone seemed to feel cheerful and united.

For an hour we traveled as before: plodding along, easing across gullies and straining through sand.

McVey trotted up beside me. "Grass is burning," he said, and pointed. To the north, a smudge of smoke lay on the prairie. I judged it a long way off, but it was hard to estimate distances out there. I nodded and Bob rode back up ahead of the wagon. In a few minutes Hopkins came up from behind. He'd seen McVey point.

"The lightning must have started it," he said. Again, I nodded.

For about another hour I kept my eye on that smudge. It didn't seem to come any closer, but it grew a lot wider. When I looked at it, the wind was in my face. Finally I rode up beside the wagon.

"See that?" I said to Joel.

"I've been watching it."

"It's spreading."

Just then Drum halloed for a halt and the Quaker drew in his mules. The guide came trotting back. "There's a fire over there," he said, "and it's spreading."

"We were just talking about it," I said.

"I don't much like the looks of it. It's upwind of us and I'd say it's got a good start."

The others, except for Hopkins, came up from behind and we sat our horses with their heads together and talked about it for a little.

"Fire travels fast on the prairie," said Drum. "That one's about four-five miles away. It's a good thing the wind's no stronger than it is."

"We can back-fire it," said McVey.

"How's that?"

"Set our own fire, let it burn, then get on the burned ground and let that other fire go around us."

Drum snorted and pointed to the ground. "Strike fire in that dry grass," he said, "and the flames will leap as high as the wagon. You'd never hold onto your horses."

"We can go downwind a ways on foot and start it."

"That's a risky idea, Mr. McVey. No sense in taking a chance when that fire may burn itself out without even coming near us. We're not far from the river, anyway, you know. We're on a course angling into it. If we just turned south right now we'd hit the river in about four miles."

"Are we turning?" asked Bob.

"We aren't in any danger yet. If it looks like trouble we can turn. I'd rather not. We'd lose time and we'd be down there in a valley where the traveling is mighty poor. I'll keep an eye on the fire," he said. He licked his lips and smiled, and he wheeled his buckskin about and trotted out to his place.

We'd covered less than a mile before he stopped again. He trotted back and sat his horse in silence beside the team, squinting northward at the fire. I'd been staring at it so hard all along that I couldn't tell whether or not it was any nearer.

"I think we'd better go to the river," he said calmly.

McVey growled loudly. "What's wrong with a back-fire?" he demanded.

"It's against my judgment," Drum answered primly.

"Suppose we come to one of those gullies and get stuck?"

"The washes run into the river. We'll be going parallel to them."

"Your judgment!" Bob said hotly, but Drum turned away from him.

"Mr. Tyree," he said, "just guide on me, and move them along." He looked once again around at the whole lot of us, and gave an encouraging smile. "It's not so far," he said. "But don't let them lag." Then he trotted his horse to the south, swinging his arm in a starting signal.

I grabbed the bridle of the near mule and helped Joel get them turned. Then he clucked them up and we fell again into our positions. With our backs to the smoke, it seemed everything was just as before, except that the sun was no longer in our faces. One direction looked pretty much the same as another out there. We kept looking back, though— all of us. Now and then Drum would stop for a moment, turning his horse so he could look us over like an officer reviewing troops. Then he'd glance again at the fire and trot back out in front. He seemed very pleased and excited and— defiant. I rode up beside McVey and said: "That man loves excitement."

"Anything that scares us tickles him."

It wasn't so long after that that I smelled smoke. I knew the horses wouldn't like it, so I tried to hurry them as much as I could; but the wagon set our pace and Tyree had his hands full as it was. The next time Drum stopped and turned, I cantered out to him. Bob was right behind me.

"The horses are getting the smoke," I said, and he nodded with a judicious frown and eyed the fire.

"For God's sake, Drum!" Bob burst out, "Stop playing soldier and set a back-fire!"

Drum gave us both the sort of look you use on unruly children. "Tell Mr. Tyree to push them right along," he said, and he left us. Bob cursed and grabbed me as I started to turn away.

"He's just pig-headed, now, because it was my idea. Let's stop this."

Suddenly our horses shied as a big hare went loping past us. Bob pointed at it. "He's running," he said, "and he's going to be fried rabbit as soon as he's winded. The same goes for us."

I looked at the smoke. It was still a long way off. "Drum knows what he's doing," I said.

I rode back to the wagon and fell in beside the team. Tyree was anxiously clucking to them and worrying at the reins. He looked confused.

"We have to speed up," I said.

"I can't speed up much," he answered, but he gave them a slap with the reins and they responded by throwing their heads angrily and jingling their bits.

I went back to Hopkins. Behind him, I could now see little flickers of red in the smear of smoke that lay along all the northern skyline. "Keep them close to the wagon," I said. "Don't let them lag. I'll give you a hand."

Then I tried to take my place in the train, but I couldn't do it. I put Hoecake into a canter again and overtook Drum.

"Ned," I said, "This is serious."

He gave me a startled look. "Of course it's serious!" he said, outraged. "I should say it's serious."

"The fire's gaining on us. How far have we got to go?"

"I'd say another two miles."

"Look back there."

"I've been looking." I heard the sound of McVey's horse as he came up, and I damned him silently. There was just the chance that he was right, that Drum didn't want to change his mind in Bob's favor. "We're going to have to spur them up," said the guide.

"What about the wagon?"

"The wagon too," he said calmly.

"The wagon?" I cried.

"He can get a trot out of those mules," he said firmly. "It won't do the team any good, but that can't be helped."

McVey had pulled up with us in time to hear this last. "If that wagon hits a rock at a trot," he said, "it's good-bye Quakers."

"Your job is to stay in front of them, Mr. McVey, and see they don't hit any rocks."

"What the hell is your job?"

"There isn't time to quarrel, Mr. McVey." Drum turned to me. "I'll stay ahead of the wagon and point out a trail for him. Tell Mr. Tyree... No. I'd better tell him myself." He wheeled about and trotted to the wagon. I sat where I was with McVey.

"Let him run," said McVey. "Let's start a back-fire while we've still got time."

"The stock's already spooky," I said. "Let them stand for a minute and God knows what they'd do."

"I know what I'm going to do," he said, and he jerked his horse viciously around and put it into a run to the south. He was going out ahead and try to set a fire.

I looked to the north. The odor was stronger. Suddenly the distances came into focus. The rolling smoke confused it all, but those flickers of red were no more than two miles away. The fire had covered four miles while we were covering two. Tyree was nodding his preacher's beard as Drum stood in the stirrups and gave him directions. I looked for Bob. He was flogging his horse along at a run. He pulled it to a sliding halt and threw himself off. He was quite a way off, but I could see that he was taking something from his saddle-bag. Flint and steel, I guessed.

[135]

Drum came past me at a trot and as he went by he called: "Same order of march!"

Tyree smacked his mules hard and yelled: "Heeee-awww! Up, mules!" and the team threw themselves into their collars. As they got the wagon moving Tyree never let up on them and they fought the harness and then settled into a jerky trot.

James Pierce, hauling on the lead pack-horse, gave me a startled look of question.

"We're going to run, Jim," I said. "Lead them out to one side. Don't get right behind the wagon."

He nodded and did as he was told. Hopkins came jouncing up with the rear of the line and once again I blessed that nerveless gray gelding. I think you could have blown a horn in his ear without startling him. "Willis," I said, "just hang on to your saddle and trust that horse. He'll take care of you." Two more of those big rabbits came past us, galloping all out.

As for the loose horses and mules, they were on their own. The best I could do was try to head them in the right direction while they were still steady enough to be driven. Already, wisps of smoke, like huge phantom snakes, came writhing and curling along the ground. I got in behind them and shouted at them, and they went eagerly into a trot and then a canter. They gained quickly on the pack horses, and as they got the excitement of the race they began to scatter and gallop. They went thundering past the pack line and the wagon and then I reined in. They were well started and they'd probably follow Drum's horse. If any of them should turn, I would be more useful back where I could head him off.

The wagon was bowling along like a surrey, bounding from one tussock to the next, crashing and groaning as if every nail in it was popping out. Martha was lying flat, crosswise, just behind the box, and I guessed her husband had made her get back there. He was white as he leaned out over the laboring haunches of the mules, slashing them with the reins and yelling like a fiend.

I saw McVey, standing stock still on the prairie with the reins of his plunging horse in his hand. Grimly scowling, he watched the wagon careen past him. The fire he had tried to start was feebly licking at the grass beside him. It had burned a tiny patch, not big enough to shelter a single man from the fire behind us. I pulled up beside him.

"Better get going," I said. "Don't ride that horse too hard. You want him to last. Just keep him headed right."

"I couldn't do it alone," he said bitterly.

"It's too late now. Let's go."

He climbed into the saddle and rode beside me after the wagon. "Let's stop the wagon," he yelled, "and get the woman off."

"What about Joel?"

I pulled out ahead of him and began to overtake the others. Jim was riding steadily along at a good canter, half-turned in the saddle to watch his pack-horses and keeping a firm line on them. That boy had sense. He was pulling the leader just fast enough to make the line string out. They were jerking at the leads a little, but he had them working too hard to frighten.

Hopkins was sticking by his post at the tail of the line, and the gray was rolling along like a rocking horse. There was a horse you could give your grandmother. I fell in on the other side and looked back over my shoulder. It was close. I didn't even try to guess how close. I could not only smell the smoke, I could feel it in my eyes and taste it on my tongue. I shouted to Willis: "If I tell you to, just leave the packs and ride for the river as hard as you can." He nodded grimly. He had hold of the saddle.

I tried to account for the loose ones, but they were all over creation. At least I didn't see any of them turning back toward the flames. All around, rabbits came bounding through the grass, and soon there were lizards and snakes and little scurrying rat-like things. There was a terrible crash from the wagon, but it was still in one piece and still rolling, although our supplies were bouncing and rolling and I saw a sack of some kind fly up and fall behind it on the ground. I marked the spot and rode to it. It was a ten-pound

[137]

sack of meal, and it had landed without bursting, so I swung down and picked it up, then remounted with it on the pommel of my saddle. That left me between everyone else and the fire. I sat there a minute to get a clearer idea of how close it was, and right away I heard the crackle and growl that it made. I put Hoecake into a run and she laid down to it with a good will. I overtook the wagon first, for the boy had led the pack horses on past it. Martha was still flat, hanging on to the seat struts with both hands. Tyree was leaning so far over his team that he was almost riding them.

"Run!" I shouted. "Hit 'em!" Then I took out after the leaders. I passed McVey and caught Drum. That buckskin horse wasn't running, but he was eating up the ground with a smooth single-foot gait. "How much farther?" I yelled.

"Not far," Drum said. His face was placid, confident, and determined.

"Listen," I said, matching my pace to his, "that fire's getting close. Let's stop the wagon and cut off the mules; then some of us can stay with it and fight fire. We can keep it from burning."

"It's all right," he said. "We'll make it. Push them along. Ground's sloping ahead."

I peered out ahead, but with the smoke twisting along the ground you couldn't see clearly for more than a hundred feet or so. The wagon, behind us, sounded like a house being torn down, but Drum never glanced back. I turned around.

Jim was still steady as a rock. He had the pack line in an easy gallop, still orderly, and he watched them with a cautious, judicious concern. Hopkins was pounding along, legs flopping, his hat gone and his yellow hair streaming in the wind. McVey, a little in front of the mules, was scanning the ground ahead, but it was an absurd effort. He would point to a bump as he rode over it and then the wagon would hit it with a shattering jolt. The smoke boiled everywhere.

No better rider than he was, Hopkins might have a fall any minute, and I realized that with his bad leg and its thick boot he might have trouble mounting in a hurry. The more room he had, the better, so I got beside him and said: "You can't do any more. Run for it as hard as you can, and hold on tight. Put your arms around his neck." His face was set. Every time he plopped down on the saddle his teeth rattled. He grunted, never taking his eyes off the ground just ahead of him, and pulled ahead. I looked back again, and I was looking into the flames with thick smoke boiling all around me. Hoecake sidled uneasily, so I patted her neck and said: "We're going now," and turned.

I got behind the wagon. I figured that if Martha were thrown off I had a chance of picking her up. I wished I had a horse to lead in case the wagon broke down and I had both of them to help. We thundered on and the smoke crept in billows around and then past me, so that I could no longer see the running, riderless horses spread out up ahead and Drum, the leader, still straight in his saddle. I could just make out Hopkins, flopping along, and Tyree's straining back. I tried to guess how far we had come. Four miles? It seemed like ten.

Hoecake was beginning to blow a little, and she didn't like being held down to the pace of the lumbering wagon. I began to worry about what I would do if I really felt the flames at my back. Could I spur on past the Quakers and the wagon and save myself? Maybe I could at least take the woman off if it looked as though the wagon wouldn't make it, but how long should I wait? Glowing ashes were drifting past me already. That was when I became frightened. I didn't want to have to stop and help anyone. It wasn't fair that I had wound up behind the wagon to begin with. This wasn't my post. I didn't have to stop for them. To my horror, I knew I would. I would try to get that damned Quaker woman onto my horse, and that would cost me my life.

I was so bitterly absorbed in this idea that I rode right into the tail of the wagon. How, I didn't know, but Hoecake and I went crashing against the wagon and she went down on her forelegs. As she came up I was on her head, stirrups lost. I clutched frantically at her mane, her ears, her bridle, but she plunged away and I fell clear.

I fell into a foot of water. The wagon had stopped in the river and I had ridden right into it. The meal bag that I had saved was in the water beside me. I fished it out and stood up.

9

THE oozing, soggy bag of meal I tossed into the wagon.
Then I splashed off after my horse. She was standing shaking her bit angrily, but she didn't appear to be hurt. She let
me take the reins, and I led her up to the front of the wagon.
Joel Tyree was down in the water to his thighs, talking to the
mules, who kept shifting to find a firm footing in the sand
of the river bed. Martha was crouched on top of the wagon,
peering dazedly down at us. I couldn't see anyone else for
the smoke that lay upon the water all around us. From the
shore came the crackle of the fire, and now and then the
clouds of smoke opened for an instant to let the red glare
through to us.

"Did everyone make it all right?" I asked Joel.

"I think so," he said. He was completely drained, and I
didn't blame him, but he kept petting and soothing his team.
A rabbit came past us, swimming! It was the only time in my
life that I ever saw a rabbit swim. Then I noticed that
the water was full of things: snakes, lizards, shrews, little
prairie foxes, and a sneezing, angry badger.

"I ran right into the wagon," I said. "Old Hoecake must
have lost her head there."

"She wasn't the only one. That was a near thing, Garvin
Cooper. There, boy, steady."

The flames hissed at the river's edge and the wind made a

[141]

rent in the smoke. The glare turned the water red around our legs for a second.

"Are you far enough out?" I asked.

"We're far enough."

"I'm going to tie Hoecake to the wagon. Keep an eye on her, will you?"

I left the wagon and headed for the far shore, even though I couldn't see it for the smoke. I'd gone no farther than a couple of yards before a great splashing came toward me and I was almost run down by one of the spare horses, plowing along like a side-wheeler and walling his eyes. I caught his halter and the feel of a firm hand reassured him, for he stopped and stood by me, fretting and puffing. I led him on, for there wasn't much else to do with him. The water came as deep as my waist, and then dropped as the smoke thinned ahead of me. I heard the sound of a man talking and headed for it. Then I saw the bank ahead and the huddle of horses. It was the pack train, with Jim Pierce walking among them, talking to each horse as he soothed them and went over our goods. He had brought them all the way without breaking the line or losing a pack.

"Have you seen the others?" I asked him.

"Mr. Hopkins was right ahead of me," he said. "Is the wagon all right?"

"They made it," I said. "Jim, you did a good job. You're a cool man." He regarded me sternly, rigidly showing no emotion, but he gave an embarrassed little nod to acknowledge my praise.

The smoke was beginning to clear and we could see others of our horses and mules standing uncertainly in the grass off at a distance. I took a length of rope from one of the pack harnesses, fastened it to the halter of the loose horse as a hackamore, and climbed on him. "I'll go round up some of that stock," I said. "As soon as the smoke clears a little more you'd better start unpacking those horses. We'll want to look them over."

I got them together without much trouble. There were three horses and one mule, which left one horse and one mule unaccounted for. They were nervous, but they let me herd them slowly back toward the river. McVey came riding out to meet me. The smoke was almost gone, and I could see Hopkins helping Jim unload the packs and Drum up on the wagon with the Tyrees. Everyone was safe then.

"Quite a ride," I said to McVey. He shook his head wearily.

"Lordy, Lordy, Lordy!" he groaned. "I thought I was a goner."

"At the worst, we would have had to leave the wagon."

We picketed the stock near the pack horses and went to help Jim. Drum, standing on top of the wagon, called to us: "Anything lost?"

"No. Anything there?"

"Can't tell until we straighten it all out."

While Hopkins opened packs, Bob and Jim and I set to work unloading the rest of the string. As Bob and I heaved at a saddle Jim, holding the horse, said to me: "Mr. Cooper, how come we didn't just set a back-fire?"

Bob let the pack-saddle fall back onto the horse. He looked at me and said: "That's right, Cooper. Why didn't we?" He grinned viciously.

Jim looked uncertainly from one of us to the other. "It might have spooked the stock, Jim," I said.

McVey said: "Jim, how'd you like a job as a guide?"

"Sir?"

"Oh, quit it, Bob!" I said. "Let's finish this job."

As we finished up, McVey whistled softly to himself, and now and then he would glance out where Drum and the Tyrees were climbing about on the wagon. When we had everything set out, Hopkins and Jim Pierce began sorting and stacking the supplies and Bob pulled me aside, down to the river bank. "Let's have a cigar," he said, "and give this thing a think." We lit up and he squatted and pulled a handful of reeds. "Did Drum lose his head?"

"Nonsense. He was calm as a cow all the way."

"Right. Too calm." He began dexterously plaiting the green reeds.

[143]

"What do you mean?"

"He got a big thrill out of that little run we took, Cooper."

Just then Drum hailed us from the wagon. "We're coming over," he called. He and Tyree were in the water, at the bridles of the two mules, while Martha handled the reins. Hoecake was tied to the tail of the wagon.

"This just makes the big adventure a little bigger," said Bob, "in his damn' fool imagination."

"He could be right about the stock," I said. "We had to take a chance either way."

Bob peered at me scornfully and gave a chuckle. "You still want him to take care of you, don't you?"

"I'm not judging him; that's all."

"Well, I've already judged him."

"And what do you want to do?" I asked.

"Fire him, and go on alone. We just follow this river."

"What about him?"

"Give him supplies and food to get him back to the settlements."

"You're the one with too much imagination," I said.

"I don't want to wind up dead."

"We're all safe and sound," I said. "Don't overlook that."

We had to break off and leave it there, for the wagon came to the bank and we all waded in to help them heave it up. When it was on level ground Drum and Tyree unhitched the team and picketed them with the rest of the stock. The mules were reeling with fright and exhaustion. I unsaddled Hoecake and then we all assembled at the wagon. Drum, soaked to the waist, presided from a seat on the wagon tongue. It was getting dark, and a fine, fiery sunset was spreading across the western sky, but we had had enough fire.

"We lost an ax," Drum said, "and a bag of beans and a little box with some of Mrs. Tyree's belongings in it. The wagon feels to be rolling sort of peculiar. What about the stock, Mr. Cooper?"

"A mule and a horse still missing."

"I don't think they'll go far in the dark, and tired as they are. We'll find them in the morning." He sighed and looked around at us. "We came off pretty well," he said. "We'd better get a fire going, though, and dry off before we chill. Let's all scrape up what fuel we can find while Mrs. Tyree fills the kettle."

As we wearily scattered to look for twigs and dry grass, McVey hesitated only a moment and then came close after me. He overtook me out of earshot of Drum and said: "Listen, we can't put this off, and we can't just talk about it. If I put my opinion up for argument Drum and Hopkins and those Quakers will hold a debate and that'll be the end of it. We've got to get together and lay down the law. Will you stand with me?"

"I can hardly stand up," I said. "I'm tired and I'm still scared and I can't think. There's too much to take into account. Let's sleep on it."

"Will you stand firm with me if the others will?"

"Not until I've thought about it. I tell you, Drum could be right."

"You're supposed to know all about horses. Is he or isn't he right?"

"For God's sake, leave me alone for a little! Can't you let it lie?"

"Hell, no, I can't!" He turned away from me and headed for Hopkins, who was listlessly scraping up grass in the dusk. I watched him as he went up to Willis and saw Willis rise and turn glassy eyes upon Bob. They talked and Hopkins seemed to be agreeing, nodding his head, and then shaking his head to something else.

I stumbled around picking up twigs and leaves and made my way back to the wagon. I dropped the fuel where Martha pointed and sat down heavily next to the wheel. In a moment Hopkins came up with his gleanings and added them to mine. I stared at him in the gloom, but his face showed nothing but shock and fatigue. After a little Tyree came in with McVey at his side. They stopped talking as they reached us. Pierce brought a huge armload of tumbleweed, dropped it and

[145]

squatted on his heels near me. None of us made a move to start the fire, although Martha's kettle was ready. We waited until Drum came in with his findings and let him prepare and light the fire.

"There," he said as the flames took hold. "A little better than that one, eh?" He looked back toward the far bank. We could see only a few smouldering spots in the burn there, but off to the east there was a hot glow where the fire was marching off downriver.

We sprawled weakly and watched Martha put the kettle on and start mixing meal and salt and water. The fire glinted in McVey's beard, and his eyes above it glittered too, as he stared stonily into the blaze. He must not have got what he wanted. I couldn't care very much, or even think about it, but I was glad he was being silent, at least for now.

We took our coffee eagerly, and it was a bitter disappointment to taste it—scalded and oily as usual. Martha was an awful cook. She couldn't work much damage on side-meat, beans, meal and syrup, but the coffee hurt. We bolted down the meal cakes as she passed them around, but no one had anything to say. That was all she offered, and no one complained. We wanted sleep more than food. As the fire died Drum rose and went rummaging in the supplies. In a moment he came back with a sack of dried apples. He thrust his hand in and brought out a clutch of them.

"Better have some apples," he said cheerfully.

"God damn your apples!" Bob shouted. We all nearly toppled over. He shook his head wearily and threw himself back full length in the grass. There he lay panting softly. He said: "Oh, the Devil!" and that was all.

Drum stood staring down at him, stupefied. "What's the matter?" he said. "You gave me a start." He looked around at us in that way he had. "Nothing to swear about. Well, here they are, for anyone that wants them," and he carefully set the bag on the ground beside the dying fire. "All pretty edgy," he said. "I'll just have a look at the stock. We can go over things better in the morning. I guess you'll want to sleep now." He looked once again at Bob, and then at the bag of apples, and walked off toward the horses.

Drum let us sleep the next morning well into daylight. We rose stiff and dirty and hungry and had to scout again for scraps of fuel before we could even have coffee. The grass fire had either gone out, somewhere down the river, or it had moved so far during the night that we could no longer see it. Across from us the blackened prairie still smoldered and smoked. The burn extended as far as we could see north of the river in an incomprehensible desolation. You could see the curled, scorched forms of little animals that had burned to death on the bank, hesitating at the water, and more floated drowned in the milky, slow-moving river. If you forgot about our side of the river, still alive and growing, it looked as if the whole world had been dipped into fire.

We were a pitiful sight. We were smoke-stained and grimed and plastered with dust, all on top of our sun burn, and our clothes looked as if hounds had been sleeping on them. We gathered at the fire and Drum helped Martha fix a big breakfast for us. We all felt a lot better after we began to eat. We even began to laugh wearily at our sad looks, and then we started talking about what had happened to us.

"How far was the fire when we reached the river?" asked Joel.

"Quarter of a mile," I guessed, "or a little more."

"I don't think it was that near," said Drum.

Martha shook her bedraggled head. "From the wagon," she said, "it looked very near."

"I was riding behind you," I said, "to pick you up if anything happened, Martha. You looked like you might fly off any minute."

"I was ready to let go," she said, "when I finally saw the river."

"You know what I was thinking?" I said. "I was wondering if I would be killed stopping to help you." It was not a very good thing to say, but I was too giddy with fatigue and let-down to care.

She smiled palely. "Thee would have stopped to help us?" she asked.

"Oh, yes. I knew I would, and I regretted it."

"Would *thee* have stopped for me, Robert McVey?" she said with the same smile.

"I tried to take you off before we started," he said coldly. "That was after I tried to keep us from starting at all."

"Thee wanted to stay and see the fire?" Joel said.

"I wanted to burn a clear place and get on it until the fire passed." Joel started to say something, but Bob wouldn't listen. He went on. "In fact, that's what we should have done. The boy, here, thought of it too. But our guide wanted a thrilling dash for the river." Bob looked narrowly at Martha. "You know, he might have killed you and Joel—*would* have, if that wagon hadn't held together."

Drum said: "Now, Mr. McVey, I think you're too quick to strike fire. You say hard things. We're here, all well and sound and with our gear."

"Drum, I hereby suggest that you be fired from your job of guide." He rose and struck a truculent pose, his hands loosely on his hips as he glowered over us. "I put it to these people: Aye or Nay?" He looked around at our faces; then he said: "Cooper?"

"It's not that easy," I said quickly. "You're rushing things." Drum turned to me in stunned confusion. He must have been expecting an instant "Nay" from me; and I realized that he had the right to expect it. I tried to mend the wound by adding: "This isn't called for."

"Hopkins?" Bob demanded.

Willis said, "Aye," very calmly, but his face was pinched at the mouth. I hadn't been prepared for that.

"Jim?"

Pierce shook his head. "It ain't for me to say, Mr. McVey."

"You're betting your life on him, Jim. You've got a vote." The boy shook his head again, very firmly.

"Joel?"

"Does thee wish us to turn back?" Tyree asked.

"We can settle that after we've taken care of Drum."

[148]

"Nay," said Joel softly. "Thee is wrong, Robert."

"Martha?"

"Nay."

"Two for and two against, and two not voting. One of you two has got to vote."

"If either does," I said, "both must."

"Fair enough," said Bob. "All right, Jim?" Pierce said nothing, but he didn't shake his head. He seemed to be trying to think. He looked at me.

"I vote Nay," I said.

"Jim?" Bob demanded.

"I'll do what everybody else wants to do," said Pierce. "I'm not the one to say Mr. Drum is in the wrong."

"Then you vote Nay?"

"Thee cannot force him," Martha suddenly cried. "If he does not wish, thee cannot make him. Let him be!"

We had practically forgotten Drum. Now he took off his hat and wiped his pale scalp with his palm. "You people must have already talked about this. What about me? What do you accuse me of, Mr. McVey?"

"Foolishness. There was no need for what happened yesterday. We could have held the horses until the fire passed. We could have blindfolded them."

Drum grunted. "You ever blindfolded a horse?" he asked angrily.

"There is no need to argue," said Martha. "The question is not horses or blindfolds. The question is whether we have trust in Ned Drum, to lead us."

"Do you?" Bob asked calmly.

"Yes, I do. And I have trust in us all together, if we but work together."

"She's right," said Drum. "We'll get nowhere unless we pull together. And someone has to be in charge." He clapped his hat back on his head and stared solemnly at McVey.

Bob hesitated for a moment. Then he spread his hands. "You've all voted," he said, "and the vote goes for him."

"It cannot be left on who won and who lost," said Joel with unexpected firmness. "We must agree."

[149]

"All right, then, I agree!" said Bob. He smiled down at Joel, who was still squatting by the fire at his wife's side. "Ned Drum is the smartest man on the prairie and we're a brave band of pioneers, and I'm King of the Mountain."

"You can go back," said Drum. "It's only a two-day ride to Salina. You just stay with the river."

"Why the hell should I go back? I paid my fare. No, Drum. I'm going where I want to go. But I tell you this: the next time you get too brave for me I'm going to let you get brave by yourself. Understand?"

"No. Say what you mean."

"I mean I'm not going to let you risk my neck for me. I can do that for myself. If I don't like the looks of what you're doing, then I'm on my own."

"What you mean is that we can't count on you to pull your traces and do your share. Isn't that it? You refuse to take your part."

"Call it that. Don't count on me."

"All right, Mr. McVey. If your friends here will put up with that, there's nothing I can say. If they're willing to have you along, knowing how you feel, that's their concern. My advice to them would be to leave you and let you make your own way back."

"Robert McVey shall come with us," said Martha. "He is our friend."

Joel nodded. I cleared my throat, but said nothing, letting Martha's words stand for me.

"Mr. Hopkins?" Drum asked. "Are you satisfied to come along?"

During all this talk, Willis had remained sitting, staring down at the ground before him. Now, he nodded slowly. "I only want the best chance," he said. "I voted against you because that seemed the safest and best thing. I'm candid about it. My concern is my own safety. I don't stand on my honor or on principle. I'd be a fool to leave you, or to say that I'm against you. Now, my best interest is to put my trust in you. I tell you this frankly. You can count on me, because I have to count on you."

[150]

"That's fairly spoken," said Drum. "I wish Mr. McVey could feel the same way. I'm ready to give you my hand and forget the thing, Mr. McVey. That's how I am."

He waited, but Bob hesitated, making no move to offer his hand, and finally said: "Why should we shake hands? You don't like me, but you want to pretend you do. I don't trust you, and I won't pretend to. Is that fairly spoken?"

"Not by my way of thinking, it isn't. But if that's the way you'll have it, there's nothing I can do." He turned away from Bob and scanned the southern, unburned horizon, in a businesslike way as if the whole ugly matter were now forgotten. "I don't see anything of the missing stock," he said. "I hoped they'd come in during the night. It seems we'll have to look for them." Bob squatted and poured himself another cup of coffee. "Jim and I and Mr. Cooper and Mr. Hopkins can ride out to hunt them," Drum said. "Mr. Tyree, you and Mrs. Tyree can start spreading the wet things to dry and you'd better check over the harness. We may be out all day, though I doubt if they're far." He looked at Willis. "Feel up to the ride, Mr. Hopkins?"

"I think so, but I need a hat."

"Lost yours?"

"Yesterday."

"Well, you'll have to have something on your head, all right. A handkerchief might do. I could make you a cap, if we had any leather. Mrs. Tyree, why don't you see what you can rig up, while we get ready?"

I went to saddle Hoecake, and while I was doing it I looked over the horses to see which one was missing. When I realized which one it was, I went to Drum, who was examining the feet of his gelding, and told him. "No need to look for the horse," I said. "It was the mare with the cracked quarter. She probably pulled up lame and the fire got her."

"Eh? Oh, yes. Too bad. Sure it's her missing? Too bad. You're most likely right. Pitiful."

He told Jim and Willis that it was the mare and not to worry about her, as long as we could find the mule. With our two teams, we had been working the mules one day in harness and one out. With a mule missing they'd have to work two in and one out. With the kind of going we had, that would be a terrible grind on them. Drum gave each of us one of his three small compasses, with instructions to ride due north if we got lost. He was to head south and then make a swing westward. I would go a little way with him and then swing east. Hopkins, meanwhile, would work to the east closer to the river and Pierce would do the same thing to the west. We took each a leather water-bottle and a rifle, on the chance of finding game. Martha had stitched together a sort of sun-bonnet for Hopkins, out of brown silk. It was a kind of peaked helmet with a visor, and made him look wildly absurd and very uncomfortable. Still, it was better than nothing. Just before we mounted Martha gave each of us a johnny-cake and a handful of apple, twisted in a piece of cloth. Pierce set out at a trot, his feet dangling, and Hopkins started the other way, stiff and self-conscious in his outlandish hat. Drum and I rode side by side straight out onto the vast, gently rising prairie to the south. I turned once and looked back at our camp against the smoking, tortured landscape of the burned northern shore. Martha and Joel were already at work. McVey stood with his hands on his hips, watching us ride away.

10

"MR. DRUM," I said, "Bob's a good man. He's an honest man. He feels strong, and he doesn't hide his feelings."

Drum worked his lips thoughtfully for a moment. "Might as well be hiding them from me," he said. "I tell you straight out that I don't know what goes on in his head."

"Ned, you always try to see the best in people, and you're disappointed when you don't. I hope you'll remember that sometimes it may be there even if you don't see it yourself."

"I try to make allowances," he said.

"Well, Bob would like to see the best in people, but he asks a lot of them and he's angry when they don't measure up, the same as you."

"How is it that I don't measure up, may I ask?"

"That's not what I meant. He thinks you're too optimistic."

Drum thought about it, then shook his head. "I don't see that," he announced. "With all respect to you, Mr. Cooper, I don't see that. But don't you worry; I've been at this job for twenty-six years, and I've seen some touchy ones and I've got them across. You'd never dream some of the things I've come up against, Mr. Cooper. That's the truth. I was hoping that this time it wouldn't be like that. I was hoping that everything would be kind of better this time because we're breaking new ground, in a manner of speaking, and I

[153]

had hopes that everybody would catch fire from that, if you see what I mean, and pull together. But it doesn't matter. We'll be all right." He turned to me, with a serious face, and said: "You know, I was once shot by a man in a party I was leading. That's the truth. I was riding through some brush. He was out hunting and he shot me for a deer. Shot me clean through the neck and I ran things from the back of a wagon for the next two weeks. You can still see the scar, when I take off my shirt."

"Where was that?"

"On the Humbolt Trace, going into California."

"How'd you happen to get into this business?" I asked.

Drum did not immediately answer. He gathered his thick beard into the fingers of his free hand and tugged at it. Then he slowly shook his head.

"I just did," he said. "It seemed like what I was cut out for, you might say."

"Did you just decide you'd be a guide?"

"No. My folks moved into Illinois when I was a boy," he said, "and there was a lot of coming and going up there. When I got big enough to take work I hired as a wagon driver with some people going to Missouri. You know how a boy is. I wanted to see the Indians, and all that. The train broke up because of smallpox in the party. I picked up another job after a bit and went up the Missouri on a flat boat. Then I guided some up there, for the government, and after that I went to Oregon as second man in a wagon party run by a fellow named Joe Stallman. I made two trips with him, as second man, and Stallman taught me navigation and how to organize a trip. He was a fine man, and an able leader, but he had bad luck. Something was forever happening to him: stock getting sick, wagons breaking down, fights starting— just one thing and another. I learned a lot from him.

"Stallman was the one that got me to set up on my own. He thought a sight of me. He said: 'Ned, you've learned the trail as fast as any I ever saw. Why don't go on your own?' He even got me a party. People from Ohio, they were, going to California. I took them there. That was a cold year. We lost a lot of time because of snow in South Pass. Of all the guides I know, every one said that was the earliest snow they'd ever seen in South Pass. We were held up quite a while, what with the snow, and one thing and another.

"I hauled some freight out in California, but the business you could get back then didn't amount to anything, so I came back and took a party from Council Bluffs to California. Fine people. Family named Heinz, German people, got them together. We had to make two starts because the grass was scant. Through the mountains, we took the Cobb's Pass route. We were the fourth party ever to take Cobb's Pass."

Drum fell silent, and I thought he was going to say something more about that trip. Maybe he was trying to think of something, but if he was he couldn't find it. He went on:

"I was wagon master for Tom Rutherford after that. I led some people down to Santa Fe. I made a number of trips through this part of the country for Rutherford, both freight and emigrants, and then I was a scout for the cavalry for two years. Too much writing reports and tell just what you did and where you went. 'Why did you do this and why did you go this way instead of the other?' Anyhow, I quit.

"I made another California trip, and came back on my own. My next trip was guiding a party bound for those mountains out there, that we're going to. They were good people, religious people, but very close with money. They wouldn't buy what all I told them to buy and we ran short of everything you can think of: powder and ball, flour, salt, grease, everything. The wagons weren't fit and broke down all the time. I was glad to see the last of them, but they were fine people, you understand. They just had no idea of what to expect."

Once again he paused. I waited. He seemed deep in thought. "Then what?" I asked.

"Well, then I got back to Whitaker and met the Tyrees."

I didn't know what to say. I didn't know what I'd been

waiting for. *Something.* I tried to recall one detail of all those trips he'd told me about, and all I could remember was that he'd once been shot by accident, for a deer. The rest was already melted together into a vague picture of dull, petty woes and meaningless achievements. Was that his twenty-six years on the frontier? Wasn't he any more than the fourth guide through Cobb's Pass?

"You've done a lot," I said.

"I've traveled a lot of ground," he said, but there was nothing ironical or grim about his tone.

"Have you ever been East?"

"No. Never even thought of it. Whitaker's too much for me; I reckon Boston would kill me."

"Why's that?"

He smiled. "You make a fellow answer up, don't you? You've got the lawyer's style, all right. Nothing wrong with that. We ought to answer up now and then. Helps a man to think. I couldn't really say, though, what it is. I just feel like I was cut out for this life out here. What I've done hasn't amounted to much, so far, but you put it all together, and I can say I've pulled my weight."

"Mr. Drum," I said, "do you mind if I ask you where you got that horse?" I had been watching the flow and gather of the yellow gelding's pace.

"Not at all. I bought him from a man from Independence, Missouri, a man named Luther Jones. He was a big man, in his day. He took the very first party into California on the Singleton Trail. He was a famous guide. A well-respected man." He sighed. "Well, we ought to split up, I guess. I'll bear off a bit and you do the same." As I started to pull away, Drum drew his horse to a stop and I reined in and waited.

"Mr. Cooper," he said, "it seems to me that Mr. McVey has had a good lot in life. He's well-spoken and well-dressed and he has an education and a trade that's what you might call a profession, even. He's a nice-looking young fellow, and in good health. How does he come to look on the dark side?"

"I don't know, Ned."

[156]

Drum sighed and frowned unhappily. "I don't imagine he knows himself," he said.

I rode alone into the great prairie, looking for our lost mule. It was pleasant to be alone for a change, even though the sun was fierce and the glittering distances hurt my eyes. As Hoecake and I ambled along I was thinking, or trying to think, about the vote that McVey had forced me to cast for Ned Drum. I wondered if it had cost me Bob's friendship. I hoped not. I had a lot of respect and sympathy for the man, but that was not a case against Drum.

I rode for about two hours, weaving in a big loop to the east, without seeing anything of the mule. The country down there was a little rougher than north of the river, the gullies running often seven and eight feet deep. Standing down in one of them, the mule would be invisible to a man fifty feet away. The constant peering into deceptive distances and into the shimmering waves of heat soon had my head aching. Every mile or so I would stop and stand in my stirrups for a careful look in all directions. Half the world was a gray-brown disc and the other half a gray-blue vault. There was not a thing to focus your eyes on. When I glimpsed a movement on the plains sometimes I couldn't tell if it were a hundred yards away or a mile. It could be a ground-squirrel, a hare, a bear, or a buffalo herd, for all I could tell.

With my eyes playing tricks on me, I must have stopped heeding them, for I did a foolish thing. I came to a deep wash through flinty ground. Hoecake paused on the bank and, without even looking down, I urged her forward. When she felt the footing a little doubtful under her, she lost her head and tried to turn back to the flat. I had a loose rein on her and she got sidewise on the bank before I could stop her and, when her hindquarters lurched beneath me, I knew that we were going into that creek-bed flatways. As she fell I got up onto her neck and tried to push clear and fall above her. I lit on my arms and face in a bed of flints and tumbled down the slope with her shoes clattering on the rock all

[157]

around me. I rolled and scrambled to get clear and managed to reach the bottom a few feet from her flailing hooves. After I'd got up and picked the flint out of my palms I went to have a look at her.

Hoecake was shaken, but unhurt except for a couple of scratches. She stood up and shook herself, walling her eyes at me reproachfully. I patted her and crooned to her until she quieted down, and then I looked over my gear. The saddle was wrenched around onto her side. The dragoon rifle I had been carrying in a holster on the saddle skirt had lost its stock, broken off at the trigger when she rolled on it. I pulled my saddlebags off and looked into the side where I kept my two pistols. One of them was bent up beyond using, but the other was all right and nothing else seemed to be damaged. I started to unbuckle the girth, to take the saddle off and remount it, and when I pulled at it the buckle-tongue, which must have been bent, snapped right off and I sat down under Hoecake with the saddle in my lap. I swore mightily and got up. I had heard several horsemen say that they'd never use a buckled girth. Now I knew why. With the tongue gone from the buckle, there was just no second-best way of tightening it. I threw the saddle back up on my mare, ran the strap through the buckle and tried to twist it around to tie it. The leather, which I had oiled only once in three months, was just too stiff to make a hitch. If I had had wire, I could have made a hook to go into the belt-notch, but I had no wire. I wasted some time poking among my things for a piece of metal that might work, until I realized that all I really needed was a leather thong small enough to thread through the hole in the strap and long enough to make a girth-hitch in the buckle. My saddlebags were closed with thongs, but they were too wide to go through the holes. After trying, with no luck, to force one of them through, I decided I'd just have to split it the long way with my knife.

I tossed the reins over Hoecake's head so she could graze while I worked. Then I sat down against the bank of the gully, opened my knife and began paring at the brittle leather thong. The sun was straight overhead. Sweat poured down my neck and into my eyes and around my ears, and my sweaty fingers soon could hardly hold the leather. I fussed and muttered and tried to squeeze myself up under the shade of my hat brim. I worked for perhaps ten minutes, then I stood up and looked desperately around me for a spot of shade. On the opposite side of the gully, just at the edge, two Indians stood watching me in silence.

For a moment I simply stood gripping my knife as hard as I could and staring at them. Then I nodded at them as pleasantly as I knew how, grinned at them, and tried, without taking my eyes off them, to size up my position. Hoecake was cropping grass along the far side of the wash and a few yards down. She was just a little nearer to them than to me, but I was down in the gully with her while they were up above. My saddle bags and my broken rifle lay against the bank almost at their feet. I carefully transferred my knife to my left hand and then I made a gesture of friendship with my right. The two stared down at me, scowling slightly.

They were a young man and an old one. The young one was naked except for leggins and moccasins, but the older man was wrapped in a robe of wolf-skins. Neither one seemed to be armed, but the old man grasped a long, heavy staff in his knotty hand. They wore no paint, and their hair hung in heavy, greasy hanks on their shoulders, bound back from their faces with decorated bands of buckskin.

I said, slowly: "Do you speak English?" They regarded me coldly and finally the old man started off in what I thought was some Indian dialect. After some words I recognized it as Spanish, but all the Spanish I knew was *por Dios,* and it didn't seem a time for profanity. I shook my head. We stared at each other for a long time. There was only one thing to do, though, so I did it. Keeping my eyes on them, I began to walk slowly toward the loaded rifle which lay against the saddle bags. The instant I moved, the old man sat down on the edge of the gully, pushed off and slid to the bottom on his heels and his rump. He fetched up right on top of my gear and when he stood up the barrel of the broken rifle was almost touching his leg. The other one stayed where he was. I stopped and wiped my right hand on my trousers. He was watching the open knife in my left hand, and now and then his glance flickered down to the rifle.

"You friends?" he said.

"Yes," I said, quickly. "My friends. Near." I pointed to the north.

"You friends," he nodded. "Many friends."

"Yes," I said, "Many."

He thought for a moment. "You hurt," he said, pointing at my left hand. I glanced quickly down and saw that there was blood all over my fingers. I had cut myself, somehow, without even knowing it.

"Not bad," I said. He nodded. He was an evil looking man, with squinty eyes and a face carved into ruin by a thousand deep, hard wrinkles.

"Horse fall," he said. They had been watching me for a long time, then.

"Yes." I pointed at the rifle. "Rifle broke. No good. See?"

He looked down in mild surprise, as if he had not realized there was a rifle there. Very carefully, he picked it up with one hand and looked at it. Then he said: "You give me. I fix him all good, soon. Yes."

"No," I said. Something told me that the best pose was firm, confident dignity, so I said nothing more.

He stared at me for a couple of seconds. Then he very carefully laid the rifle at his feet. He stepped over it and came toward me. I moved just a little to let him by, and he went toward Hoecake. I couldn't get between them, much as I wanted my hands on that rifle. If he jumped on my mare and rode off I would be lost, with nothing to gain by shooting either him or her. I stayed a little behind and below him and followed. He stopped near Hoecake and stared at her. His hard old eyes took in the trailing reins, the loose saddle and the hanging girth straps. He turned to me and pointed to her near foreleg.

"Horse hurt," he said.

I glanced at the leg, and as I did he swung his club at my head.

His staff was too clumsy for a quick smash, and I saw it coming in time to duck, but the ground was bad and as I dodged I went tumbling on my hands and knees and dropped my knife. If he had gone right after me, he might have clubbed me dead before I could get up, but he jumped for Hoecake, she bolted away from him, and by the time he turned back to me I was on my feet again. He cocked the club in both hands, dropping his robe, and began to shuffle toward me. I glanced at the other one. He had jumped down into the wash and was already busy looting my saddle bags. There was a pistol in the bags, but I didn't have time to worry about it. The old man was on me. I poised to dodge, and he stopped, afraid that if he swung that long cudgel and missed I would have a chance to close with him before he could bring it around again. He shouted for the other one to come help him as I feinted to the right, then he feinted a swing with the club, shouting again. He squinted at me and came slowly on again. "I'll give you the pistols," I said breathlessly. He swung the club. I dodged back, it swished past me and I stepped in behind it and kicked him with all my strength square in his old belly. He went on his backside with a squawl and I snatched the staff from his hands. The young buck had found the two pistols, but one was broken and the other wasn't primed. The rifle was loaded and capped, and he could have killed me with it if he had realized that the broken stock didn't matter. Instead, he dropped the pistols and raised the rifle by the barrel, as a club. But my staff was two feet longer and I went at him with it like a bayonet, frantically. He dodged and hit at my hands with the rifle, skinning my thumb. Then he tripped and before he could roll away I smashed him over the head. Blood spurted and he came up running. I looked around and saw the old man just getting up. Hoecake stood beyond him, his for one quick dash, but he didn't look as if he could walk, much less dash. He just stood and faced me and waited, his jaw hanging slack as he gasped and heaved.

I grabbed up the rifle, cocked it, and ran for my horse. The old man, when he saw me coming, fell to his knees and put out both his hands toward me, but I ran on past him and grabbed Hoecake's reins. I led her to my saddle bags and held the reins in one hand as I grabbed up my belongings, scattered by the young brave, and crammed them in the bags. I tossed the bags across Hoecake's withers, in front of the loose saddle, and then sprang up myself behind the saddle, as if I were riding double. Holding the cocked rifle in one hand, like a pistol, I spun Hoecake about and kicked her up out of the gully. There I paused and looked around. The prairie was empty as far as I could see. Down in the wash, the old Indian had got up again. He stood holding his stomach and panting up at me. I turned my horse north and put her into a fast trot.

After I got a mile or so from them, I slowed down and began to tremble. I had had the vision of dying alone in a strange land at the hands of a strange people.

"Thieves," said Drum, shaking his head. "How did they wear their hair?"

"Long, with no feathers, Just a head-band."

"Then they weren't Kaws. Delawares, maybe. Could have been Comanches on the way up to trade at Salina, or Pawnees. Pawnees would have been more likely to sneak up and steal your horse and all your gear before you knew they were around. You should never get separated from your horse on the plains—not for a minute. Your horse is your life, out here."

"How come they couldn't have been these Cheyennes of yours?" I asked peevishly. Drum had irritated me by taking the whole matter very lightly. In fact, he had even chuckled a little as I had told my story to them, squatting by the wagon.

"There wouldn't be any Cheyenne down this far without horses."

Martha had warmed a pot of water. Now she dumped a handful of salt into it, then a strip of clean rag. "Give me thy hand," she said. I obliged, gritting my teeth, and she wrapped the rag, soaked in hot brine, around my mashed thumb, the one the Indian had hit. I groaned as the salt bit the raw flesh, but she said firmly: "It will keep thy hurt from mortifying."

"Feeling good?" McVey said with a smile.

"Just grand."

"Cooper," he chuckled, "What's the matter with you? Can't you stay on a horse?"

"You can be damned," I said, and he laughed. I smiled as well as I could and said, "How about getting me a cigar out of my coat, and one for yourself."

Hopkins said. "Suppose these Indians get some friends and come looking for us?"

"I told them there were a lot of us."

"They could still have a look and find out that's not so."

"The man's right," said McVey, handing me a cigar. "It might be best for us to get out all the rifles and load them."

"It might be even better," said Joel, "if we hid all the rifles."

"Think they might leave us alone?" asked Bob.

"I don't know. What matters is what we do, not what they do."

"Not if we're dead," said McVey, and Hopkins sniggered.

"Ned," I said, "don't you think we ought to have a guard awake tonight?"

"Oh, I sleep pretty light."

McVey cocked an eye at Drum and said: "Those Indians weren't after Garvin's scalp; they just wanted to admire it."

"We can keep guard, if you like," said Drum. "It might help people to rest easy. As a matter of fact, it was the horse they were after. A scalp's a war-trophy, but a horse is like money to an Indian—better than money. Like I said, a horse is your life out here. It's horses that the Indians fight over, most generally.

"I was a scout you know, for the army. That was up north of here. Whenever the Indians fought among themselves it was usually over horses. The Kiowas and the Comanches were allies, fighting the Cheyenne. We went among them and tried to make peace. When a quarrel broke out, the army would send someone in. Then we'd offer to hear both

[163]

sides and if they agreed they'd be bound by our decision. It was generally horses. A bunch of young Kiowas would steal four or five Cheyenne horses and the Cheyenne would ride after them, or maybe try to steal them back, plus interest. They had no way to settle their grievances, outside of war, until we came along. I think they were glad when we offered to help."

"Blessed are the peacemakers," said Martha.

"Amen," said Drum, "but we had a hard time of it. You never knew what might happen." He shook his head.

"Why did thee leave that work, Ned Drum?" Martha asked.

He smiled. "I couldn't get along with the army way of doing things," he said. "I wanted to be on my own again. Guiding is a good life, once you get set up in it. You can take a job or turn it down. You can even quit and then take right up again. You can move your business whenever you want. All the stock in trade that a guide needs is a good horse and his knowledge, and his reputation. Reputation is the most important thing, when you come down to it. Shouldn't be, but it is. People often count more on what they hear than on what they can see with their eyes." He looked at me, for some reason, and then rose. "Too bad, but you can't let it worry you."

I was afraid that Bob was going to put a sharp word into the opening Drum had given him, so I quickly asked if anyone had found the mule we'd been looking for.

"Oh, yes," said Drum. "Jim Pierce found him, not far away. Mile or so, eh, Jim? Good doing. Suppose you and I go feed the stock, Jim."

Pierce rose and went with Drum toward the picket-line. The rest of us sat or sprawled about the wagon as Martha began to fix our supper. Hopkins watched Drum walk away and said, gloomily: "A man is what he thinks he is."

"Stuff," said McVey. "He's what he does."

Hopkins sat up and turned to me. "What do you think a man is, Garvin?"

[164]

I didn't intend to be drawn into any more talk about Drum. "Man is a legal fiction," I said lightly.

Hopkins laughed, suddenly delighted. "Bravo!" he said. "Well said." He came closer to the fire Martha had started and began to feed it little bits of grass. "I've got an idea," he said with a smile. "When we get to the mountains, why don't we establish our own government, like everyone else out here? Garvin will be the lawgiver. Give us a law, Garvin."

"We'll have only one law," I answered, "and that will be: Behave yourself."

"Excellent! Simple! And what about criminals?"

McVey said: "Give them an hour's start and hunt them down with hounds."

"Better and better! You can be Master of the Hunt. I'll be Grand Inquisitor. Joel Tyree, what about thee?"

"Thee'll need citizens," smiled Joel. "I'll be a citizen."

"And what about Drum?" asked Hopkins.

"Let him be queen," growled McVey. "His horse is King, isn't it?" Hopkins showed his teeth in a happy grin, but McVey rose abruptly and turned to glare out at where Ned and Jim were moving among our horses. "Him and his horse and his reputation!" he said.

"It's a damned good horse," I said.

"Thee is unkind, Garvin," said Martha.

"No," I said. "I just meant to say that his horse is the one thing I can know about for sure. That's all."

"I'm the one that's unkind," said McVey.

She looked up from her work and smiled at him. "Thee need not brag to me, Robert," she said.

He laughed, and Martha with him. "You're feeling a lot better since you washed your face, aren't you?" he said, and she laughed again.

"I hope I look a little better," she said.

"You had a bath!" I cried, noticing for the first time that she and Joel and Bob all had scrubbed faces, clean hair, and fresh clothing. I sprang up. "I'm going to wash before I eat," I said. "How about you, Willis?"

"I'll wait until I've got something in my stomach," said Hopkins.

"There's a nice pool up there," said McVey, pointing a little above camp, "if you don't mind company. Of course, some people want the whole river to themselves."

Martha chuckled again, shaking her head as she stirred briskly at a bowl of hoecake batter. "I nearly died of fright," she said.

I glanced at Joel, who was smiling affectionately at his wife, and then back at Martha, who explained.

"I went to bathe," she said, "when Joel and Robert had finished. I was standing in the water, scrubbing away, and suddenly something furry touched me from behind." She put a hand to her breast and rolled up her eyes in mock terror. "I almost died on the spot. I shrieked for Joel and jumped out of the water and ran up the bank. I was almost back to camp before I remembered I hadn't any clothes on." She laughed. "So I jumped back in the river and starting *screaming* again."

"What was it?"

"A drowned wolf," answered Joel, "floating along."

Martha shuddered, still laughing. "Poor thing," she said, "but it frightened me so. I don't know what I thought it was, but it was cold and hairy and . . . ugh!"

McVey grinned at her. Joel smiled blandly.

"Well, I'll risk it," I said. "If I scream, somebody come running."

I got some clothes that were rested, if not exactly clean, from my belongings, and went down to the river. McVey sauntered along with me and pointed out the pool, a little above camp, behind a steep bank. After a glance back to make sure that I was properly out of sight, I stripped and waded in. McVey sat on the sandy shore and watched me.

"No wolves so far," I said, and began to rub the grime from my arms with a handful of soap that Martha had given me from her bucket.

"You know," he said very solemnly. "Martha's not a bad figure of a woman, under it all."

I looked up at him sharply and he laughed. "I thought you'd jump!" he grinned. "Don't worry. I didn't see anything I shouldn't. But Martha thinks I did. By the time I looked around she was back in the water. Why *did* you jump, when I said that?"

"The way you said it," I answered, returning to my scrubbing.

"Where did you get the idea I'm after that woman, Garvin?"

"I didn't. Are you?"

"I might as well be," he said. "She thinks so, and so do you."

"What do you have to keep baiting Drum for? We've got another month on the trail, Bob. Why make it unpleasant?"

"For who?"

"For all of us."

"Oh, hell, I don't know, Garvin. Am I as bad as that?"

"It's all right with me if you want to despise Drum. But there's no reason to take it out on the whole lot of us."

"Am I doing that?" he asked.

"That's how it looks."

"You believe he's a fool, don't you? Just like I do."

"Not altogether," I said.

"You respect him, though. I don't see how you do it."

"He's trying to make something out of himself, Bob."

"He's got mighty poor makings to go on."

"That doesn't matter."

"Maybe not. I've been voted down."

"Was that what you wanted?"

He shook his head. "You're scared of me, aren't you?" he said.

I grinned. "Don't give yourself airs."

"You're scared I'll take it into my head to diddle Martha, I know. She told me you advised her not to try to save my soul."

"Oh, did she?"

"You scared I'd take it the wrong way?"

"You did once," I said. "I was listening that night when we slept together back by the Solomon."

"I see," he sighed. "Maybe you're right. I suppose I wouldn't turn her down, if it came to that. Would you?"

"It won't come to that," I answered, "and there's no reason to wonder if I would or you would or she would or anything like that. Is there?"

"I *always* wonder," he said.

11

SINCE the easiest going, according to Drum, was on the north side of the river, we forded at first light the next morning. We climbed the far bank in a billowing, drifting cloud of fine, powdery ash. The smell of the burned prairie was suffocating. On the wagon box, Martha Tyree raised her hand and pointed. Out above the seared, smoking grassland, vultures were circling and gliding—hundreds of them. Every second or so, one or two of them would dip down and come to a clumsy, running landing. They were in little huddles and clumps all over the plain, croaking and crying mournfully.

It took us all the morning to get out of the burn, but we made pretty good time, since the footing was good and fairly level as we moved along a shelf-like ridge, never more than a quarter of a mile from the stream. There was no wind to carry off the ash we stirred up, and within an hour we were all gray with it: horses and men and gear. It was a nuisance, but we could see that Drum was right about choosing the north bank. The valley on the other side rose steeply in crumbling ledges and folds, cut by deep washes.

The number of dead things on the burned ground was surprising; I had never realized how much life there was on the prairie. Hundreds of little ground rodents lay where the flames had caught them. Rabbits were stretched as if they'd died mid-stride. Scorched, dried snakes cracked like twigs beneath our horses' hooves. Partridges and little song birds had fallen into the fire or been caught on their nests, and their eggs had burst and charred. The smell of burned flesh, sweetening into decay, was over it all. "Poor things," Martha Tyree would say to the burned bodies of the little animals as the wagon passed over them. "Poor things."

When we came out of the burn we stopped to shake the ashes out of our things and have a bite to eat, but we made quick work of it. For the first time in weeks, it looked as if we might have a day's trip that would come up to the "average" of twenty-five miles. McVey had taken his usual place in the line that morning, riding just in front of the mules to test the ground for Tyree. That afternoon, however, as soon as we got out of sight of the burn, he pulled out of line, and rode around to the tail of the wagon. He took the Tyrees' fowling piece, which always lay within reach there, and then trotted up to call to Joel.

"I'm going to ride out and have a look for some game," he said. "I'll be up ahead. If you need me, someone fire a shot."

He said this just a little louder than he need have, but Drum, plodding along up ahead, gave no sign of noticing. Bob put a fresh charge in the shotgun, checked his long rifle, which he always carried slung across the back of his saddle, and cantered out past the guide without a look or a word for him.

In the next couple of hours, as we rode peacefully along, I counted Bob's shots as they rang out faintly from the valley ahead. He fired seven times, and not long after the seventh shot he came riding back with half a dozen partridges. Seven shots for six birds.

That night we feasted. To go with Bob's partridges, Martha made a pudding of flour, brown sugar and dried apples. With the river at hand, we had plenty of coffee, too.

We traveled for a week along the slow, cloudy river with no difficulty beyond an occasional dry gully to cross. We made as much as thirty miles in one day, but the average was nearer twenty. The shallow valley flattened out even more as we moved west, and before long there wasn't any valley, just the river winding erratically along across the wide prairie. With little fall to the land, the rivers of the high plains run "a mile wide and an inch deep," and often we saw long stretches of the Smoky Hill where at least the second part of that saying was true. Bars of dazzlingly white sand lay dry in the riverbed, and there were places where you could cross dry-shod by leaping from one to another. The water was there, but it spread out mighty thin.

For the first couple of days after we left the big burn, Drum and McVey did not talk, but they couldn't very well keep that up and Ned came around to his old, polite manner once again. McVey dealt drily with him: no friendliness, but no insults. Drum still left McVey out when he detailed jobs for us, but he left the meat-hunting to Bob, and Bob seemed to enjoy it. He rode out almost every afternoon and was gone for an hour or two. Usually he brought us partridges or rabbits, but as the cover along the river grew more and more scant he began to return with lighter bags. One day he brought in a half-grown pronghorn antelope but there were a couple of days we had no meat at all.

One morning just after we set out we came on a herd of buffalo. Drum gave a hail and we all rode up for a look. There were between fifty and seventy-five of them, watering at the river, huge and ragged, with scraps of their winter pelts still hanging. We came within a hundred yards and they paid us no heed at all, but went on splashing and drinking and wallowing heavily in the shallows.

"Ned," I said, "I thought you told us the buffalo were gone from out here."

He snorted. "A pitiful herd that is, Mr. Cooper. Fifteen years ago they ran in the thousands. One herd might cover the earth as far as you could see in two directions. These probably wouldn't be here now, except that the white man hasn't reached this far."

"He has now," I said. "We're him."

Drum nodded. "We could kill them all," he said, "from

[171]

right here. All you have to do is keep still and shoot them down one at the time, picking off the outside ones first. As long as you kill each one, don't just cripple them, they'll stand around and watch while their friends fall dead. They have no fear. I've heard of men shooting into one herd for four days, all day long, and keeping ten skinners at work for a week."

"Shall we take one for meat?" I asked.

"We can get other meat. These may be all that the Indians out here have left. I look at it that the few buffalo left are like a private herd. The Indians depend on them. Let's leave them go."

"We could dry the meat," said Joel, "and have a supply. It would not be wasted."

"I know," said Drum, "but I wouldn't feel right about it."

"If they're as dumb as you say," said Bob, "they won't last long anyway. Let's take one."

"Well, I suppose we could kill a young bull, if you people are set on it. Just one won't matter, I guess."

McVey dismounted and unlimbered his long rifle.

"Best lie down and take a good aim, Mr. McVey," said Ned, "a wounded buffalo can run fifty miles. You want to kill him clean. Remember he's got a hump on his shoulders, and don't shoot too high. That bull there, coming out of the water, is a likely piece of veal. See if he gives you a shot."

McVey walked out in front of us and sat down. He used his knees as a shooting-rest and leveled the rifle. The rest of us all watched the bull that Drum had pointed out. He came rumbling and grunting up out of the water and stood in a perfect position with his broad side turned to us. Bob put his cheek to the rifle and took aim. The bull bobbed his head and blew into the dust. The rifle banged and he fell heavily to his foreknees. He stayed like that for a moment, feeling around with his hind feet as if he were going to rise. Then he rolled clumsily onto his side, throwing up all four hooves, and lay there stiffly. He didn't make a sound. He didn't struggle. Not one of the others in the herd so much as looked at him.

"Cleanly killed," said Drum.

"Silly brutes," said Hopkins wonderingly.

"See what I mean?" said Drum. "We'll have to shoo the herd away before we butcher him. I'll ride down and try to move them. Stay mounted, in case they stampede this way. If they do, stay close to the wagon and keep your horses facing the herd. A buffalo will go around you if he can, and if he sees you."

McVey silently reloaded his rifle as Drum rode down to move the buffalo. He mounted, and we gathered around the wagon to watch. As Drum neared the herd he put his horse into a canter and took off his hat to wave it. He shouted and rode straight at them, but at first they just raised their bearded heads and stared stupidly at him. Then a couple of them turned and went off at a trot and soon the whole herd was moving up beside the river in a lumpish gallop. As small as the herd was, their hooves made thunder and they raised enough dust for a regiment of cavalry. Drum dismounted by the fallen bull and approached it cautiously. Satisfied that it was dead, he waved for us to come on and we stirred ourselves. By the time Joel got the wagon up beside the dead buffalo Drum had opened its throat to drain the blood and was sawing away at the heavy hide.

We gathered around on foot and stared at the thing; muddy and rough, it was more like part of the very earth, like a hillock or a stone, than a dead beast ... except for its great, round, watery eyes and the thick tongue trailing in the dust and the dark, clotted blood soaking the ground.

"A cow makes better eating," said Drum, "but the cows are needed for their calves. This one will be all right. He's young. I wonder if you could give me a hand with this, Mr. McVey?"

Bob nodded and began to roll up his sleeves. It was a good sign—on both sides.

That meat lasted us only a few days, for the part that we tried to preserve by hanging in strips along the wagon, for the sun to dry it, went bad. Bob spent more time on his hunts and returned always with poorer and poorer bags.

[173]

McVey was the only one of us who stayed busy during this time. When he wasn't hunting he was scouting around the prairie or stopping for a few minutes to sketch: sitting back in his saddle with one leg cocked across the pommel as a rest for his sketch book, or squatting with it on his knees while his horse grazed nearby with trailing reins. He sketched the river, the birds, the strange, prickly plants we came across, the horses, the wagons. He was still apart from us, just as he had declared himself from the beginning, but at least he seemed no longer at odds with us. That was how it seemed, at least. He was pleasant with us all, but after his outburst against Drum, back at the burned ground, no one was willing to risk setting him off again—not even Martha, although I still saw her watch him, sometimes, in that calculating, pitying way. The traveling was so easy and uneventful that we got the feeling that our trip was over, or as good as over. I know I felt that way. I was thinking ahead, all the time, to the mountains we were soon to see: the new country waiting for me, friendly, virgin, full of promise.

It continued hot and dry, but the sun no longer bothered us; we were all tanned to gunstock color. One thing that began to get on our nerves was the dried apples, for Drum was very strict about everyone eating one handful every day. When we began to grumble, he taught us a trail song that he had learned on the emigrant routes:

> Dried apples I loathe, I detest, I despise.
> Dried apple pudding and dried apple pies!
> Dried apples I loathe, I detest, I abhor.
> In Oregon's valleys I'll eat them no more.

We sang that one with deep conviction.

Joel and Martha seemed always to have things to say to each other. Besides talking all day long as they sat side by side on the wagon box, they chatted together earnestly through the evenings and through our Sundays, when we stopped to rest the stock. The animals continued to do fairly well, but the grazing was poor, dry stuff and they didn't like it. We agreed that as soon as we found really good grass we would stop, Sunday or not, and let them have a couple of days on it. We did not worry about it, however. We didn't worry about anything. The vast, featureless prairie; the unchanging weather and the days that were all the same; the cloudless sky; the dull, automatic moving-on; began to prey on us. You could feel laxness and boredom in our campfire talks. McVey was not the only one who drew apart and into himself. We all did it. Even Drum seemed satisfied and disinterested. For myself, I read, worked with the horses, engaged in long, pointless conversations with Willis, or just lay around and daydreamed.

Hopkins kept his journal for a while, but when that palled he began—of all things—to collect rocks. He had gotten the idea that the country we were crossing might hide unknown riches: gold or silver or God knows what. He sat around in his spare time stitching little sacks that he cut out of Martha's empty flour sacks. Soon he had a whole saddlebag full of them, each one holding a handful of sand or gravel or clay and tagged with the approximate location where he'd found it. When we got to the mining country, so he told me, he intended to have them all assayed.

Jim Pierce listened—he listened always to everything, without a word. The boy just didn't know what to do if there was no work under his hands. He whittled and repaired harness and fussed with the wagon and was positively elated when I asked him to see if he could make a new stock for my broken rifle. He stayed busy on that for a week.

Drum remained as cheery as he could, in the atmosphere of all this boredom, and often rallied us for being "kind of glum." He would bustle about our little fire of grass and twigs, saying: "It's not very exciting, is it? this putting one foot after another? Well, that's the way you get where you're going. One foot after another. You'll settle down to it. We're better than halfway there now, you know. Maybe two-thirds of the way. I guess they'll sit up and think then! Those that said there was no trail this way! We'll show them a little something, eh?"

[175]

He was very disturbed when he noticed that Hopkins had given up his journal.

One evening when McVey came in from a fruitless afternoon's hunt, he brought Drum a curiosity: a strip of untanned leather, decorated on one side with beadwork. We gathered about as Drum turned it over in his fingers before speaking.

"Indian work, all right," he said. "I can't say that I know the pattern. Some men can tell the tribe by the beadwork. This is a piece off a war shirt."

"What's that?" McVey asked suspiciously.

"Sort of a vest that a chief wears in war and in ceremonies. It's like a medal, in a way. This strip runs down the side, under the arm. See where it was stitched?" He turned it over and peered closely at it again. "Where did you come across this?" he asked.

"I'll show you tomorrow."

The next day, when we got to the place, McVey pointed out where he had picked up the piece of leather. Drum dismounted and walked about for a bit, then he went down to the river's edge and began to walk along peering at the ground. He motioned for us to come look, and he pointed out the tracks of horses.

"I make it five horses," he said. "Braves. No women or gear. They watered here three or four days ago and then crossed. They may have been down here hunting those buffalo that we saw."

"I thought you said they wore these shirts for war," I reminded him.

"Generally, yes, but if a man had a war shirt he might carry it along with him when he went on a long hunt."

"In case he met whites," said McVey.

"To keep it near him," Drum replied. "Magic, sort of."

"How far are we," Hopkins asked, "from this Indian village you told us about?"

"Maybe a hundred miles."

"How close will we come to it?"

"We'll pass within forty, fifty miles of them."

Joel had been looking at the hoof-prints, the river, and the stretch ahead. "I can see why they came here to water," he said. We looked, and he pointed upstream. At first, it looked as if the river ended right above us. Then we saw that there was a channel—perhaps three feet wide and six inches deep—winding through the glittering sandbanks.

"They run thin, sometimes," said Drum.

"Couldn't get much thinner," I said.

We looked at it for a while, gazed at the tracks of the Indian ponies, and went slowly back to the wagon and our mounts.

That afternoon, Bob went out as usual for his hunt. He was gone a long time, and he came back empty-handed just at dark, when the rest of us had eaten and were beginning to worry about him. As soon as he strode into our circle I knew that something had happened. His eyes were snapping darkly.

"This river's about to quit," he said. He hitched his thumbs in his pockets and stared at us.

"How's that?" asked Drum.

"I rode up as far as I could and still get back. There's no game, and no brush up there. Just rocks. The river's about to peter out. Five miles from here it isn't enough to wet your hat."

"Dry?" said Joel incredulously.

"Damned near. Just a trickle."

"It's low, all right," said Drum. "There's no denying that."

"Low isn't the half of it!" Bob cried. "It's running out!"

Drum smiled indulgently. "I know, Mr. McVey," he said, "there'll be a pool and then a little wet stretch and then another pool, and so on. It gets that way."

"Drum, I tell you the river's almost dry. *Bone* dry! Absolutely dry. We're going to have no water by tomorrow night."

"Bob," I said, "is there grass?"

"A little. It gets pretty rocky, though."

"Enough to graze the stock?"

[177]

"I don't know. Doesn't look like it to me."

"We'll see," said Drum serenely, "as we go along. It's too soon to throw up our hands, Mr. McVey."

"Well, suppose it turns out I'm right. What are we going to do for water?"

"We've got barrels. We can carry two days' water, if need be."

"Where can we get in two days?"

"Fifty miles, if we have to. In fifty miles we can find water."

McVey stared coldly at Drum. "You'd better be right," he said. "You'd better be right."

McVey had not exaggerated. By noon the next day the river had shrunk to a pitiful dribble. But Drum was right, too. There were still little pools of hot, clear water, connected by threadlike channels. We stopped at one of those pools just after midday and watered the stock. By the time they had all drunk there wasn't more than a soup-bowl full of water left. Joel and Jim and I stood and watched the tiny stream refill the hole. It seemed to do it very slowly.

And there was enough grass for the animals—or would have been, had they not already been on short rations for a week. Joel, Ned, and I talked it over. Drum estimated that it would be a hundred miles yet before we found really rich pasturage.

"Let's rest them every third day," I said, "until we get to decent grass."

"It'll mean that much longer before they get it," Drum pointed out, and I had to agree with him. After all, a hundred miles was five days, at the rate we'd been going. It would be hard on the horses, but not killing.

The river kept on shrinking, until McVey's gloomy predictions began to seem worth listening to. By the next evening we had traveled one stretch of it that was completely dry for a quarter of a mile. The channel between two pools had disappeared, and the higher pool was standing water. At Drum's directions, we filled both our water-barrels and all the canteens.

That night as I was consoling Hoecake for the poor grazing, Drum came out and joined me. He was very thoughtful and a little nervous.

"Mr. Cooper," he said, "I'd like to ask your advice, in confidence."

"All right, Ned."

"How do you think the spirit is, in these people?"

"Good."

"They've been kind of talking worried today."

"It's the water," I said.

"I know. I don't want them to lose heart."

"I don't think they've lost heart—not yet."

"The water's all right, Mr. Cooper. Even if the river goes plumb dry, we can make it over to Sand Creek, by pushing a little."

"Sure that wouldn't be dry?"

"It's spring-fed," he said. "Not likely to dry up. This river here drains rainwater off the prairie. Different kind of a thing."

He stood silent by my mare, absent-mindedly stroking her neck.

"What's the advice?" I asked.

"Eh? Well... that's it. I just wanted to know how you thought everybody was coming along. Don't want anybody to think about giving up, you know. We've got to push on. It isn't far now."

I felt sure that he had come out to ask me more than that, but he patted Hoecake once more and left me. The more I thought about it, the less I liked it; and yet, I believed him when he said we could reach water.

Just before noon the following day, we came to a place where the riverbed lay dry for as far as we could see. McVey spurred his horse ahead and Drum rode out right behind him. The rest of us let our animals graze as we sat in the shade of the wagon to await their return. They were gone an hour, and came back on lathered horses.

"A few little puddles," said McVey calmly.

Drum dismounted and came to us, pushing his hat back on his head. He squatted, and Bob stood behind him in the sun. Both of them were soaked with sweat and plastered with dust. They'd been riding hard.

"How far did you go?" I asked.

"Five miles or more," said Drum. "It's quit on us, all right. We're going to have to make a dry march, as fast as we can, to reach Sand Creek. We'll water here as well as we can, and give the horses a rest. We'll set out at sundown and travel until dawn. That'll be easiest on everyone, even though we won't get much sleep."

"Give up, Drum," said McVey.

"No, Mr. McVey. There's no reason to give up."

"Why not ask somebody else what they think?" Drum made no answer, so Bob turned to me. "Garvin?"

"There is no need for more voting," said Martha firmly. "We have put our faith in Ned Drum. Can't thee accept that, Robert? Can't thee believe it?"

"I can't understand it," he answered. "Garvin?"

"She's right," I said.

"Joel?" Bob asked. "You've got a wife to worry about. What about you?"

Joel hesitated. "I have faith in Ned Drum still," he said, "but Martha is wrong when she says there is no need to talk of this. I hope that we will not do anything foolish just because we feel committed to it."

"I agree," Drum grunted. "If we come to the end of our line, why, we'll turn back. But this isn't it."

"What if we're dead at the end of the line?" asked Willis.

"It's not that bad, Mr. Hopkins."

"I don't want it to get that bad, either," said Willis.

"No one does."

McVey shook his head. "Drum, you just don't believe it can get that bad. Well, it can."

"Mr. McVey, what makes you think I'd tell you to go on if I didn't know it was safe? Do you take me for a fool?"

"No. I thought you were a fool once, Drum, but I've changed my mind. I think you're crazy. I think you want to be a first-timer so bad that you're willing to die trying. I'm not. Garvin probably is, and Jim doesn't know any better,

[180]

and Joel and Martha will trust in God to the last gasp. But I'm not and Willis isn't."

"You told us once not to count on you, Mr. McVey. It seems you were right."

"I meant it. Willis, how about you and me turning back right now?"

Hopkins stared at McVey and wet his lips nervously.

"Thee cannot!" cried Martha.

"Why not? Give us one pack horse and some food and powder and shot. We can follow what's left of this river back to that trading post. Then we'll decide what to do."

"All right," Hopkins blurted suddenly. "I'll do it."

"Good man."

Drum had been watching McVey thoughtfully and doubtfully. Now he rose and set his face sternly. "I wouldn't do that, Mr. McVey. Wouldn't be safe."

"Safe! How do you know what's safe?"

"There's something I haven't told you people. Maybe I shouldn't have kept it from you, but I didn't see any reason to frighten anyone." We waited as he drew a deep breath. "There's Indians watching us," he said. "They've been about for three days now, almost all the time. I've seen signs, and I spotted one of them yesterday. I think it's the same five whose tracks we saw. They won't bother us. But two men alone, I don't know."

There was a moment of silence. McVey said: "These noblemen of yours?"

"Cheyenne, by the look of the one I saw."

"I don't believe you. Where would they be hiding close enough to watch us?"

Drum chuckled. "Believe me, Mr. McVey. They're out there. Do you believe me, Mr. Hopkins?"

Willis nodded slowly.

"Then why don't we try to get some sleep?"

"Drum," I said, "you should have told us."

"Why? There's nothing we can do but go along and not worry about them. They won't bother a party, but if they

[181]

saw a chance to get a horse or two they'd take it. I doubt if they'd kill you, Mr. McVey, but you'd have a long, hot walk."

There was really nothing to say. We all looked hard around at the prairie. You could see where they might hide: little cracks and crevices in the ground, clumps of brush, a stone here and a bank there. We settled thoughtfully to rest in the shade of the wagon, but we did not sleep.

12

WE started out as soon as the sun was below the skyline. It was nervous going at first, since the horses didn't like it and all of us kept thinking about Indians even though Drum had assured us that they would lie low during the night. It was better when a half moon came up just before midnight, and the cool night breeze made a welcome change from the blistering days we were used to.

We traveled hard, even though horses and men alike began to get sleepy toward morning. Martha actually dozed off on the wagon box and would have fallen over the dashboard if Joel hadn't got a handful of her skirt and heaved her back. At the break of day we stopped and scraped together brush for a fire. The gray light showed us the riverbed of gleaming sand, dry except for one shallow puddle the size of a wagon wheel. We made the most of it, though, for it held enough water for two of our horses. We each had only a couple of swallows from a canteen before we spread our blankets.

Our terrain had changed during the night, too. Once again the ground was noticably rising to the westward, and getting a little rougher and rockier. The western horizon was no longer so knife-blade clean, but was broken by little hills and washes rising from the river on either side.

We slept like the dead for the first couple of hours of

daylight. About mid-morning I was awakened by Drum gently shaking my shoulder.

"I've been keeping watch," he said. "Would you be next, Mr. Cooper?"

"Watch?"

"Just keeping an eye on the stock. Nothing's liable to happen, but I thought it would be best."

I nodded and crawled out from under the wagon. Drum crept wearily into the shade and subsided with a mutter among the others sleeping there. Joel and Martha had their tent, but I soon knew that the rest of them weren't going to sleep for long. It was just too hot, however tired they might be. I climbed up into the back of the wagon and sat on our supplies, shaded by the canopy. The horses and mules were restless on their lines and weren't doing much sleeping. After a while, when I began to think I was liable to doze off, I hopped down and went to have a look at them. They were doing all right, considering the distance they'd come and the fare they'd had. So far, only their dispositions had been affected by the poor forage; they were nervous and sulky-acting and put their noses out to me in an anxious, questioning way. I patted them and hummed to them and then brought a bucket from the wagon to let each one wet his muzzle. The very smell of the water excited them, and I had a time keeping them from knocking me down to get at it.

When I went back to the wagon, Hopkins was sitting up blinking at me, his downy blond hair plastered to his forehead with sweat.

"I can't sleep in this," he whispered, and James Pierce raised his head groggily and frowned at us.

They both got up and we walked down by the river bed to see if we could find any more of those little pools. We scouted both upstream and down, but found no more water, though much of the sand was moist underfoot.

"I bet we could dig water," said Jim.

"We may have to," said Hopkins nervously. "Garvin, what do you think about this? Shouldn't we turn back?"

"I don't feel much like going either way," I said, "but

I'm counting on Drum. If we go back, I haven't got enough money to make another start."

"Neither have I, but this is serious."

"This trip means a lot to Ned," I said. "He isn't going to let it fail if he can help it. He may drive us hard, but I don't think he's going to be careless. He just can't afford to be."

"Do you think he's telling the truth about the Indians?"

"He's got no reason to lie."

"Except to keep me and Bob from turning back. That would be a failure for him too, you know."

"I don't think he'd do that," I said.

"Mr. Drum knows about the Indians," said Jim Pierce. "I believe him."

When we returned everyone but Ned was awake and grumbling at the heat. We spent the rest of the heat of the day in drowsing fitfully and unhappily in the sun. Toward late afternoon I managed to sleep once again, and they woke me at nightfall for a bite to eat before starting out.

McVey waited until we were all mounted and ready to go before he said, loudly in the darkness: "Which way?"

Martha gave a little groan. Drum snorted impatiently. Bob sat his horse out in front of the team, just visible in the night, and when no one answered him he gave a little laugh.

"Here we go," he said. "Six fools and a crazy man. Lead the way, Brother Drum! We're going to the promised land."

The rough, rising ground made that night's travel a lot harder. We had two bad gullies to cross along toward morning, and in the dark it was a nightmare job. The sun caught us as we struggled up out of the second one, and we unhitched and watered the animals in our sleep. Drum again took the first watch, and he must have waked someone else for the second one, for when I was beaten out of sleep by the sun it was almost noon and everyone else was already up. There was no longer any river at all: just the winding trail of flat sand marking its course; and we were leaving the prairie for sure, for the land ahead was rolling and broken and to the north lay a range of high, pale, clay hills. Those,

[185]

Drum told us, were the Smoky Hills that gave the river its name.

"Then thee knows where we are for sure?" asked Joel.

"Of course, Mr. Tyree."

"And how far to the water?"

"About thirty miles, at the most."

"We'll not make it tonight," said Joel, pointing west and squinting into the heat that shimmered on the rocks out there.

"No, I doubt if we will."

Jim asked: "Are the Indians still following us?"

"I think they've given us up, Jim. They don't like moving at night."

"One barrel left," said McVey.

Drum nodded. "It will do."

"Grain getting low."

"Mr. McVey, there's water and there's grass, within our reach. Tomorrow, or tomorrow night, we'll reach it."

"Suppose we don't?"

"No supposing to it," said Drum obstinately. "We will."

"Why? Because that's the way your daydreams all come out?"

Later, as the day cooled and we began settling to another nap, I said to Bob: "You better forget about turning back."

"What do you mean?"

"Back that way, it's two days to water and four days to decent grass. The horses wouldn't make it—not on one barrel and the little bit of oats we have left. We've got to keep going."

He thought about that for a moment. Then he began to chuckle. "The brave pioneers," he said. "The brave pioneers! Garvin, what a story we'll make in the history books!"

That night's travel will stay with me as a vision of Hell's torment. With balky, angry mules and horses, we struggled up through tumbled, rocky ledges, crumbling banks and shifting sand. Numb with fatigue and driven by our growing fear, we worked like madmen. We would have been ready to pick that wagon up and carry it, if Drum had told us to. He himself remained calm and soft spoken. When the sun discovered us toiling over a waste of dry shale, he called a halt and addressed us.

"Another ten miles," he said to us. "If you feel like going on, we can be there by afternoon. We've water yet, and if you're too tired, we'll rest; but I'd advise pushing on."

We looked up at him stupidly as he stood before us.

"Ten miles," he repeated, "at the most."

"Why not let someone take one of the barrels on a pack horse," said McVey, "and bring water back?"

"By the time he could go and come, we could get there with the wagon. That wouldn't save any time."

"Oh, I forgot. You want to set a speed record, don't you? Forty days. Excuse me."

"Mr. McVey, you mustn't give way to despair."

"Despair!" yelled Bob. *"Despair?"*

"That's what I said."

"I was right, Drum. You're out of your head! You're raving mad! You tell me when to get worried, will you?"

"Shall we go on?" asked Drum.

"For God's sake let's not stop," I moaned. "If I lie down I'll never get up."

Martha nodded.

"Good, good," said Drum. "That's the stuff that moves mountains—and crosses plains. That's the spirit. We'll have something to eat and pass around a little water, and then go on. Just a little further! You've good as done it now! After we reach the creek, it's easy going and only another hundred and fifty miles. Tomorrow, you'll see the mountains in the distance, maybe."

We made a fire, yawning and groaning, and gathered about it while Martha made meal cakes. We washed them down with a mouthful of water apiece and prepared to start up again. Bob went to the wagon and began to unlash one of the water barrels.

"Mr. McVey," said Drum. "Don't waste your time."

"Don't you waste your breath," said Bob. "I'm tired of

listening to how fine and dandy everything is. I'm going to take this barrel and try to find water."

"How do you think you're going to do that? Do you know where it is?"

McVey stared at him, then looked out ahead of the wagon. He hadn't realized, apparently, that somewhere in the last couple of days we had left the dry bed of the river.

"You tell me," he said.

"No, Mr. McVey. You'd best stay with us."

Bob looked at him wearily and shrugged his shoulders. "All right, I'll die your way," he said.

"No need to talk of dying," said Drum gently.

"That's right. Let's be cheerful." McVey went to his horse and rode out ahead.

"Where are you going?" Drum called hoarsely.

"I'm going to see what's ahead!" shouted Bob, and he kicked his weary horse into a trot.

"Mr. McVey!" Drum bellowed. "Come back!" Then he shook his head. "The devil with him," he said. "He's just going to wear out that horse. Everybody ready? Let's go."

I remember very little of that morning. I was reeling in the saddle, bringing myself around now and then to give them a hand with the wagon, then clambering back onto my horse someway. Bob rode out ahead whenever he saw a high spot or a hill that might give him sight of whatever lay before us. I guess he just felt he had to be *doing* something. Anyway, he seemed more alive than anyone else except Drum, who kept plodding along, cheering us and encouraging us and wheedling us onward. We took a short rest around noon, too tired to try to eat, and McVey crouched by the wagon staring coldly to the west.

"Bob," I said, "don't wear yourself out."

"I always knew that it would be somebody with ideals that would do me in, Garvin."

"Oh, stop it!"

"What do you want on your tombstone, Cooper?"

"Bob, you're very dramatic, but you're not being any help."

[188]

"I tried to be a help, three days ago."

As I tried to think of something to say, I dozed off.

It was about an hour after our rest stop that I was riding along like a sleep-walker when the sound of a shot jarred me to attention. I looked around and saw that I was back near the tail of the pack-line, with Willis. He looked like living death.

"What was that?" I asked him.

He shook his head, so I rode up past the wagon just as Tyree pulled his team to a halt.

"Who shot?" I asked.

"I think it was Robert. He rode up ahead."

Drum was sitting out there on his yellow gelding, standing in the stirrups and craning his neck to see up into a jumble of rocks and dry brush. I looked the same place, but could see nothing. Drum turned his horse and trotted back to us.

"He wouldn't be hunting," he said.

"Hadn't we better go find out?" I suggested.

"Let's wait a minute."

Just then Bob came into sight, leading his horse down out of the rocks. His rifle was in his hand. He glanced once down at us, then he sprang to his horse and came crashing toward the wagon, pell mell. He brought the trembling horse to a halt and sat looking at us. He seemed to be trying to swallow, and get his voice, and his face had a surprised and uncomprehending look as if he'd seen something not of this world.

"I shot an Indian," he said.

13

He was an old man; not an ancient, but older than I had expected. His long, glossy hair was streaked with gray. He lay on his back in a narrow, sandy gully that was too small for him so that it hunched his shoulders together and pinned his elbows in against his ribs. The indrawn shoulders and arms and the way his head fell back, exposing his sinewy old throat, made it look at first as if he were in a spasm of agony, but he was unconscious, motionless except for the quick heaving of his chest. His skin was an ashy brown. His thick hair was spread like a halo beneath his head, and a band of beaded hide had slipped askew over his forehead. He wore a sleeveless shirt, and both his lank arms were ornamented with bracelets of twisted iron wire. Floppy leggings covered his legs, and about the middle he wore a sort of apron of skin and a belt with a fur pouch fastened at his waist. One of his hide moccasins had fallen off, showing a dusty, stringy foot on which the yellowed nails stood out like flat claws. His waist and his right thigh were smeared with blood. I stood and tried to look steadfastly at him and still not to see him, and not to see the bruised, blue, ragged wound in his right side.

"He'll have a horse nearby," said Drum. "Mr. McVey, why don't you try to find it? Jim, you help him."

Bob mounted, not looking at any of us or at the Indian,

and trotted off up the wash. Jim Pierce ran to his horse and followed. Drum squatted in the dust and took the Indian's hand in his, feeling for the pulse. "Cheyenne," he said, "and an important man."

"How can you tell?" I asked.

"His gear and his clothes. Mr. Hopkins, will you bring his weapons? Mr. Cooper and I will carry him down to the wagon."

Hopkins picked up the Indian's short, stout bow and the handful of arrows that lay by it in the dust. I got around by the Indian's shoulders and waited for Drum, but he just squatted there, looking down at the man's face, and then he passed the fingers of his hand across his eyes as if to brush away a cobweb.

"All right," I said. Drum nodded and gathered the man's thighs into his arms, ignoring the blood that smeared his coat. I took him under the armpits, flinching a little as his face rolled against my shirt, and we lifted. We got a grip and started carrying him, with Hopkins limping nervously along beside us. Joel Tyree came to meet us and gave me a hand. We laid him in the shade beneath the wagon and Martha knelt beside him.

"Moisten a cloth," she said, and her husband went to do as she'd said.

"He's a dead man," said Drum. "The bullet is in his bowels." He was still staring down at the Indian's face, and once again he brushed distractedly at his eyes. "Mr. Cooper," he said, "do you see anything of Mr. McVey and the boy?"

"No."

"They must find that horse," he said soberly. He seemed to be trying to think at once about many, many things. "This had to happen!" he cried suddenly. He bent his head, burying his chin in his beard, and he crossed his arms on his chest, clasping his shoulders, as he said again: "This had to happen!"

"How did it come about?" asked Joel, handing his wife a dripping cloth. She began to sponge away the blood on the

Indian's stomach. Drum shook his head, slowly, ponderously. I saw that there were tears in his eyes.

"I don't know," he said, and he meant it.

"Why did Robert McVey shoot?" said Martha.

"Ask him! Don't ask me. He just saw the man standing there, and shot him."

"Did they attack him?"

" 'They'? There wasn't any 'they.' There wasn't but this old man, standing there."

Martha went on wiping away the blood, and the blood kept flowing back until the bit of rag in her hand was drenched with it, and still she kept dabbing. "We must bind it up," she said, but none of us moved. She sprang up and clambered into the wagon, where she began digging into her goods for cloths.

Drum raised his head and set his jaw. He seemed to have hold of himself. He took my arm and turned me away from the wounded man. "Listen to me," he said. "Mr. Tyree, Mr. Hopkins. You too. Listen to me. We must decide what to do. No, No. Leave him. He's a dead man. Come here and listen to me." He led us out into the sun and stood with his hands clenched at his sides. "If they don't catch that Indian's pony," he said, "it'll be running home. The Indians will backtrack it and find us within a day or so. If they do catch the pony, we've got a little longer, but not much. We must decide what to do."

"What can we do?" said Willis numbly.

"If we leave the wagon," said Drum, "and the packs, and ride hard on our best horses, we can be at Bent's Fort, on the Arkansas, in three days."

"Then that's what we have to do, isn't it?" I asked.

"I don't think we'd make it," said Drum. "They'd run us down in no time. If I'm right about where we are, they're almost between us and Bent's. They'd catch us, unless we had the best luck there is. Remember, our horses haven't had rest in a day and a half."

"Have we any other chance?" asked Willis.

"I'm thinking," said Drum. "Even if we get to Bent's all

right, the Indians will complain to the Indian agent, and we'll still be in trouble."

"How?"

"Mr. McVey will have to be charged, of course, and tried."

"What would they do to him?" I asked.

"Who knows? Put him in jail, I expect. The Indians have to be satisfied. There are treaties. Mr. McVey would have to be punished, but it probably wouldn't be much. He'd get off with a year's sentence and then he might be pardoned after a few months, if somebody carried it to the governor." He sighed. "We'd be called to witness, too," he said.

"What if we go on to the creek, get water, and then go back the way we came?" asked Joel.

"They'd catch us, that's what."

"Ned Drum," called Martha. She had stopped dabbing, and the ground around her was littered with stained rags. Drum went to her and leaned over the Indian.

"Yes," he said, "he's dead." He lifted the old man's hands and laid them on his bony chest. "If he had lived, we could have taken him to the village, and it might have been all right. We could have told them that it was an accident, that we were hunting, or something of the sort."

There was a clatter of hooves up in the rocks and we all spun about in a fright. It was Bob and Jim, leading a shaggy, cow-hocked gray pony with a padded saddle. Drum went to them as they dismounted and took the pony's bridle. He unhitched a little decorated role of hide, a sort of satchel, that hung on the pommel.

"His pipe and tobacco," he said. He carried it over to the dead Indian and tucked the roll into the crook of his arm. Then he turned to McVey. "Your man is dead," he said. McVey did not take his eyes off of Drum, or change one muscle of his face. "Why did you shoot?" Drum asked. "What happened?"

McVey cleared his throat. "He was crouching down, watching me. He had his bow ready with an arrow in it. He had me cut off from the wagon. I just shot."

[193]

"Did he make any move to fight you? Did he threaten you?"

"No," said McVey, speaking a little louder, "he didn't threaten me. He didn't do anything. He just looked at me."

"And so you killed him."

"You said they were liable to attack."

"I told you not to go off on your own!" cried Drum in a rage of frustration. "I told you that to keep you from doing a foolish thing. Did you think this old man was going to attack you—him with a bow and you with a rifle? Were you that scared?"

"Yes, I was scared."

"Then why didn't you call for me? Why didn't you run? Why didn't you do anything but shoot?"

"Ned, Ned," said Martha. "This is no good, and no use. What must we do?"

Drum shook himself like a hurt animal. "Give me a hand," he said, "and let's wrap him in something. The tent will do. Get the tent, Mr. Tyree."

Joel and Jim wrestled the heavy canvas down from the wagon. Hopkins and Martha helped as they spread it on the ground beside the Indian. Drum rolled him on it and folded it neatly over his head and his feet and tucked the sides under. The neat package made the old man deader and more horrible than he had been even in his stringy flesh and his sticky blood. When that was done, Drum straightened up and turned to us.

"We've going to take him to the village," he said.

We didn't understand. We stared at him.

"We'll face it out," he said. "That's the only way." He pointed down at the body. "Among these people, when one man kills another in a quarrel or by accident, they pay damages. The widow and the man's brothers have to be paid. Usually they give horses or goods of some kind. That's the way they generally do. We'll go there and tell them he was killed by accident. We'll offer to pay whatever's fair." He looked from one face to another.

[194]

Joel said, "Will they accept that?"

"Their chief is a fair man," he said. "I told you about him. I think he'll agree to it."

"Suppose he doesn't?" I asked.

"We've no choice, Mr. Cooper. We can't run, without leaving the wagon and all our belongings, and we'd have a poor chance even then, what with Mrs. Tyree that isn't used to being horseback, and Mr. Hopkins here that doesn't ride too good to begin with. We can stand and fight. Is that what you want? We're better armed than they are, and better mounted. We could kill some more of them and probably get away if our powder held out. But we'd have to answer for that, too, in the end."

"You mean to hand me over to them?" said Bob. He seemed embarrassed.

"What will you choose?" demanded Drum. He pointed to Martha. "Shall we let them kill this woman?"

"I'll take my horse and some meal and find my own way. I'm on my own. I can take care of myself."

"And have us answer for your killing? No."

Martha began: "Ned, we must not do..." but Drum interrupted her fiercely.

"We'll have no more talk, Mrs. Tyree! And no more voting. We're going to do what has to be done. We're going to do as I say. I've been too easy; that's my trouble. Well, no more! I'm not going to stand and see everything brought to ruin! I'm going to take hold, you understand? Now let's pack this man into the wagon. Put his pony in with the others, Jim."

"Ned," I said, "why don't we parlay with the Indians? We can..."

"No! I'm tired of arguing with you people. You must understand me! I'm in charge. Get ready to move out. Give me a hand, Mr. Tyree."

Joel helped him lift the body of the Indian into the wagon bed. Then he went to his horse and mounted. McVey had not moved, and neither had I. Martha was hesitating. Pierce had mounted and Hopkins was walking slowly to his horse.

Drum looked at us, trembling. "You talked of letting me go," he said. "Suppose I let *you* go? What then, eh?"

Martha went to the front of the wagon and climbed wearily to the seat. Joel followed her. One by one, the rest of us mounted. Drum's gelding started off at a willing trot, but the rest of us had to kick our mounts out of their weary stupor to get them moving. I fell in beside McVey.

"I'll talk to him when he cools down," I said. "I've got an idea. We can stop outside that village and call the Indians out to talk. We'll tell them it was an accident, and offer to pay. If they want to make trouble, we'll offer to fight."

Bob shook his head. "Garvin," he said, "to think that I've ever called a man a fool."

"Anyone might have done it," I said. "Particularly after Drum tried to scare you with his Indian stories."

"There's something wrong with me, Garvin. You know that?"

"Don't start thinking that way. We've got to worry about what's coming, not what's past."

"I've always had an idea that someday I'd kill a man. Some fool, I thought, would be more than I could bear, like my father, and I'd kill him. It didn't even take that much."

"Anyone could have done it!" I insisted.

"That's right. But I killed this one." He beat his fist on his thigh. "I shot him down."

"Forget that. Think about what's ahead, and think clear. And don't get scared. I'm not going to let Drum do anything wild."

"You're too late. You could have stopped us all from doing wild things, Garvin, maybe. But not now."

We crashed along through the boulders and the gullys for over an hour before we came in sight of a line of stunted trees and brush, marking the line of a stream. It was the creek, just as he'd told us we'd find it. The horses caught the scent of water and broke into a trot. Joel barely kept his team from hauling the wagon straight into the trees, and they were frantic as he and Martha unhitched them. We pulled them away as soon as they'd drunk enough to wet their bellies

[196]

good, and tied them where they could browse on the green leaves and shoots. Then we filled our water barrels and last of all we lay down on the bank and drank for ourselves, slowly, blowing into the water, dunking our dusty heads and bathing our tired, hot eyes.

"We're further north than I thought," said Drum, "but this is the main fork of Sand Creek. About twenty-five miles south of here is where Rush Creek branches off. The village is just above that fork. We'll take an hour here to breathe the horses, but before we camp we have to cover another ten miles. Then tomorrow we'll reach the village in daylight."

"Ned," I said, "the horses can't go any more today. They haven't rested since yesterday, and they've been working hard."

"They'll have to go more, Mr. Cooper. Don't you worry. I've got my eye on them." He was talking to me, but he was watching McVey as Bob crawled wearily into the shade of a clump of little willows. Bob had tied his little gelding by its reins, leaving it saddled. He lay in the shade on his back and slowly closed his eyes, breathing deeply. Drum marched over to Bob's horse and quickly drew Bob's rifle from where it was lashed against the saddle-roll. He went around the wagon, putting it between him and Bob, and there he drew the charge. Then he climbed up and stowed the gun under some of our supplies. I watched him, and so did Pierce, but I didn't see anyone else notice what he was doing. When he was finished he went to his big yellow horse, slipped the girth and lifted the saddle to the ground. He took a handkerchief from his pocket and began to wipe the gelding's back and withers. I walked over beside him.

"Ned," I said, "as soon as it looks like those Indians mean to harm Bob, I'll start a fight with them. I promise you that. And I'll give Bob another gun, too, to defend himself."

For a moment, he went on swabbing his horse. Then, not even looking at me, he said, "I don't think you will, Mr. Cooper. If you do, you'll be dead. There's thirty lodges in this camp. That's anywhere from sixty to ninety braves,

[197]

you can figure. You'll not fight them in their own village, unless you're more fool than I take you for."

"You're going to let him die because you don't like him."

"I'll do everything I can to reach a settlement. But if he does die, remember that it was him that killed this old man in the wagon." He patted his horse and looked around at me. "I've had enough trouble, Mr. Cooper. Every time I've tried to do something, I've been tripped up by someone like this McVey fellow. Every time. I've gone along thinking that if I treated my fellow man right, he'd treat me right. I've tried to be like the Lord's pillar of cloud to you people, like a guide going before, to show the way. Now it seems I must put on the ways of the pillar of fire." He nodded primly. "I can do that, too."

Drum was beyond anything I, or anyone, might say to him. He was a righteous man outraged. It wasn't us; it was his whole life, of which this trip was to have been the capstone. Now he was going to lead us straight into the lair of Fate, and demand of her why she had cheated him.

He couldn't even wait out the hour he had granted us. We had barely got our breath when he saddled up and called us to form our march. We moved because we were too numb with fear and weariness to fight him. He struck out south along the sandy creek at a good pace, and Tyree had all he could do to make his mules keep up. Luckily, the land opened up as we traveled downstream, or I don't think we'd have made it. The creek wound through shale and sand, nourishing a strip of greenery a few yards wide on either side, while farther out the land flattened into the familiar, parched, yellow-brown prairie. After the first mile, the wagon had fairly easy going, but there were some bad spots. Drum never looked back, and when Joel stopped the wagon to ease over a gully I'd have to ride Drum down to make him wait, and then he would sit there looking patiently back, his hands crossed on the saddle horn.

We stopped to water the animals again late in the afternoon, but Drum pressed right on. We didn't even get a chance to sit down. As he started out, and Joel called up

[198]

his team, I put my foot in the stirrup, swung to the saddle and felt Hoecake reel under my weight. She took two limping steps and stood still. I swung off for a look and saw she was pawing uneasily with her off forefoot. As the wagon rolled out past me I shouted to Joel to stop, and he reined in. He sprang down, while Martha stood up and yelled at Drum to wait. Jim Pierce came up and the two of them watched critically as I explored the leg with my fingers. The cannon was tender, and there was a swelling that ran all down the inside of the leg.

"Tendon," said Joel.

Drum came back to us at a trot and looked down at me from his tall buckskin. "What is it, Mr. Cooper?" he asked patiently.

"She's bowed a tendon," I said.

"You'd best pick out another then," he said, "and change your saddle."

"She can't keep up like this."

"You'll have to leave her. Some Indian will pick her up, and be glad to have her."

"She's a good horse. Let's stop here for the night. I'll soak this until the swelling goes down, and in the morning I'll wrap it so she can travel with us. We've covered six or eight miles."

"Nearer five. We'd better keep going."

"Drum..."

"I'll bring you up a fresh mount. Pull the saddle."

He rode back to our dusty, straggling pack of loose stock and started to look them over.

"Joel," I said, "we don't have to keep going. If we stop, he has to stop. And if we don't stop, every horse we've got is going to go lame or fall dead."

"He's right," said Hopkins. Willis was still pale and shaky, as he had been while we watched the Indian die.

Drum came back leading a bay mare that looked about as strong and fresh as any we had. When he saw that we still had not unsaddled Hoecake, he pursed his lips thoughtfully.

"We're going to camp," I said.

"Eh? Going to camp? Mr. Cooper, I thought you were the man that didn't believe in putting too much store by a horse."

"It isn't just the horse. It's everything."

"Mr. Cooper, you must keep your head. We're in a bad position, but you were the one I thought would not go off half-cocked. You have to face the facts, Mr. Cooper. I know how you feel about your mare. She's a good one, all right. But an hour or two can make all the difference now. We'll just have to keep going." He swung down and came to the other side of Hoecake. "Here," he said, "I'll give you a hand," and he began to loosen the girth.

I just stood there while he took the saddle from her and put it on the bay. Then he slipped the bay's halter and replaced it with Hoecake's bridle and bit.

"There you are," he said. "This one here isn't such a bad horse, Mr. Cooper."

He remounted and trotted out in front of the wagon. Joel looked at me and I shook my head in tired resignation. Then I mounted the bay, and we set out again.

Hoecake tagged along with us for a mile or so, back with the loose animals, but finally the pain became too much for her and she stopped and stood, her forefoot lifted, watching us as we went on. We kept going into the dusk and pulled up in the pitch dark on a sandy bank above the stream. Tyree started scraping around in the brush for firewood, but Drum called out: "No light. We'll make a cold camp tonight." We found our blankets by touch and laid them out around the wagon. The Tyrees slept in the open with the rest of us, now that their tent was the coffin for the dead Indian. Martha passed around dried apples and that was our supper, for we carried little else that could be eaten uncooked. As we ate the moon came out, showing us the stream below, now broad and fast-running, and the prairie on each side beginning to fall in rolling hillocks toward the valley of the Arkansas, south of us.

As the camp settled down, I looked for Bob's blanket roll. He had made his bed a little apart, and he was sitting on it, his arms around his knees, with Martha Tyree beside him.

As I hesitated, they looked up and saw me, and Bob said, softly: "Sit down, Garvin. Martha says she loves me."

I sat down, saying nothing. Martha smiled gently at me. In the moonlight, she was pretty.

"And Robert doubts me," she said. "Does thee not love him too? I think thee does."

"Martha," said Bob, "you think you're cheering me up, or something. But you aren't. You're trying to whip me when I'm down, and I'm not going to let you do it. What do you want to do? Baptize me in that creek, there?"

"Oh, Robert, I want nothing of thee. That is all I want thee to believe."

"Then leave me alone and I'll believe you." He smiled at her rather weakly. "The trouble is," he said, "that Drum wants something out of me and it looks like he's going to get it. As long as I had to kill someone, I don't know why I didn't kill him."

"Thee did not have to kill anyone," she said. I wondered if she realized how cruel that sounded.

"Bob," I said, "as soon as Drum goes to sleep why don't you take that horse of his and leave? On that gelding, you can cover some ground. We'll see that you get a good start, if we have to hog-tie him."

"Where do you want me to go?" he said. "I'd starve in a week, Cooper. Besides, I don't want Martha killed because of me, or the boy or that fool Hopkins, or even you."

"When we get to the village," I said, "we can tell them we tried to bring you in and you got away. I don't think they'll bother us; not if we pay up."

"Don't start thinking now, Garvin. It's too late for you to think."

"Thee must not despair!" said Martha sharply.

"Oh, Martha, go to bed, go to bed! If you want to love me, crawl into this blanket with me. Otherwise, leave me alone."

"Thee cannot shock me, Robert, or deceive me. Thee is good. Thee knows the kind of love I mean."

"Leave me alone, Martha!"

She sighed and rose, brushing her long skirts. "Good night," she said. "Good night to thee, Garvin," and she rustled off toward the wagon, where Joel was waiting.

Bob was silent for a moment. The moonlight on his beard made it look silvery, like an old man's. "She's decent," he said. "She's a pretty good woman. But she thinks that everyone's just like her."

In the morning, I found Hoecake standing with our picketed stock. She must have trailed behind us and caught up late in the night. The injured leg was hideously swollen and every time she touched that hoof to the ground she winced and trembled. She looked like a living, walking piece of pain, and I couldn't bring myself to go near her, but stood watching from a distance. She lifted her ears a bit at the sight of me. Pierce came up and shook his head solemnly.

"She's ruined for good," he said.

I just nodded. He stood nervously beside me until, in a moment, Drum came marching out to see what was the matter. The guide went up to her and stroked her muzzle while he bent for a closer look at the leg. I flinched as he ran his fingers down the swollen tendon, but he had a good touch, and she barely winced. He came back to me shaking his head.

"A shame," he said. "She'd best be shot, Mr. Cooper, but you might as well wait until we're ready to pull out." Then he went back to where Martha was fixing breakfast.

When we were all ready to march, he turned to me and nodded. The others watched as I took my one good pistol from my saddle bag.

"Use this," said Drum. He was wearing a percussion revolver in a hip-holster, and he drew it out and offered me the butt. I took it, looked to the caps, and walked out to Hoecake. She turned her eyes on me and whickered.

I'd heard a lot about shooting injured horses, but I'd never had to do it before. I decided that it would be best not to stand in front of her, so I walked around to the side and she turned her head to watch. I raised the pistol quickly, feeling the eyes of the whole party on my back, and fired. Her head snapped back and she fell heavily on her haunches, only to spring up and lurch past me in a crazy, three-legged gallop. She went fifty feet and fell on her forelegs, then her haunches folded and she lay down, still holding up her bloody head and feeling with her hooves for the ground that had somehow got out from under her. I ran to her, thumbing back the hammer of Drum's big pistol, and got as close as I dared. The first shot had gone too high, smashing a gouge into the flesh and the skull between her ears. Splinters of bone showed in the torn hide and the bloody forelock. I aimed below her ear and fired again, and she stretched her neck on the ground, shuddered, and died. I walked back to Drum so sick that I seemed to have no wrists and no knees. As I handed him the hot pistol he said: "I'm sorry, Mr. Cooper." I nodded, and turned to my horse.

The horses were fairly willing, at the start of that day's ride. The rest and the water had freshened them; but they still had no reserves of strength. They'd been too ill-used in the past week. By noon, when we had done fifteen miles, the mules were laboring pitifully and the horses were so fractious we could barely control them—all but Drum's gelding, which never faltered. Hopkins had never had very firm knees, and when his gray decided to take the bit in his teeth Willis was helpless. It took the reins away from him, bounced him and balked, and when he had worn himself out fighting the stirrips, it threw him. McVey and I stopped for him, as the wagon went rumbling on, and he rose from the rocks with a rent in his pants and blood on his face. He said absolutely nothing, but when he remounted his jaw was set so hard it looked as if he'd crack his teeth. We didn't stop for long at noontime. Drum kept pacing about, working his mouth thoughtfully and staring downstream. As we prepared to mount he said: "It won't be long now. Let's keep close order. Don't let the stock straggle, Mr. Hopkins. We'd better have our rifles showing and wear all our pistols. It's wise always to give an Indian the impression of your strength."

[203]

I hung my short rifle upon my saddle and put my loaded pistol in my waistband. Drum gave the other dragoon rifles to Jim and Willis and took one himself. His second pistol and holster he gave to Hopkins. He asked Tyree if he'd drive with the fowling-piece across his knees, just for the effect, but Joel refused. While the rest of us rigged for war, McVey sat his horse and watched.

"What about me?" he said. "Don't I get to play soldier?"

It was the first admission anyone had made of Drum's taking Bob's rifle. Ned ignored it, but it set off something in Willis. He came up beside the wagon, dusty and flushed and exhausted, and still with dried blood on his chin.

"I have something I want to ask," he said, "and I would rather Bob didn't hear it."

I looked at McVey. He scowled and narrowed his eyes at Hopkins.

"All right," said Drum, "if it's that important. Will you ride off a bit, Mr. McVey?"

Bob turned his horse about without a word and rode some yards apart from us, beside the creek. There he dismounted and sat upon the ground with his back to us.

"I don't think he's to be trusted," said Willis, "even unarmed." He was very determined and grim and very frightened. "Back in Whitaker," he continued, "I saw Bob go berserk, and so did Garvin. That day, he nearly got us killed, when he started raving at the militia. I don't think there's any telling what he may do when he gets among the Indians; and if he should suddenly go out of his head we could all be killed."

"What's this happened in Whitaker?" demanded Drum.

"I think Willis is exaggerating," I said angrily. "It wasn't 'berserk.' He just lost his temper."

"Call it what you choose," said Hopkins. "If it happens in the Indian village, it can cost us our lives. He's completely rash. I think he's proved that."

"Mr. Hopkins," said Drum, "there is no turning back. We are within five miles of that village and we've got to go on. You leave Mr. McVey to me."

"I didn't mean that we should stop," said Willis.

"Then what do you want?"

"I think Bob should be bound."

Martha said, "Oh, no! No!" and came tumbling angrily down from the wagon box. I sprang from my horse and went to back her up. Drum frowned at Willis, who was glaring defiantly at us all.

"How do you mean 'bound'?" he asked gruffly.

"His hands bound," said Willis. "We're taking him to the Indians to save our lives. We can't take any risks."

"I don't think that's necessary," said Drum.

"It is not!" said Martha.

Hopkins, his mouth trembling just a little, said to her, "You're just ashamed to admit what we're doing. You want to give him over to them half way and make them take him the other half way. There's no telling what he may try. If we do this thing we'd better not do it without doing it right."

"Willis," I said, "you just hold on to that rocking horse."

"You saw him that day," he said to me.

"Willis, don't you understand what happened to him in Whitaker? Didn't you see what made him so wild?"

"Is there something to what he says, Mr. Cooper?" asked Drum.

"Nothing! That day in Whitaker Bob was mocking the mob. It was foolhardy, but he couldn't stand to see men acting like animals. That's all. Let's go on."

Drum said: "Mr. Hopkins, I believe there's no need for what you ask. But I want you satisfied." He turned in the saddle and called to Bob, waving for him to return. As Bob came back to us, leading his horse, Drum got down and stood to meet him. Willis swallowed nervously.

"What are you going to do, Drum?" he said urgently.

"I'm going to put it to him straight-out, and ask his pledge of good conduct."

"Ned!" I cried, but Bob was already upon us and Drum faced him with a firm, businesslike expression.

"Mr. McVey," he said, "you might as well know that

there's been talk of tying your hands before we go any further."

Bob stared at him and I died inside myself with shame and fear for him, but I knew that there was no right thing for me to say now.

"We must make the best impression we can," Drum went on, "and show the Indians our good faith. That's one thing. The other thing is that if you should cut up when we get to that village it would be bad for us all. Now what I ask is that you give me your word you'll not make any trouble."

McVey shook his head. "No," he said calmly, "I won't give you my word. I don't owe you anything for killing that man. You're trying to kill me, now, and I guess that's fair enough, but I don't have to help you do it."

"Your word is good enough for me," said Drum. "No one's out to kill you. We'll do all we can to save you, but you ought to do the same for us. You understand?"

"Ned Drum," said Martha sharply, "Robert will not do anything to hurt us. Thee can know that without asking any oaths. Thee is only torturing him now. Let it be, and go on."

McVey suddenly dropped the reins of his horse and thrust his hands out side by side, balled into fists. "Tie me, Drum," he said. "I think you'd better."

"It isn't needed, Mr. McVey," said Drum, "as long as we can be sure that you won't cause any trouble at the village by doing something rash."

"I give you no promises, Drum."

Ned hesitated, and I thought that Bob had bluffed him down, but Drum was just too dense. He felt nothing of what was before him. He shuffled his feet and said: "As long as Mrs. Tyree vouches for you, and Mr. Cooper..."

"I don't promise them anything, either," said Bob coldly. He thrust his hands at the guide.

Still Drum wavered. He hadn't expected it to come out this way, and I realized that Bob was frightening him.

"Quit it, Bob," I said. "Don't push it."

But Drum's mind had turned over and clicked into its

ratchet. He said, "Mr. McVey, I'll do it, if I have to. Now, I ask you once again to give me your word."

"No."

Drum turned about and went to the wagon. He reached up under the seat and pulled out the halter he had taken off the horse I was now riding. Very deliberately, he opened his clasp knife and began to cut the headstall loose from the cheek straps, to make a single long piece out of it. Martha put her hand on his and he threw it angrily off. He turned upon the whole lot of us.

"I'm through fooling with you people!" he cried. "Do I ask too much? His word. If he'll have it the hard way, then I can be hard. If need be, I'll drag you all to that village by the hair of your head. I've let you ruin me, very near! but now it must stop. I'm going to do what I set out to do!"

He sawed savagely through the strap and strode back to Bob, folding the knife into his pocket. McVey still held his hands out, wrists together. Drum grabbed Bob's red hands in his pink ones and crossed his wrists. Then he took two turns with the strap and knotted it. He stepped back, breathing hard, and McVey stood blinking at him, his hands still held out as if he didn't know it was over.

"Now mount up," ordered Drum, and he turned back to his own horse. Bob went to his horse and mounted clumsily, holding the saddle-horn with his bound hands.

Martha's eyes were full of tears and she groped blindly for the footstep on the wagon.

"This is best," I said hoarsely, not quite sure who I was talking to. "From here on, Bob owes us nothing. Bob, this means that if you can get away you're free to go, and I, for one, won't try to stop you. That's for Ned to worry about."

"I can do it, Mr. Cooper," said Drum. "Now let's ride."

14

For the next miles down along the widening, sparkling creek, I sat my horse in a stupor of fear and self-hatred. I felt, too, bitterly resentful that this had fallen on me unfairly, when I was so heavily weary and sun-parched and lonely. I kept trying to get things together and understand what was happening to us, to weigh it out and find my one right course; but hard as I tried, my mind kept falling apart in simple, complete exhaustion. I kept looking ahead at Drum, his broad, black shoulders bobbing along as his golden horse paced the prairie in fast, swinging strides.

Martha sat the wagon box, swaying, face of stone, her hands clenched in her lap. Beside her, Joel leaned over his reins, his cheeks streaked with sweat and his whiskers powdered with dust. Hopkins clung like a drowning man to his saddle. Jim Pierce kept his head up and looked only straight ahead with a kind of wonder in his eyes, as if life were just now unfolding itself awesomely before him. McVey held the reins clenched tightly in the fingers of his bound hands. All of us, glassy-eyed and slack limbed, grayed with dust and bleached in the sun, seemed like the wake cast up by Ned Drum's solid, black form—the one solid thing among us.

I remembered where it was we were going, though. I kept my eyes on the prairie ahead and tried to imagine the people waiting for us, the little, wizened brown men like the one in our wagon. As we rode down toward the valley of the big Arkansas River, the prairie turned greener, and on our right, to the west, the roll of the plains deepened into gentle hills. The strip of brush that bordered our creek broadened into a shallow green valley, and beside the stream there were taller trees now: oaks and poplars and straight cottonwoods. The ground underfoot was grassy once more, and we rode sometimes for minutes under shade as we twisted along.

After a couple of hours Drum led us into the creek and we forded it, the water belly-deep on our horses. If the wagon had bogged we'd never have got it out, but the bottom there was clean, brown pebbles and hard packed sand. We came a little later to another creek, almost as big as the first one, coming down out of the hills to the west, and we turned to follow it. The valley down which it flowed was forested with clumps of cottonwood and in some places the brushy hills on either hand fell back to make little meadowed coves. It was as we came into one of these that I saw Drum, ahead of us, pull his horse to a stop on a little rise of ground and stand in the stirrups. For a second he shaded his eyes with his hand. Then he plopped heavily back into the saddle and put his heels hard into his gelding's ribs. The buckskin reared and came down at a run. Like a wild man, his coat-tails flapping and his elbows waggling, Drum galloped down to the creek and into the water in a burst of silvery spray. He crossed, urging his horse frantically on, and disappeared into the trees on the far side. I rode up to the wagon.

"You wait here," I said to Joel. He nodded.

I looked back at the others to see who I could ask to come with me. Jim caught my eye and calmly came up beside me. "All right, Jim," I said, and he rode with me after Drum.

On the far side of the creek, we passed through a little grove of oaks and then came out into a wide clearing, perhaps a half mile across, with the hills rising sharply on three sides and the creek on the other. Drum's horse was standing with trailing reins a little way from us. Ned himself was squatting on the ground and he seemed to be digging at something. Suddenly he sprang up, ran a few yards on, and plucked something from the grass. We rode toward him and as he heard us come up he threw down whatever it was he had in his hand and came toward us at a stiff, heavy trot. He spread his hands and stared wildly at us in choked fury.

"This was it," he said. "This was the camp. They've been gone for three or four days."

"Are you sure?" I asked.

"Look there," he cried, gesturing behind him and shaking his head. He went toward his horse and Jim and I rode to the place we'd seen him feeling the ground. There was a circle of bare, hard-packed earth about twenty feet across. For yards around it, the grass was trampled and dead, and in the center of the circle was a rectangular hole, a couple of feet long, full of ashes and charred wood. The circle of packed earth had been the floor of a tepee, and the hole had been the firepit.

"Go back to the others," I said to Jim. "Tell them to pull the wagon and all the animals into the trees, out of sight."

He nodded and rode toward the creek. Drum was sitting on his horse, looking around at the great ring of tepee sites on which we stood. I went to him.

"They go north," he said, trying to make sense of it, "and hunt in the mountains during the summer. Sometimes they don't come back for a year. They wander. That man we killed was probably one of their journey-scouts." He said "we killed." He put his fingers to his eyes. He had tracked Fate to her den, and it was empty.

"What do we do now?" I asked.

"They've been gone three or four days and maybe a week. The fire stones are cold and all the food leavings have been cleaned up by animals. They're probably fifty miles away by now."

"We're well rid of them," I said. "Now let's get away from here, as soon as we've rested the horses."

"I guess there's nothing else we can do," he said softly. He turned his horse back toward the stream and I followed him. As he rode, he kept shaking his head slowly. We crossed over and found the others waiting for us in a thin clump of cottonwoods. McVey, alone, was still on his horse. I was looking straight at him as we rode up from the water, so I saw him watching Drum's face and I saw him smile when the guide drew near.

"Why don't you follow them, Drum?" he called.

Then I got close enough to see the wild glint in his eye and I realized that he, too, had been cheated.

"You lost, Drum?" He grinned. "Get out that old compass! Come on! Let's find those Indian friends of yours and have us a war dance." He leaned back in the saddle, gripping the pommel with his bound hands while the dun sidled uneasily. "Don't worry, folks! Drum will take care of us. Trust Drum!"

"Well, Mr. McVey," said Drum as he dismounted, "it's all turned out for the best, so far." He seemed unperturbed now, but strangely vague in his voice. "I'll help you with that strap."

"Better not, Drum," said Bob with a grim smile. "You'd better just leave me tied."

Drum had started toward him. When Bob said that, Ned stopped and gave him a look of weary confusion. I think that if he had not stopped, if he had simply gone to Bob and cut him loose, everything would have been all right. But Drum hesitated.

"You turn me loose," said Bob fiercely, "and I'll kill you as soon as I get my hands on a gun." With that, he sat back in his saddle and glared at Drum.

"That's no thing to say," Drum told him gruffly, but he went no closer. "It came out for the best, didn't it?"

"That's not your fault. Stay away from me, Ned."

Ned wet his lips and walked to Bob's horse. McVey leaned over and held out his bound wrists. "Go ahead. Turn me loose. I swear to God I'll kill you." He was livid. "I'd sooner kill you than any Indian."

"Bob . . ." I said.

"Why don't you untie me, Cooper? Come on and let me loose so I can shoot this stupid hound."

I went to them and got between him and Drum, who was just standing shuffling his feet and working his brows. Bob held out his hands to me, but as I took hold of the strap he said: "Garvin, I'm telling the truth. I'm going to kill Drum, if I can. I swear it to you. Before you decide to let me go, you'd better believe that."

I looked up into his face, but his gaze never wavered. He seemed too calm, suddenly. His breath came very slowly and heavily, and his eyes were dead. "Decide," he said softly.

"I'm about to believe you," I said.

"You'd better."

"Stop it. Get the idea out of your head that you're going to kill someone. It's over. Now we've all got to pull together to get out of here."

He straightened and laid his hands on the pommel of his saddle. "All right," he said, "leave me tied. I'm not pulling anything but a trigger. I don't want Drum's blood on your head. I'll get loose, sooner or later, and when I do I'm going to kill him."

I didn't believe him. I had the firmest possible belief that he was making a frantic, terrible joke—perhaps as much a joke on himself as on us. Still, I stood there. I didn't want to take anything more on myself. I was worn out and frightened and angry with Bob for what he was doing: now demanding a gesture of faith from me. As I wavered, he gave a hoot of derisive laughter. "Cooper, I wish you could see yourself," he said. "You look just like Drum. And Drum, you know what you look like? You look like a dead man. I'm going to kill you, you . . ." and he went into a tangled string of breathless obscenities.

I took Drum's sleeve and made him come with me away from the hooting, howling McVey. "Leave him alone for now," I said. "He'll be all right."

"The man's out of his mind," said Drum indignantly.

"Just leave him alone," I said. Martha had come to us and was listening. "I told you there was no need to tie him. If

[212]

he's half crazy, it's no wonder. How would you feel? Leave him alone and he'll come out of it."

Martha said: "He will be calm in a little while, Ned Drum. For now, leave him. He might injure himself or thee if he were loose now. He was ready to die. Now he must get ready to live again."

Drum nodded, touching his fingers to his eyes.

"Right now," I said, "we've got to rest, feed and water the stock and then get moving. Which way do we go from here, Ned?"

Joel said, "The man must be buried."

"Burial the Devil!" said Hopkins breathlessly. "Dump him in the river and let's go."

"The horses have to rest," I said, "and so do we."

McVey, as we talked aside, climbed down from his horse and went to the water. He took off his hat and threw it aside. He lay down, clumsily, on his belly beside the stream, and tried to cup his hands to drink from them. The way they were tied, he couldn't manage it, so he just plunged his face into the water and sucked it up in noisy gulps. When he had slaked his thirst he rolled back onto the bank, his beard dripping, and crept into the shade of a little tree. He propped himself against the trunk and watched us, smiling contemptuously.

"Let me know when the meeting's over," he called.

Drum ignored him. "Jim," he said, "you and Mr. Hopkins care for the stock, and don't let them drink too much. Now, gentlemen ... No, no. Wait, Jim. We can't camp here. We should get on away from this village, and then stop."

"Ned," I said incredulously, "we can't! The horses are all but dead right now. We've got to stop and graze them. And we're no better ourselves."

He hesitated, pursed his mouth and nodded. "We've traveled hard," he said. He made no motion to do anything, though, and the rest of us stood wearily watching him. I was expecting him to drive us on, but he only said: "Not likely they'll come back here." He glanced uneasily down at Bob, sprawled in the shade.

[213]

"What about the dead man?" asked Joel.

"Eh?" said Drum. "Well, I guess we might carry him yet a while. We might run into them."

"The weather is hot," said Joel.

That thought seemed to shock Drum. "Yes, yes," he said. "We can give him Indian burial, over there by the village."

"Let's do it, then," I begged, "before we all drop."

Drum pulled himself together. "All right," he said. "Let's get him down and put him on a horse. I'll show you what to do."

Jim said: "Shall I water the horses?"

"Why, yes, Jim. If you will. We won't be long. Mrs. Tyree, you might start us something to eat."

Joel and Drum and I took the canvas-wrapped body of the old brave out of the wagon and lashed it across the back of one of our pack horses. Drum and I mounted and, with Joel leading the pack horse afoot, crossed the creek. Drum led us straight across the little plain where the lodge-circles marked the site of the Cheyenne village. It was a little eerie, taking the body through the place that had been its home just a few days before. One of these spots of hard-packed earth had been his own lodge, perhaps. The ground we walked on had been worn clear by the moccasins of his people. Drum took us to a grove of runty oaks right at the foot of the hills that ringed the village. There he dismounted and walked about looking up into the branches. It occurred to me that we had brought no shovel.

"In the trees?" I asked.

"Yes," he said. "That's the way they do it."

He selected a stout tree with three branches forking wide at about head-height. He pointed. "If you'll just climb up here, Mr. Cooper," he said.

While I got into the tree, Drum had Joel lead the horse bearing the body up next to the trunk. Then they untied the canvas parcel and Drum lifted one end up to me. It was heavy. While they boosted from below, I dragged the corpse, still wrapped, up into the fork of the tree. I balanced it there, but the body was limp and sagged horribly at each end. Drum tossed me the rope that he had used to lash it on the horse.

"Leave the tent on?" I asked.

Drum looked to Joel and Joel nodded. I was very glad. I tied the body clumsily to the branches supporting it, and then I dropped out of the tree. We stood there for a second, looking up at the thing.

"Is that all?" asked Joel.

"That's all," said Drum. "He's got his pipe with him, and his bow. That's the way it should be, according to their custom."

"To dust he returneth," said Joel. "Have mercy, Lord, upon this man's soul."

"Amen," said Drum.

We mounted, Joel bareback on the funeral horse, and rode back, quickly, through the deserted village and across the stream to our friends.

Jim and Hopkins had watered the animals and strung a picket line in the grass above the stream. Martha had made coffee and started meal cakes and fat meat. McVey was still propped under his tree beside the creek, staring. As we forded the stream he called to us: "All done? We'll have another burying as soon as I get a shot at that fat fool on the yellow horse." Drum rode up the bank past him without a single glance.

We wolfed our food in silence—all except McVey. He managed all right, despite the strap on his wrists, and made a great fuss about the food, grinning as he complimented Martha for her cooking. She took it very coldly for a while. Then she set her tin plate on the ground and picked up her paring knife.

"Give me thy hands," she said gently.

Bob smiled at her for a second, then stretched his arms toward her. The rest of us held our breath. "I thought you were against killing," he said.

"Thee will not kill Ned Drum," she said.

"Of course I won't," he laughed. "I wouldn't harm a hair of his stupid head. Come on. Cut it."

[215]

"Don't do it!" said Hopkins loudly.

"Go ahead, Martha," Bob said, affecting a wheedling tone and still grinning.

"Thy pride has been hurt," she said.

"You hurt it," he said, "when you wouldn't have me. That was good for your pride, but hell on mine." Joel winced just the least bit, just enough for Bob to see, and Bob took his advantage. He smiled at Martha. "You got me all inflamed," he said, "dancing around on the prairie naked, and then you wouldn't have me."

That didn't bother Martha. She simply sniffed at him. But Joel's mild air was too good to be true, and Drum looked as if someone had reached a hand right in through his friendly, honest eyes, into his soul, and shaken it like a rag mop.

Bob's hands were still held out toward Martha, and the knife was still in her hand.

"Cut it," he dared her.

She might have done it. I don't know. But Joel said, very coolly: "We will cut it when thee can be trusted." She gave her husband one glance, a little wave of confusion rippling in her eyes. I guess that was the first time in their life together that she had felt the need to prove something to Joel, and she didn't like it, but she didn't hesitate. She dropped the knife and took up her plate again.

"Christians!" Bob said, chuckling. "Abolitionists!"

Later, as we lay about in the shade, Bob left off his railing at us. He followed our movements with eyes full of wicked amusement, but he was as tired as anyone, and I hoped he would sleep. I closed my eyes beneath a tree and was falling uneasily into a doze when Joel touched my arm. He asked me if I would talk with him for a moment and then he led me up beside the picketed horses. There Martha and Ned Drum were waiting for us. Martha looked awfully tired. Ned was still embarrassed and he kept looking at Martha and Joel in an alarmed way, as if he couldn't guess what they might do next. Bob's gibe at Martha had cut deeper than I had realized.

Joel said: "We must have a guard for tonight."

"Aye," said Drum hoarsely. "I expect those Indians are still about."

"Not the Indians," said Martha. "Robert McVey."

Drum rumbled something unintelligible.

"Even with his hands tied," said Joel, "he could still use a knife or a gun, if he got one."

"You're beginning to believe him," I said bitterly.

"No," said Joel, "but in his state he may be dangerous to himself or to us. There is no knowing. Does thee not believe him?"

"I'm afraid of him, I guess. But we must try not to take him seriously. He's trying to believe the worst of himself, because he's ashamed of himself. We can't let him."

"I would like to trust him," said Joel, "and if it were me alone, I would. But there are others."

Drum nodded his head sadly. I stole a glance down into the trees by the river. Bob sat against his tree, watching us. He caught my eye and grinned.

"I will watch first," said Joel. "In two hours I will wake my wife. She'll wake thee Ned Drum, and thee can wake Garvin Cooper, for the last watch."

"What about the others?" I asked.

"It isn't fair to ask the boy," said Martha, "and Willis Hopkins is not reliable."

"Neither am I. I couldn't stay awake."

"I'll sit up with you," said Drum. "I don't use much sleep."

"Drum, he's not going to kill you. He's just ashamed. He's not insane."

"Mr. Cooper, I don't know what to believe. How would you feel with someone carrying on at you like that? I've seen him kill one man already, and I think there's something wrong with him. I don't know what to believe."

I saw that Drum was falling apart. He literally did not know what to believe, what to think, what to do. The world had been jerked from under him. He didn't look at anyone, but gazed at the prairie or the trees or the sky or the ground

[217]

before him, blinking his eyes as if he were seeing things he knew could not be there.

"Ned," I said. "We're counting on you. You're still the guide."

"Eh? Don't worry, Mr. Cooper. We just go up this creek a ways and then cut over and follow the next one west. Another week, maybe, or two, and we'll be on Cherry Creek. There's settlements all along there."

"We can still do it," I said.

He nodded.

"The horses are pretty bad off, of course. We're going to have to rest them soon. Is there grass up ahead?"

"Oh, yes."

He walked listlessly back down to the camp.

"He is tired," said Joel. "Something has gone out of him."

I agreed. The two Quakers followed Drum, but I went to look at the horses and mules. They were pitiful: footsore, their backs tender, their mouths cracked. They hadn't as much spirit among them as any one of them had had two weeks before. Drum's buckskin gelding was the exception. His step was still light, his head high. He was a magnificent animal.

We lay beside the creek all afternoon. Pierce and Hopkins slept. The Quakers sat in the shade, murmering together. Drum drowsed off and on, snoring and mumbling in his sleep. I tried to keep myself awake. I watched Bob. He didn't sleep, either, or maybe he did. He looked as if he were asleep with his eyes open, dreaming some black dream, as he lay there. I had the feeling that he was waiting, and that any movement by any of us would stir him again into his railing and obscenity. Toward nightfall Martha roused herself to fix us some beans and some soggy meal cakes.

As we finished, Bob grinned at Drum and said: "Don't forget your damned apples, Ned. Gotta keep your bowels open. You're gonna need 'em. Believe me, you're gonna need 'em."

As dark came down, I crawled onto my blankets and fell

into sleep as into a well of night. I was aching with weariness, but it seemed that Drum woke me in the same instant that I closed my eyes, and for a moment I was confused, and frightened by a sense of time snatched away from me. He explained that it was my guard time, nearly morning. Good as his word, Drum sat up with me for a while, even though I told him that I thought I could stay awake.

"That's all right," he rumbled softly. "I don't use much sleep."

We sat together with our backs to a wagon wheel and watched, in the pale moonlight, the sleeping forms around us, the gleaming little stream, the trees stirring in the night breeze, and the stock rumbling and stamping up on the picket line.

"Ned," I said, "don't let Bob get at you."

"How's that?"

"Things he says. Don't make too much of them."

He grunted. I could not see his face for the shadow of his hat brim.

"There's nothing behind what he said to Martha," I said. "I know the whole story, and there's nothing to it. It was just something that happened back on the river, the day after the fire."

Drum was silent for a moment. Then he said: "A guide should know what's going on in his party. He should keep his eyes open."

"Your eyes were open. There was nothing to see."

"If you say so, Mr. Cooper, I'll certainly take your word for it. But I was surprised that Mrs. Tyree didn't have anything to say."

"What could she say? She had nothing to apologize for. Why should she defend herself against him?"

I could make out his slow, thoughtful nod.

"Ned, you don't defend yourself, do you, when he calls you these names?"

"No."

"Neither does she."

"That's right," he said, but he said it with no conviction.

He wasn't really worried about what Martha might or might not have done. That wasn't it at all. He was worried about what she *was,* and what Bob was, and Joel, and probably all the rest of us. Suddenly, he had found that it wasn't the plains and the rivers and the hills that he had to know, but *us*—and he didn't.

He fell asleep, with his face in his beard. To keep myself awake I got up every few minutes and moved softly about the camp. Over in the deserted Indian village a fox began to bark excitedly and an owl scolded him. Out in the prairie around us were the furtive slithering sounds of small things hunting and hunted. As the first light of the dawn washed up from the plains I even saw little animals, or perhaps their shadows, flitting across the sand and scurrying among the stones. Toward sunrise a flight of partridges came down from the hills to the south, whirred overhead and settled beside the creek. I could hear them down there purring and clucking as they drank and bathed in the shallows.

A little later a bitch fox, with heavy dugs, came up from the creek bed and, when she saw the wagon, sat down in surprise and lolled her tongue at me. She looked right into my eyes, curiously, with her foxy grin spilling her pretty tongue. A terrified marmot broke cover near her and ran, squeaking, for his hole. The fox watched him and grinned. Her hunting was done for the night. The marmot scrambled safely into its den. When she was rested, the fox got up and trotted briskly around us, making a detour, but keeping her eye on me. When she got beyond us she slid like mist into the prairie and was gone without a sound. I wiped my eyes and stood up. There was just enough light for me to make out the forms and faces of the sleepers. Drum was slumped with his face on his knees. Underneath the wagon Martha and Joel lay side by side. The woman's face was puffy and sulky in her sleep, and very unpretty, but her hair had come loose and one warm brown tress was beautiful, curled upon the yellow sand. Hopkins slept all in a knot with the blanket drawn over his face. Jim Pierce lay on his back with his mouth open and snored very softly. This was the way we had been meeting our days: with foxes coming past to grin at our helplessness and our untidy, private selves, while we slept on unknowing. It was a wonder that the morning, coming upon us like this day after day, was not tired of us.

Bob lay a little apart from the rest. In his sleep he had squirmed into a little hollow between two trees, and there he was curled with his bound wrists twisted up beside his chin. As he slept you could see, behind that fiery beard, the simple, human face—curiously innocent and unformed in the safety of sleep. The light was coming up fast; they would wake soon. Stepping very carefully, I went to McVey and squatted beside his blankets. I put my hand upon his shoulder and gave it a gentle pressure. "Bob," I whispered. "Bob?"

He woke slowly, opening his eyes and looking all around and finally up at me as he drew his face together, putting on the man that he was. He started to stretch his arms and felt the strap that held them, and then he became still another man.

"You can sleep pretty comfortable this way," he said, wiggling his fingers to show me what he meant.

"Listen," I said, "we've got to talk sense."

"Don't talk to me," he said, "just cut me loose. You'll do it sooner or later, Garvin; why not now? Go ahead." He grinned. "You're like a hound on ice," he said. "You're scared to run and you can't stand still."

I couldn't risk it. If I had cut the strap as he slept, while he was innocent and free, he might have been saved. Now, I didn't know.

"Hello, Drum!" Bob shouted, calling past me to the wagon. "Wake up, you dumb, fat sow. Garvin nearly got up his nerve to let me loose. You almost slept your life away that time!"

Ned groaned. McVey chuckled and pushed himself up against his tree.

All that morning we followed the creek, and by noon we could see that it was going to go the way the river had gone.

It got lower and lower and then was just a lot of puddles strung together by tiny, trickling channels. I pointed it out to Drum and he stared stupidly at the shining sandbars.

"What water there is," I said, "seems to be coming from those hills south of us. We're heading away from it."

"This is the way," he said.

We were sitting on our horses, out in front of the rest of the party, and McVey called: "What's the matter, Drum? Lost your way? Get out that old octant!"

Drum pulled his horse about and headed on upstream, leaving me sitting there. He was finished. We had no guide. He had been our pillar of cloud and then he had tried to be the pillar of fire. He had no more than that in him, and he couldn't go back to the old way. Bob wouldn't let him.

We toiled along steadily up the shallow valley, the creek dwindling and the grass growing coarser and drier, the trees runtier, as we headed back into the wastelands. We stopped and ate at noon, and rode on in the blazing white sun of the afternoon. Drum rode stolidly, his big horse seeming never to change its flowing pace. Drum didn't look back, but that didn't save him from McVey. Bob yelled at him now and then just to let Drum know that he was not forgetting. The rest of us rocked along, just trying to stay in the saddle, and Bob didn't neglect us. "What a sorry lot," he'd laugh. "You look like a sinners' bench. Sing, you god-damned Christians! Sing 'Old Elijah'! Strike it up, Martha!"

Once Hopkins drew up beside me and said: "We haven't got two weeks of this in us."

"We'll rest soon," was all I could say. He shook his head and went back to his post.

I felt as if all the marrow had been drawn out of me by that malignant western sun. I caught myself slumping in the saddle with my mind wandering back to Georgia or back to the College of William and Mary and evenings in the cool, dark common room playing cards and drinking ale. I remembered my little room at school and getting out of bed on a cold morning and ringing for the servant to come and fire up my stove while I dressed, prancing on the cold floor. I remembered the mock trial in my last year, when I defended Socrates and won acquittal. I made a drama of my summing-up for the philosopher—a spectacle, with table-thumping and pirouetting and sudden lunges at the jury, with ringing cries and hoarse whispers. Afterward as I walked to the common room I met one of my teachers, a wrinkled, ugly old man. "I won my first case today, sir," I said to him, laughing.

"A friendly jury," he smiled, and as I started on past him he laid his boney fingers on my arm. "Your client was guilty," he said. "You must remember that, Mr. Cooper."

He was a humorless old man. He had been secretary to President Madison after the president's retirement, and we students felt that he was haughty about it.

"Perhaps he was guilty," I said, "by the letter of the law."

"The letter preserveth integrity, Mr. Cooper; the spirit destroyeth reason. You're an attorney, and should know that."

"I won my case, sir," I insisted.

"And very noisily, too. There's nothing wrong with that. But let me ask you this: In Athens, in the year 399 before Christ, would you have been so bold as to take that case? Eh? And if you had, could you have won the jury that rejected the *Apologia?* This was a game you played today. Don't make a game of the law."

He took his hand away and scurried off. A very learned man. He was the only one of our faculty who still wore his hair long, and nothing was good enough for him. "Humility!" was the refrain of his lectures. I can still hear him croaking: "Suspect yourselves, gentlemen! Suspect your reasoning, your judgments, your senses. Hold your own motives base until proven otherwise." His cry of "Humility!" amused us, coming from so arrogant a man. A few may have understood that he was humble before no man, only before the law. I was not one of those few.

We camped by a little pool in the creek bed. The horses

[223]

found little browse, and poor stuff. As the creek had dwindled, the valley had closed in on either side of us in sharp, sandy bluffs broken by crumbling stone shelves. The little cliffs, not more than thirty or forty feet high, were painted in red and yellow and gray and umber where layers of chalk and soil and quartz showed through the surface rubble. We'd left the trees behind us. Here there was nothing but spikes of reedy grass and a few dusty bushes and clumps of cactus. I didn't like what we were going into.

As soon as I could get alone with Drum, among the horses, I said: "Ned, didn't you tell me that this creek runs into the Arkansas?" He nodded. "Why don't we just follow it down to the river, then, and take the Santa Fe route?"

"We've come this far," he said. "Let's finish what we set out to do." To my surprise, his voice, that had been so vague and listless, was once again almost hearty. I looked at him closely. He had something on his mind; there was no doubt of it.

"We're in no shape to cross this kind of country," I said.

"You never know what you can do until you've done it, Mr. Cooper. You may surprise yourself."

"How far is it?"

"Not much more than a hundred miles."

"We'll never make it."

"Oh, you leave that to me, Mr. Cooper. We're going to make it all right. We're going to do just what we set out to do, and then you'll be proud of yourself. We'll have reason to be proud."

As we went together to the fire, McVey looked up and grinned at Ned. "Drum," he said, "why don't you just lie down and die?"

Ned gave him no heed. He bent over Martha's cookfire and wrinkled his nose as if the familiar, sickening odor of sputtering fat were something rare and strange. There was a strange, sly little smile on his lips. I didn't like that smile. Drum had found some secret comfort to shield him from Bob, and I wanted to know what it was. McVey saw it, too, and I think it must have frightened him, for all during

[224]

supper and as we bedded down, his gibes were louder and wilder and more obscene than ever.

We tried to ignore him. Drum came to me as I settled for sleep, and said, "You'll have the same watch tonight, Mr. Cooper. I'll wake you."

"Ned," I said, "we've got to get him go. His hands will rot with that strap on them."

"We won't have to worry about him much longer. Four or five days."

"We can't do a hundred miles in four or five days," I protested. "We'll be lucky to do it in ten days. On top of that, I tell you these horses have got to have rest on decent grass. Besides, we can't take him into the settlements like this. What are we going to do when we get up there?"

"Turn him over to the authorities," said Drum blandly.

"Authorities?" I was stunned. "What authorities?"

"The army. Or the Indian agents. Whoever we find. This trip is nearly over." So that was his secret.

I sat up and grabbed his arm. "Drum! Why can't we just let him go? Why can't we let him go his own way, once we're up there?"

"Let him go? Not a bit of it! You leave it to me, Mr. Cooper. I've seen this kind of thing before. He's got to be delivered to the authorities."

"Drum," I said, "you can't do that. It isn't that kind of thing."

"Well, I'd like to know what kind of thing it is, then. He's killed a man, and threatened us all. We'd have been there by now, but for him. I know how to handle his kind."

"Ned, if you're thinking about punishment, the man's been punished enough."

"We'll let the authorities decide that."

"I thought you could stand alone," I said. "This is for us to settle. Listen, if I tell Bob, and get him to agree to drop the thing, will you do the same?"

"I don't see how I can," he said.

With that he left me. I slept badly. The prairie seemed a seething hive of night creatures. Owls and foxes and chitter-

[225]

ing mice talked all around us in the darkness. I was not awakened by Drum, but by Bob's railing. Ned had let me sleep right through the night and had taken my guard turn himself. I didn't need to ask why. I had put myself on the other side. He didn't trust me to guard Bob now. It didn't matter. He couldn't stay awake forever and I'd get my chance to tell McVey what Drum planned.

We got ourselves together to travel. The pack horses sagged under their loads. When I threw the saddle on my bay it almost knocked him down, and I knew he was finished. Instead of taking another horse, I picked out the stronger of the two spare mules and saddled him. He was a chunky brute with a mouth of triple-tempered carbon steel, but he had some heart left in him and he moved easily.

"Look at the Georgia gentleman!" laughed McVey. "Hang on tight, Cooper!"

To Hopkins, as Willis heaved himself painfully into the saddle, it was: "You know what's wrong with you, Willis? You're sorry for yourself. Well, I'm sorry for you too."

When we get to the mountains, I thought, I'll set him free. He can't keep this up—not when he gets up there and sees roads that need building and ravines that cry for bridges. I've got to tell him, and remind him of his profession. He still has that. If anything can get to him, that can.

Martha Tyree was climbing wearily to the wagon box. She paused and said: "Listen. A thrush."

"It's not a thrush," said Drum. "It's what we call a mountain robin. It's like a thrush, you might say."

I was standing looking at Drum, waiting for him to start out. Beyond him, in the brush along the creek, an old Indian stood up and leveled a musket at us. The musket flashed and smoke hid the man. Then there were Indians everywhere.

They came out of the ground like swarming locusts: naked, howling, waving spears and clubs and sabers, and at first I thought we were overrun, massacred, cut down.

Drum drew his big pistol and fired at one brave who came

bounding in among us and the Indian kept on running, right past us. Then he aimed at another who came splashing across the stream, but the Indian ducked into the brush on the near bank. For a second, I spun like a top, trying to decide which way to run. Then I went for my rifle. My mule, with the rifle and my pistol, was in a frenzy. I got the reins, but he reared and kicked at me in terror. I pulled his head down and tried to get hold of the rifle. A painted Indian brave with a feather in his hair hit at me with a something—a lance or a tomahawk—and missed as the frantic mule jerked me off my feet. I scrambled up, still clutching the reins, but the Indian had disappeared. I didn't bother with the stirrups. I climbed that mule as if he were a tree. When I got him between my knees he quieted down.

"Our horses!" I shouted. "Get the horses!" It was too late. Our loose animals had all stampeded and up on the hillside the Indians were dashing after them. Jim Pierce had the pack-line in hand and he brought them to the tail of the wagon. Bob's horse had thrown him and gone with the others. Drum had mounted and gone to the head of the team, where he sat quite coolly with his pistol in one hand and the off mule's cheek-strap in the other. Hopkins' horse had stayed with us, but Hopkins himself was underneath the wagon where he lay with Bob's long rifle poked out between the wheels. Tyree was standing beside the wagon, but he still had the lines of the team and he was fervently begging them to stand. His wife crouched beside him. McVey came up beside the wagon too, and leaned there with his hands tied, watching Drum.

We were not overrun at all. There were about twenty of them. In that first instant, I had thought they were every one of them running straight at us, but now they were mostly just capering and whooping on the hillside, dashing out to yell and shake their weapons at us, then ducking into cover.

15

"Don't waste powder!" Drum shouted. "Wait until they get close. They're trying to provoke us!"

"Provoke us!" I yelped. "Great God!"

He was right, though. They didn't make the concerted rush that would have bowled us over. They just kept hooting and prancing. They caught most of our runaway stock and led them one by one up the valley and out of our sight into a fold in the bluff. We just had to watch the animals go.

"Mr. Tyree," Drum asked, "can you drive this team?"

"I think so."

"Good. We're going to have to move. This isn't a good spot we're in."

An arrow cut the turf near me and for a second I seemed to feel it in my flesh. I could feel it tear and cut. It was more horrible than any bullet.

Drum sidled his horse back along the wagon and leaned over to Hopkins. "Let me have that rifle, if you please," he said. I've never heard anything finer in my life. Hopkins handed it to him and Drum looked to the cap. "Hold my horse, Mr. Hopkins." Willis crawled out from under the wagon and obeyed. "Now we'll see," said Drum, dismounting.

He stepped out into the clear and raised the long rifle. "Mr. Cooper," he called, "you and the boy tie those pack horses to the wagon tail, and tie them good. We're going

[228]

to cross the creek and take the wagon up beside that ledge of rock over there. We want to be ready to shoot if they rush us."

An arrow hit the wagon body, stuck and then fell out. Drum fired and a howl went up from the Indians. On Drum's signal, Tyree started the team and the rest of us edged along with the wagon as it lurched down into the creek bed, across, and then up toward the rocky shelf that Drum had chosen as our shelter. The Indians kept scampering and shrieking at us, but they didn't get too close. We brought it off nicely. When we stopped we had the wagon on one side and the ledge on the other, just about chin-high. The pack horses milled around at one end of our little fort, uneasy but still standing, and the mules were pulled around at the other. Inside there were the seven of us and two horses and a mule. All the short rifles were loaded and made ready and Drum's two pistols and my own.

"Now," said Drum, "we'll shoot only if they come close enough for bow-shot. But when one man shoots, the others hold fire until he starts reloading. Mrs. Tyree, will you load for us?"

Martha shook her head. Drum blinked at her. He looked at her husband and Joel shook his head. Drum said, "You mean to tell me . . . ?"

Joel said, "We will not fight, Ned Drum. Thee knows that."

"That's foolish!" shouted Drum.

"Call it what thee will."

Drum looked down at McVey, squatting against the rock. "Well, Mr. McVey," he said, "you're going to have to help."

Bob, too, shook his head. "I've killed my Indian," he said. "It's your turn. You turn me loose and I don't shoot anybody but you. Don't you understand that?"

Drum howled like a dog. He hurled both his pistols to the ground and shook his fists wildly.

"Ned! Ned!" I cried. "Hold on! There's four of us."

The old Indian with the musket appeared again. That one blunderbuss must have been the extent of their artillery.

He raised up in the brush by the creek and boomed at us and disappeared. The rest gave shouts of glee and pranced a little closer. "Shall we shoot?" I asked Drum.

"Do as you like!" he moaned. "The whole lot of you! Do as you like! I'm finished."

"Willis," I said nervously, "I'll shoot first. When I get partly loaded, you shoot. Then you, Jim, the same way."

I pushed my rifle over the edge of the rock, feeling my head the size of a side of beef. I picked out an Indian capering in the brush about fifty yards away. He wouldn't hold still, so I just sighted at his middle and fired. He ducked into the rocks. As I loaded, I heard Hopkins' rifle go off. By the time it was my turn again, Drum had pulled himself together and the four of us were firing in turns.

We fired about five rounds apiece and the Indians withdrew. Jim had knocked one of them down and Drum believed he had hit another. None of us was hurt, but one of the pack horses had an arrow in his haunch and was going crazy with pain. Pierce went in among them, pulled off his pack and cut him free. It was the only thing to do. He dashed down to the creek, bucking and kicking, and an Indian came from cover to run after him. That was about the time that the whole lot of them started trotting over to the break in the bluffs where they had taken our horses. When they were all out of sight up in the gully, I asked Drum: "Have they gone?"

"Not likely," he said.

We stood our places, the four of us greasy and blackened with powder and smoke.

"Martha," said Bob, "why don't you just go out there and preach to those Indians? They're good at heart."

"Don't mock me, Robert McVey," she said coldly. "Thee may be near thy death."

"It may be. Drum may be near his, too."

In a few minutes, the Indians came back. This time they were all mounted on rough, nondescript ponies. They rode slowly down to the creek in a mob.

"Why did they leave the horses up there?" I asked Drum.

"Horses are hard come by, for an Indian. He doesn't risk one if he can help it. They knew we had guns."

"Are they going to try a cavalry charge now?"

"I don't think so. They don't fight that way."

"They don't need to," said Hopkins. "They can starve us."

We watched the Indians deploy into the valley until they stood in a ragged line just at the bank of the creek. There was some talk among a bunch of them in the middle, then one man rode out toward us. He was unarmed, and he sat a tall piebald horse. He held his arms above his head with his palms toward us to show that he was empty handed, and he stared straight at us without expression. He was not much to look at, and neither was his mount, but that man was a horseman. With his knees and his seat he brought that horse slowly across the creek and up the rough slope toward us. He halted about fifty feet away and just sat there for fully a minute. Then he slowly lowered his hands.

"Soldiers!" he shouted. "Let me talk, soldiers!"

"Flag of truce," said Hopkins. "Does he think we're soldiers?"

"To him, men who fight are soldiers," said Drum.

"Ned," I said, "is he one that you know? That chief?"

Drum shook his head.

"Will you talk?" the Indian called.

Drum did nothing, studying the man, but while he hesitated Tyree climbed over the wagon tongue and came around the far side of the wagon. He walked down toward the man with his hands outspread.

"Look at that damned peacemaker," said Bob.

"Ned?" I said. He paid no attention. He just stayed where he was, staring out over his rifle. He wasn't afraid. He must have felt ashamed to face the Cheyenne now. Maybe he just didn't see any point in it.

Tyree talked with the Indian for several minutes, standing by his horse. We couldn't hear what was said, but twice the Indian made a gesture of chopping one palm with the side of the other hand. It was a gesture I didn't like. Finally

[231]

he turned his horse and rode back to his comrades the way he had come up: slowly and with dignity. Tyree watched after him for a moment before coming up to us and pushing in through the horses.

"What does he say?" asked Hopkins.

"They want our rifles. If we give them the guns, he says, they will leave us alone."

"That sounds like a sharp bargain," said McVey. "Drum, you better take him up on that before he changes his mind."

"Did he say anything else?" asked Drum.

"I didn't want to ask him directly about the . . . man we buried. But he didn't say anything about that. I asked him about this chief that you mentioned, this Bear Walks Around. He said he didn't know him, and that he doesn't know you."

"Was that all?" Drum asked.

"No. He doesn't speak English very well. I couldn't get much more out of him, but he said that many more of his men are coming, and that they will kill us all. I told him that we mean no harm and that we only want to go in peace."

We were all silent for a bit. Then Hopkins said: "Do you think he believed that?"

"I don't know."

"Ned," I said, "are these men relatives of the dead one?"

"They're Cheyenne, like he was," Drum answered.

"I see."

As we talked, the Indians spread out. Half a dozen of them rode downstream, crossed and came up toward us from below. Another bunch went the other way and some of them circled far and came out on the rim of the valley above us. The rest scattered along the creek, some dismounted and others just sitting their horses and staring up at us.

"We can't just wait here," I said. "Maybe he does have other men coming."

"Maybe," said Drum, "and maybe he's sent for them. But that's what an Indian always says."

"We have very little water," said Joel.

"Enough for two days," Drum murmured. "It's powder that we have to worry about, most of all." He licked his lips carefully. "Bent's Fort is no more than about fifty miles from here." We waited as he continued to stare out at the Indians. "A hard ride could get a man there by to-morrow sometime. They'd send help."

"We haven't got a fit horse," I said, "except yours."

McVey chuckled.

"I couldn't go," said Drum. "It would have to be you, Mr. Cooper. You'd have trouble finding your way, and even if you got there it would take them at least a day to get to us. And with you gone, we'd have only three men to hold them off." He turned to Joel. "Are you still of the same mind?" he asked.

"Yes, Ned Drum."

Drum nodded and turned back to face the Indians below us. "I tried too much," he said quietly.

"I hope you die!" said McVey. He gave a hoot of laughter. "Die, you fool!"

Drum spun about and bent toward Bob. "I'm going to cut you loose," he said. "And then you can do what you like. If you want to turn against your own kind, you can."

The Indian on the piebald horse came along the creek at a canter. It was no truce this time. He had a lance in his hand and a little round hide shield on his arm. Below us, he turned the pony and put it into a run. "Mr. Cooper, you shoot first," said Drum. The Indian was flying. I stuck my rifle around the tail of the wagon and waited. As he neared us he veered the pony in a curve around the back of the wagon and he slid around on his mount's neck so there was nothing to see of him except one hand and one foot. "Shoot the horse," said Drum, but it was against all my instinct. I hesitated just an instant too long. The Indian swung up, spun his pony like a circus horse and threw the lance. I ducked. Drum shot. When I raised my head the Indian was galloping off along the slope, flat on his horse's neck. The lance had gone over me and shivered on the rock beside McVey.

[233]

"Showing off for his men," said Drum calmly. "That's their way."

"If ten of them came like that all at once," I said, "we'd never stop them."

"We'd stop some. In the army they used to say: 'One Indian will always take a dare. Fifty Indians never will.'"

"Was that the chief, Mr. Drum?" Pierce asked.

"He may be a chief. They have different kinds. Usually a chief leads a war-party."

"He's a fine man, isn't he?" said Jim.

McVey said: "Why don't you join up with them, Jim?"

Drum whirled on him. "*You* already have!" he bellowed. Bob grinned at him. "I was going to let you go," said Drum.

"Hold on, Drum," I said nervously.

Drum grabbed Bob's bound wrists and hauled him to his feet with one heave. Bob stood there trembling and glaring as Drum tried to untie the stiff leather strap. He couldn't get it apart. "A knife!" he cried. His face was purple and contorted. He dropped Bob's wrists and jammed his hand into his pocket. He brought out his clasp-knife, but his fingers shook so that he could hardly open it. I looked down at the Indians. They were watching us.

"Drum," I said, "we've got trouble enough."

He finally pried open the blade. "Now," he said, panting, "we'll see." Bob offered his hands and Drum, sweating and biting his lip, began to saw at the leather. I looked again to the Indians, but they stood there like stones.

"There," said Drum. He stepped back and the strap fell from Bob's wrists. Drum closed the knife with a snap and dropped it into his pockets. He had one big pistol in the holster on his side. The other lay in the grass by the wagon wheel. He snatched it up and fumbled at the cap. It was loaded. Bob just stood and waited. With a quick movement, Drum stepped to McVey and laid the second pistol on the ledge within his reach. Then he backed over against the wagon.

"Now let's see," he said thickly. "Now let's see who you're going to kill."

[234]

Bob glared at him coldly and contemptuously. He looked at me and when his eyes came upon me I turned to stone. He looked at Martha. She was shrinking away from him and her eyes were full of terror. He reached for the pistol. He seemed to have trouble picking it up, and I saw his wrists were red and swollen where the strap had been. He took it in his hand and stood there looking at it. An agonized whisper broke from Drum: something unintelligible, some tortured plea. Bob did not move, and as he stood Drum shot him.

Ned drew and fired with his back to the wagon, not five yards away. Bob dropped the pistol and gasped, reeling back against the ledge. As he put his hand to his chest, his feet slid out from under him and he crumpled against the rock with his bloody breast on his knees. Martha Tyree grabbed him and began to straighten him out. I saw his face. He looked afraid and angry and I thought he was all right, but there was a lot of blood.

"You didn't need to shoot," I said, but it came out in a whisper, and I don't think anyone heard.

There was a whoop up on the hillside and a skinny young Indian came down at us, howling and hugging his horse. I thought he was going to jump the pony right in among us, but at the last chance he swerved and went crashing down among the pack horses. He pulled up, still shrieking, and began to flail at the horses with his spear as they milled and reared around him. He grabbed the halter of one and tried to jerk it loose from the wagon.

"Hey!" I cried. "Get out of there," and I pushed in among the horses after him, half hysterical. He jabbed his spear at me, but he couldn't do anything with those horses plunging all around him. I poked my rifle up at him and pulled the trigger, but we were both wobbling and rocking and I missed him altogther. Pierce came to my help, and the Indian, seeing it was no use, yanked his pony out of the herd and turned tail. I grabbed the halter of the nearest horse and began to chant: "Easy. Easy. Steady now. You'll be all right. Easy." Gradually they calmed, and I went back behind the wagon.

Martha and Joel had Bob's clothes open down the front. The skin of his belly was awfully white and soft under the blood. I knelt and recharged my rifle. "How is he?" I asked. Joel murmured something I didn't understand. Under the wagon, Hopkins fired his rifle and I heard more yelping down in the valley. I sprang to my place in time to see two Indians cantering along beside the creek shaking their lances at us. Then they turned and rode back.

I looked for Drum. He was still standing just where he had stood when he shot Bob. His pistol was back in its holster. "Proud of yourself?" I said, but he gave no sign of hearing me, and I was ashamed as soon as I had said it. Ned was watching the Tyrees work over McVey. Hopkins answered me. He turned from his rifle and said hotly: "Are *you*, Garvin?"

"No, I'm not," I said. "Martha, how bad is he hurt?"

"I don't think it is too bad," she answered. She didn't look at me.

"Drum," I said, "get your rifle. We need you, still."

He nodded and, very stiffly, he turned and picked up Bob's English rifle. Like a man slow with sleep, he looked to the charge. Then he leaned on the wagon and looked out at the Indians. All the shape and color was gone from his face.

A little later two Indians came down from the crumbling gullies above us, side by side, riding all out, and I shot the horse from under one of them as soon as they were in range. The other picked up his fallen friend and they retreated, leaving the pony thrashing and struggling to get up. My rifle was empty. "Kill it," I cried. "Someone kill that horse!"

"No. Save powder," said Hopkins. He was right, and the horse stopped kicking after a while.

"We'll tell the authorities the whole story," said Drum. "We'll lay it before them just as it happened."

"No we won't," I said. "You've done enough."

I heard McVey laugh feebly, and I flushed. I hadn't

realized that he was conscious. I waited for his mocking voice, but he said nothing. I could hear Martha talking to him—vague, meaningless, soothing words—and he seemed to be answering. Staring out over my ready rifle, I wondered what he might be saying to her. I was happy he was alive. I couldn't blame him for anything. All along, until the death of the Indian, he had tried so fiercely to be realistic and we had been so unreal.

We made our stand there all morning: the four of us at our rifles, the other three huddled against the rock. The Indians harried us constantly, charging first from one side and then from another while a few crept up through the brush for a close shot with the bow. An arrow cut Jim's leg and another stuck in Martha's skirts. We brought down three more of their horses and I shot one Indian through the neck as he stood bending his bow in the rocks near the stream. Some of his friends scuttled up and dragged him away. He must have been dead, for there was a big pow-wow down on the farther bank over his motionless form and then the Indians all mounted up and rode slowly upstream. With the stock they'd captured in that first wild melee, they had four horses to spare, so I guess they quit while they were still ahead.

When there were no more of them in sight, we waited an hour in the silence and the hot, fierce sunlight, and then we talked it over and decided that someone should ride down to scout. Wearily, I volunteered.

I went to Drum's yellow gelding, tied to the wagon-box brace, and when I put my hand on the reins he tipped up his ears and looked at me curiously. As I put my foot in the stirrup Drum spoke.

"Mr. Cooper, what are you doing? I can't let you take King. You'll have to get another. Take your mule."

I faced him. "You going to shoot someone, Ned?" He opened his mouth and shut it again and I swung up into the saddle.

"Mr. Cooper, you can't just do what you please. That's my horse."

[237]

"I need a good mount for this," I said, "and this is the only one left."

"Mr. Cooper!" He came shambling toward me and the horse shied from his waving arms. "You can't do this! I won't stand for it."

"You going to shoot me?" I repeated.

Martha Tyree said, "Oh, Garvin. Garvin Cooper."

"Now it's all on me, is it?" cried Drum. "No, sir! Not a bit of it! What about the rest of you? The whole lot of you! We could have made it! We could have done a great thing. Do you know what you've done? Do you know what's left for me?"

"I don't care."

"I know you don't. None of you do. Well, I won't be made a fool of. The authorities will get the whole story of this."

I started to turn the horse away and he ran to me and grabbed the stirrup.

"You have no right, Mr. Cooper! You have no right!"

I touched the big gelding and he sprang forward, brushing Drum aside. The guide went down on his hands and knees in the sand, but I didn't look back. I headed up the sloping bluff above the wagon, and the buckskin took it like a greyhound. Behind me, Drum called: "Mr. Cooper! You can't!"

I hurried the horse as far as the break of the bluff and there I paused for a look around. It would have been foolhardy to follow the Indians up the narrow, shallow valley, but up on the edge I felt safe, particularly with the horse I had under me. I could see from there that our valley was really no more than an extra-wide wash in a high, barren tableland. I started northward, warily, along its lip, keeping shy of any cover that might have hid a man. The rocks and washes and scrubby brush could have hidden an army, but the Indians weren't in hiding. About half a mile north I caught sight of them, still down in the valley and still at a slow pace. It looked to be all of them and there was no indication of trickery. That one man killed was all it had taken to end the battle.

[238]

I watched until they were out of sight. Then I rode down to the creek and dismounted to wash the powder-grime from my face and arms. The buckskin stood by alertly. He was a fine mount.

Back at the wagon, Jim and Hopkins were unloading the pack horses and examining them. Drum stood holding the wheel of the wagon, watching with a grief-stricken face as I rode up on his horse. Bob lay on his back in the shadow of the wagon with a thick pack of moist cloths on his ribs, and he looked straight up at the sky. Now and then his tongue came out to lick carefully at his lips. Martha was finding fuel for a fire and Tyree was straightening the twisted harness of the team.

I pulled the saddle off Drum's horse and tied it. He watched me silently.

"They're gone," I said. "They're heading upstream, all in a pack. You can see them about a mile up there."

Drum nodded. "I thought as much," he said. I turned my back on him and went to squat beside Bob.

"How does it feel?" I asked.

He looked at me and shook his head very slightly. His eyes were clear and thoughtful. "It hurts like the devil," he said in a tired voice. "Garvin, I think I'm done for."

"Nothing like it," I said. "We'll get you down to that fort and I'm going to look for some help."

"Who's going to help us?" he said. "But you look, Cooper. You look."

I left him there to go help Tyree with the mules. As I worked beside him he said softly: "Thee was cruel, Garvin Cooper."

"I was angry. I'm still angry."

"Angry with thyself, I think. To be angry with thyself is to be angry with God, in a way."

"Don't preach to me, Joel."

"You said before that Robert McVey was suffering. Now it is Ned Drum that is suffering."

"He wasn't going to let anything stop him from making his damned trail," I said.

"A slaying led to this."

"You think it's that simple?" I asked him angrily.

"I think it not simple at all. I think life is not for us to tamper with."

"One way or another," I said, "we do."

Martha said that she didn't think Bob should be moved right away, so we decided to leave the wagon where it was and make a camp against the rock ledge that had been the back wall of our fort. We spent the rest of the day repairing the battle damage and prying arrows out of the wagon. At nightfall we posted a guard up on the edge of the valley. We were lucky that the moon came up early and was almost full. At any sign of the Indians' returning, the guard was to fire the fowling-piece. I took the first watch right after supper and when Jim relieved me it was all I could do to stumble back to the camp before falling asleep.

First thing in the morning, I went to Bob.

"How is it today?" I asked him as brightly as I could.

"Look up there," he said. He was staring at the far edge of the valley. Half a dozen vultures were sitting in the rocks rustling their wings and waddling heavily about.

"They came for the horses," I said. "There's four dead horses that we shot yesterday."

"Just the same, it's not a very cheerful sight."

"We'll do something about it. I'll hitch the team and drag the carcasses up the valley."

"Thanks."

"You're bound to feel pretty low today. They say the second day is always the worst."

He nodded. "Have you talked to Drum?" he asked.

"About what?"

He didn't answer. "I guess he fixed the hell out of me, didn't he?"

"You weren't going to shoot," I said. "You had time. You could have killed him." He didn't deny that. "Bob," I said, "why didn't you just throw the gun on the ground?"

"I was thinking," he smiled.

"You're lucky you're not dead," I said.

He nodded. Then he said: "I'm not so damned lucky."

I got Tyree to help me with the team and we went down to move the horses. It was hard work: getting a hitch on the dead horse, then dragging it painfully for half a mile up the creek until we were out of sight of camp. It was early afternoon before we were done, and the mules were exhausted.

While we were working, Drum and Hopkins had gone up onto the prairie and shot two rabbits, so we got a bit of hot, fresh meat for dinner. I slept most of the afternoon, and when I woke Bob was propped up against a saddle with his sketch book on his knees. He had drowsed off over a drawing of the creek and the valley. I asked Martha what she thought.

"He is badly hurt," she said. "He cannot swallow except with pain."

"Perhaps it will be best to take the chance of moving him. We can get him to that fort."

"Perhaps," she said, "it will be best to let him be here, and be comfortable a little longer. I think that if we move him it will be great pain for nothing." Martha's eyes were full of tears. "He looked to me," she said, "when he held the gun in his hand, and I was afraid of him."

"You weren't the only one."

"I knew what he needed."

"No one knew," I said.

I looked around for Drum. He was sitting down by the creek watching his yellow horse as it grazed the sweet greens along the water's edge.

"He is hurt too," she said.

A little later Bob woke up and took a little supper. Martha had boiled the rabbit bones to make him a bit of soup. It didn't seem to hurt him so much, and I felt better. He drifted off into a deep sleep again afterward and the rest of us sat around the fire near him. We put out no guard.

"Well, Drum," said Willis. "Where do we go from here?"

Ned roused himself from a deep study to blink and shake his head.

[241]

Joel said: "We must take Robert to the fort."

"Yes," said Ned. "There's no going on now. We're finished."

"It's only a little ways to the mountains now," said Joel. "We'll get there."

"Oh, surely we will. We can just take the trail up through Pueblo and then up past the springs and on into the settlements. It's a regular trail, well-marked."

Jim Pierce said: "Mr. Tyree, what are you going to do once you get up there?"

"Find land, and make a farm. After that, we will see."

"That's what I'd like to do. You know, I thought for a while there that I'd like to join up with some fur trappers. Mr. Drum told me about them. But I believe I'd like to get me a farm, too. I reckon I could even get married." I think he expected someone to laugh at him. "Mr. Hopkins," he went on, "what about you?"

"I'm going to eat some decent food," said Willis, and Jim smiled politely.

"No gold, Willis Hopkins?" Martha asked.

"We'll see. The best future is probably in land. Or maybe in hard goods. In the gold fields, a keg of nails brings one hundred dollars, I've heard."

"But thee has no nails."

"There are ways to get them."

Jim Pierce had to finish his census. "What about you, Mr. Cooper?"

"I'm going to practice law," I said.

Drum rumbled: "You'll have to write them first. There are no laws, out here." He stared gloomily into the fire.

"Mr. Drum," said Jim, "what about you? Will you make the trip back with some more people, or what?"

For an instant, Drum sat like a stone, then he gave a little whimper, scrambled up and fled into the darkness.

As we were laying out our beds, Martha gave a little cry. I crouched with a blanket in my hand, listening, straining against the darkness. I heard Joel say: "What is it?" and she answered: "Come here, Joel." I waited. "Feel here," she said. Then: "His heart?"

Joel answered: "No."

Forms rustled and moved in the dark. Another voice—Drum's—said, "What is it? What's wrong?"

"His face is cold," said Martha.

"What's wrong?" breathed Drum.

"Robert McVey is dead."

A high, sharp cry came from the hurt night. Someone stirred the ashes of our fire and raised a feeble glow. I put my face into the blanket.

Hopkins shook me awake in the first light. I had been all night in a stuporous dose, trying with all my strength to will myself to sleep, and when Willis touched me I said: "Not yet. Not now."

"Drum's gone," he said.

I drew the blanket away from my face and made myself look at him. I had the feeling that as soon as I faced him, or any other man, I would fall apart; but Willis scarcely saw me. He was wrapped in his own fears. He was peaked and chilled-looking, although it wasn't cold.

"He must have gone in the night," he said. "What shall we do?"

"Hunt for him. Did he take his horse?" Willis nodded. "Wake the others."

I got up and pulled on my boots without ever looking over toward the rock where Bob was.

"What will we do if we find him?" Willis asked me.

"Bring him back. We won't catch him, not with that horse he's got, but we have to look. You and Jim have a look up and down the valley for some sign of him. I'll go up on top of the bluff."

"Suppose we find him and he doesn't want to come back?"

"He'll do whatever you tell him to do. Just don't take any mouth from him. He'll come back. He's still our guide."

We roused the Tyrees and quickly told them what had

happened. They didn't seem surprised. Martha shook her head sadly. "Let the man go," she said.

"We won't catch him," I told her, "but we ought to look just the same, for his own good."

"Poor man."

"You'd better keep a lookout while we're gone," I said. "If you see Indians, or have any trouble, fire two shots with a rifle and we'll come back. Two shots. All right?"

"We'll be safe," said Joel.

I saddled the mule and pushed him helter-skelter up the hill while Willis and Jim were still struggling with their gear. I had an idea where Drum was off to. He was going to that fort. It wasn't likely that I could catch him. In the first place, he was better mounted than I; in the second, he knew the ground. Still, I felt I had to try.

I kicked my mule to the rim of the valley and then I rode back and forth, casting for his trail. I found it soon enough: the fresh tracks of a shod horse, and a big one. I followed them to the west, into the dew-wet prairie with its armed, spikey plants and its raw colors. The tracks led straight. From the look of them, he had been traveling hard. In the dry ground they were easy to follow, though, and I put the mule to a sharp pace.

After a few miles, it got rocky, but I found tracks often enough to tell me that I was still following him. The sun climbed up at my back and the prairie dew was gone, and I kept at it, rocking my mule right along but riding him as easy as I could, to save him. I strained my eyes against the bleak, glittering barrens, and I carried my loaded rifle in my hand.

Before noon, I came to a shallow gully edged with withered scrubby brush: the dry bed of a creek. Drum had turned south in the stream bed, where the packed sand made easy footing for his horse. I dismounted and let my mule breathe a bit while I thought about it. I'd be lucky to get back to the wagon by dark. I'd come a long way already and the mule was not too strong. I had no food but a handful of dried corn in my saddlebag and no water except what was in my canteen. Still, I didn't want to turn back. I was sure I was gaining on him and I felt that Ned Drum still owed us something, that it was not yet over. I wet my handkerchief from the canteen and wiped my mule's nostrils and mouth. Then I remounted and set out at a trot down the creek bed.

The trail was easy to follow and fast going. In a few places the wash dipped so deep that I couldn't see over the banks, and I went through places like that in a hurry. I didn't like the blind feeling, not for even a few seconds. In mid-afternoon I reached a spot where Drum had left the gully, turning again to the west and up into a row of bare, rolling hills. I rested the mule before going on from there, and thought some more. Drum had said that it was fifty miles to the fort. It wasn't likely that he could make it in one day, not in this rough going. He'd have to camp, and if he lit a fire on this prairie it would be a beacon for miles. He had no more water than I, so he had to be heading for a stream.

I let the mule lick some water from my cupped hand. That way, I got about a cup into him without spilling any. Then I followed the tracks of the yellow horse up onto the hillside. It wasn't a steep rise, but it was a long one, and the mule made hard going of it. I was afraid, once, that I had lost the trail; but I just pressed on, taking what seemed the natural path, and before long I saw some prints to show me that I was still on him. At the skyline, I saw water and blew out my wind in a long sigh of relief. It was a tiny ribbon of a creek, about a hundred yards below me in a shallow valley. It looked to be nearly dry, but there were enough pools to water my mule and myself. Drum had known what he was doing, all right.

I was so glad to see the water that I didn't notice, at first, what was beyond it. There was more prairie, first, stretching away and away, but it had the yellow-green look of dry grass-land. Far off, I could see where it rose into dark hills. Then beyond and above the hills, against the sky, were the mountains. So far away that they seemed a trick of the clouds, they rose, first in green and then in blue and finally in purple and black and glistening silver-gray.

I stared. Then I remembered where I was, silhouetted against the sky. I urged the mule down toward the water, and he didn't lag once he scented it. I rode him into a shallow pool and let him drink while I went upstream and sucked some water from the next one. I stopped him when he'd had enough, filled my canteen, and looked around for Drum's tracks. I found them just below us. I could see where his horse had drunk, and the prints of Ned's two hands that he'd made as he lay down and dipped his head to the stream. But after they had drunk, he had not followed the stream, nor had he crossed it. He had gone right back up toward the rolling spur of land that we had just crossed. I couldn't figure that out, but there was nothing to do except follow.

The trail went to the crest of the high ground and then turned along it, heading southward parallel to the creek. This took him along the highest ground in sight either way, so I decided he must have wanted the sight advantage it gave him.

This was hard, dry ground, and trailing was difficult. I had to keep leaning forward around my mule's neck to study the ground. I followed him along the ridge for over an hour, and then I saw a thin wisp of bluish smoke rising from the creek downstream. I reined in and studied it. It seemed to be hanging above a grove of cottonwood trees about a mile from me. I dismounted and walked a little way, leading the mule as I scanned Drum's tracks. They held to the crest for another hundred yards, then they veered over to the slope, away from the creek and the grove and the smoke. I was glad to follow him and get off the skyline. We went for a quarter of a mile, staying down out of sight of the valley for most of the way but edging up here and there, apparently to dismount and have a look over. I came up to a patch of brush where he had stopped and dismounted, and I got down, holding the reins, and walked softly up to where I could peer down to the creek. As I studied the cottonwoods beside the stream, a man came walking out of them. He was hatless and wore blue britches, but that was all I could make out at the distance—except that he was white. I froze and watched him walk a bit out onto the prairie, make some motion with his arms, turn and return into the trees. I waited, but there was nothing more to see. I took the mule back a little and tied the reins to a rock snag. With my rifle in my hand, I began working along the crest for a better look.

I hadn't gone very far before I was startled by a sound in the rocks and saw Drum's yellow horse. He was standing unsaddled with the sun lighting up his coat and he twitched his ears as he watched me. For a moment he studied me, then he dropped his head and began nosing in some scrappy brush that he had been grazing. I cocked the rifle and edged toward him. He went on poking about in the rocks for something to eat. When I got a little nearer I saw the saddle laid across a stone. I crept nearer, cautiously, until I was within ten feet of the saddle. There was no sound but the gelding's shoes scraping the dry ground and his teeth breaking the brittle leaves. Then, up at the crest of the ridge, in a little notch, I saw Drum. He was sitting with his back against a stone, facing into the valley. A bullet from his big pistol had put his head all out of shape and the flash had burned the beard off one side of his face. Ants and flies were on him. I took the rifle off cock and went to him. His hat was upside down between his scuffed and dusty boots and in it, weighed down with a stone, was a piece of paper torn from his little notebook. I took the paper. Then I looked down into the valley.

In the grove of cottonwoods was a camp of dragoons. There were not many of them. About fifteen horses were picketed in the edge of the trees and back in the shade I could see the grayish humps of tents. Three men in blue britches and white shirts were working at the creek, washing clothes on the rocks, as nearly as I could make out. Another man, wearing his tunic but with it hanging open down the front, came strolling out from the trees and squatted beside them. I slipped back down beside Drum's horse and sat down. I unfolded Ned's note.

It was addressed at the top in a round, childish hand: "To Whom It May Concern."

"This is the true facts of what happened on a trip from Whitaker to Arapahoe County, Kansas Territory, starting May 25, 1858, with me in charge. The people in the party were..."

Here he listed us all. Then followed a short account, written like an army report, of what had happened. He had hung on to that last shred of faith in the authorities—but not enough to go down to that camp and try to tell them about it. His account was true enough, but only the facts were there. I had hoped to see what Drum thought of it, what he thought had been done to him, but there was nothing like that. He had simply sat down in sight of that real world to which his simple decency and his honest ambition belonged, and told the truth—as if that was all that was needed. The only hint of his feelings or his pride or his loss was in the signature: "Edward S. Drum—guide."

I saddled the golden buckskin. Then I went back and got my mule. I dragged Drum's body out of the rocks and started to try to hoist him to the back of the mule, but that wasn't decent. This was to be his last ride. I couldn't grudge him that. I put him on his buckskin, laying him across the saddle. It was a sickening job, but it had to be done. When I was through I walked off a ways and sat down for a while. Then I went back and tied him to the saddle, mounted my mule, and took the reins of the horse.

The men at the river saw me first. They stood up and stared as I came toward them. The man in the tunic turned around and yelled something and another one came from the camp. By the time I was within hailing distance there was quite a crowd waiting me. The man in the open tunic sloshed across the creek and sauntered out to meet me. He was a lank, whiskery corporal.

"What you got there?" he asked me, staring stonily at Drum's body.

"A dead man," I said. "I'm from a traveling party camped